THE ART OF PUBLIC POLICY ANALYSIS

Volume 135, Sage Library of Social Research

AND SO, MY SON, THE ADMINISTRATOR,
AND THE COMMISSIONER, AND ALL THE
ASSISTANT COMMISSIONERS SAT AND
GNASHED THEIR TEETH, AND TORE THEIR
HAIR, AND RENT THEIR GARMENTS, SAYING
UNTO ME: "WHY IS THIS SO?"
   AND IN THAT MOMENT I OPENED THE
FILE AND SET IT BEFORE THEM,
AND, LO! THEY WERE MUCH ASHAMED
AND FELL SILENT AND CAST DOWN
THEIR EYES.
   "WELL, HELL," SAITH THE COMMISSIONER,
"WE CAN'T TELL CONGRESS THAT!"

THE ART OF PUBLIC POLICY ANALYSIS

The Arena of Regulations and Resources

Peter W. House

Volume 135
SAGE LIBRARY OF
SOCIAL RESEARCH

SAGE PUBLICATIONS
Beverly Hills / London / New Delhi

To Will, Bob, and Phil. Thanks.

Frontispiece reprinted from *The Iron Law of Bureaucracy* by Alexis A. Gilliland. Copyright 1979, Loomponics Unlimited.

For information address:

SAGE Publications, Inc.
275 South Beverly Drive
Beverly Hills, California 90212

SAGE Publications India Pvt. Ltd.
C-236 Defence Colony
New Delhi 110 024, India

SAGE Publications Ltd
28 Banner Street
London EC1Y 8QE, England

Printed in the United States of America

Library of Congress Cataloging in Publication Data

House, Peter William, 1937-

    The art of public policy analysis.
    (Sage library of social research; v. 135)
    Bibliography: p.
    1. Policy sciences. I. Title. II. Series.

H61.H74   361.6'1   81-18354
                            AACR2

ISBN 0-8039-1764-3 cloth
ISBN 0-8039-1765-1 (pbk.)

FIRST PRINTING

CONTENTS

PREFACE

"Policy analyst" connotes excitement. It suggests advisor, vizier, confidant, insider. It implies power, prestige, influence, privilege. If making policy means glamor, then the policy analyst shines by reflected glory and plays the moon to the decisionmaker's sun.

In recent years, this role has grown in ever increasing ways, bringing more and more information to the policy or decision process. A few decades ago, the technicians who were developing the original techniques became involved in bringing about institutional change to integrate these systems with the decision process. With time, several of these institution builders began to suggest change in the direction of replacing the historical decision process by one that is more "rational" and less subject to human bias and error. This latter notion has been in the forefront of advanced thinking about how public policy ought to be formulated. Several elements of the public sector have embraced one form or another of these emerging philosophies in some degree. Many new analytic techniques also came into being, with the result that we are currently awash in "systems."

The purpose of this book is to look at whether this thrust in the direction of technically driven and analytically laden policy formulation is as successful as its proponents claimed it would be. The techniques that grew up in this field are now in the kit bag of most analysts. "Systems" thinking has become a normal part of our lexicon. Everybody knows what policy analysis is and what is taught in policy science programs. The question before us here is simply: Does this considerable amount of sophistication and technique really make for better policy? Does anybody use the output of these analyses? Who? How? To what extent?

The book first looks at the assumptions underlying the technical fields of systems analysis, operations research, and the like to see whether they are valid. The formal decision process is also laid out in a similar fashion, along with the modeling and other analytic techniques. After these are laid out and assessed, there is a suggestion that in the formal techniques and processes, reality is somewhat lacking.

The book next turns to defining how policy is really made. Throughout these sections I make some use of case histories and examples of federal decisionmaking and analyses, mostly in the Department of Energy, and primarily in the areas of environmental regulations (especially air) and emerging energy policies. Finally, short-run and longer-term strategies are discussed to realign techniques and practice, although some difficulties are not likely to yield to solution due to limits in our knowledge and information, and to the fact that human institutions inevitably contain human beings.

The book is designed to be of use to several audiences. One group is the community of scholars and their students who teach policy science and administration. I hope that it will be a source book that will place the techniques they train (or learn) in a proper perspective. The researchers and practitioners in the field will find the suggestions for the future interesting. For some, the distance between their analysis and the final decisions is so great that the work may help them to understand how their analyses fit into the scheme of things. Finally, members of the user community will be able to use suggestions of an organizational nature to help structure their organizations. It should also be useful to them in dealing with the analytic technician.

I wish to thank several people with whom I have worked over the years on various specific projects discussed in this work. Collectively, they have acted as a sounding board for many ideas found in this manuscript, and I am indebted to them. They include Ted Williams, Dario Monti, Joe Coleman, Roger Shull, Joan Hock, Dick Ball, and many others who make up the Office of Environmental Assessments in the Office of Environment at the Department of Energy. I would particularly like to thank Bob Ryan and Will Steger, who read and commented on the whole manuscript and helped me to smooth out and clarify my thoughts and words.

The responsibility for the content, though, is mine—and I wouldn't want it any other way.

Peter House
Washington, D.C.

CHAPTER 1

QUESTIONING THE BASIC ASSUMPTIONS

Control by Computer

It is 9:00 a.m. Monday morning, and His Honor the Mayor rushes past his secretary into his office-command center. Over the years, his office has evolved from a largely ceremonial one to an administrative and decision-making center. In addition to a desk and other standard executive furniture, the room contains an electronic map of his city showing traffic routes, hospitals, fire stations, and the like. This center is connected to a large central computer system through CRTs, and further linked to a city-wide communications system.

Out of habit, the Mayor checks on the current estimate of the city's Quality of Life Index; up .004 percent from last week. This Index, which relates tax revenues and neighborhood desires to actual city performance department by department, takes much of the guesswork out of urban administration, and is a pretty handy way to enhance chances for reelection. He next runs through an up-to-the-minute report on the traffic flow and the medical, fire, and police emergencies of the last several days, and lastly a report, by department, of the day's expected activities.

With the advent of the computer and other high-technology devices, improved software, and the commitment to collect, update, and raise to high quality the underlying information base and simulation systems, the operation of the city is considerably more efficient. To optimize revenue, the computer keeps track of things such as real property values by area, revalues the properties when necessary, and mails out and keeps track of the tax bills. To maintain services at a high level, each department of the city is constantly monitored for its performance in light of the available resources and the desires of the citizens.

Yes, the Mayor is convinced he runs a modern, efficient, responsive city.

Sound far-fetched? Well, in the 1960s, such utopian dreams were peddled throughout the nation. Experience suggests, however, that very seldom does the straight inspection of data (even from sophisticated information systems) result in an obvious policy decision. Information, whether it's electronic readings on an automobile's performance, or laboratory results on a physical checkup for a patient, usually requires that one or more experts be on hand to analyze the information and put it in a form useful for decision purposes. Often, a considerable amount of data on various facets of a problem has to be studied and melded together to provide a composite picture from which a decision can be made or an issue structured. In the public arena, as the techniques have become more sophisticated, and as more and more data have become available, a new formal discipline has come to prominence: policy analysis. [1]

Policy analyses have to be developed in such user climates as these, which determine what indices will be monitored, which level of negative impact requires attention, and what alternatives are available if action is required. At present, policy analysis appears to have become a euphemism for computer analysis, where complex political checks and balances of the type familiar to the politician are reduced to strict quantitative terms. Needless to say, the picture of this electronic city or Congress or White House never has come to pass—for a variety of reasons.

Our present interest is not so much in the study of policy analysis as an example of pure technocracy (although we shall review this phase of its development also), but more to focus on questions of how analysis can or should be used for daily public policy making. In a recent article on technology assessment, Joseph Coates describes a public policy issue as

> a fundamental enduring conflict among or between objectives, goals, customs, plans, activities, or stakeholders, which is not likely to be resolved completely in favor of any polar position in that conflict. The necessarily temporary resolution of issues by a public policy is likely over long periods of time to move closer to favoring one policy over another. Thus, the crucial question facing public policy in any given time is striking a fresh balance among conflicting forces.[2]

He goes on to say that it is important to distinguish issues from problems, for he maintains that problems can be solved, whereas issues cannot. In the public policy arena, problems are to be merely identified, and options, alternatives, and such to be studied. Issues are more difficult to come to grips with because the big ones are interlocking and consist of a nesting of subissues, so that the "key" one is not always obvious. Issues are also value-laden, evolutionary, and politically inspired, he notes. These features, which we shall return to later, make policy analysis extremely challenging. They also suggest why such analysis cannot always be highly analytical or automated.

WHY POLICY ANALYSIS CAN'T BE DONE BY COMPUTER

Policy analysis has been referred to as an art. People who practice it are usually trained to be highly analytical and yet, though conversant with sophisticated computer technology and the techniques of analysis, they hold the skill to be only a small part of their overall job, finding, as they perform more and more such analyses, that the real challenge is still people-oriented. Much policy analysis takes place in an adversarial atmosphere, meaning that the options suggested by a particular analysis will often conflict with those of another agency or group holding a different ideological position, or whose organization charter is such that they would be likely to lobby for another outcome. Sometimes the analyses compete for recognition even within a like-interest sphere, because there is always competition for the honor of doing battle in the ultimate adversary arena where the "best" analyst is chosen to defend a position from one or more analyses representing one facet of the issue. In either case, the mere technical brilliance of the analytical portion of the policy analysis, regardless of how good the data and techniques are, is only a small part of the job of policy analysis. In the end, the task is still apt to be very human-oriented, because logic and findings are joined with power, skills of an expository or debating nature, the current political climate, and other factors. The world of the policy analyst who supports the decisionmaker is not neatly described, therefore, by mechanical marvels and push-button logic. It is complex and at times byzantine, beset by situations and rules uniquely its own.

Since more than a decade has now passed since the RAND Corporation[3] launched its campaign to bring logic and rigor into the public decisionmaking process through the techniques of systems analysis, it is time for us to see how well these very formal and potentially powerful techniques have fared in the world of policy analysis. To this end, I have constructed a set of questions about the underlying assumptions and practice of systems analysis and the use of sophisticated empirical techniques in the public arena.[4]

In thinking about this set of questions, it is probably best not to get bogged down in trying to answer each specific one in an exhaustive fashion. Yet, they are clearly of a nature where answers of the "true" or "false" variety are inappropriate. Instead, it is better to try and address the questions in a rather superficial fashion. Let me suggest one way of doing this.

First, try to picture the answers to a set of questions from the perspective of "conventional wisdom" or academic principles. Then, answer the same questions from the perspective of experience, reality, or some such vantage point.

If the vector of responses using these two perspectives is not the same, then one might want to question the rigorous, analytical, mathematical techniques used in present day systems or policy analysis. These questions are presented in several groupings with a cursory explanatory discussion. More detail will be provided in later chapters.

Some Questions About the Underpinnings

As we shall see in this work, there are several places that systems analysis could be called into question. An exhaustive list of questions or problems might be long indeed. On the other hand, a look at a half dozen or so such questions and an attempt to address them in summary fashion might be instructive.

WHAT IS ASSUMED?

- What if some or many of the basic assumptions on which the whole field of systems analysis was built were false?
- What if the information on how the system operated available to those who put together systems analysis were flawed?
- What if the case studies and the oral/written history of decision-making were inaccurate?

Because systems analysis largely sprang from and was defined by members of structured disciplines such as engineering, it implies a rigor that may not actually exist in any human-based institution or organization. Conceptually, systems are usually described in a neat, parametrically definable fashion which allows one to define and bound it, to model and quantify it, to solve it for various values of the parameters, often validating the results and using it to readjust the operation of the system. This paradigm clearly assumes that it is possible to understand or to approximately define the system under discussion in a complete fashion so that the most important features can be addressed and the rest ignored or deemphasized. Further, the understanding has to be such that the relationships normally can be reduced to mathematical formulae, usually with sufficient precision that they can be designed into a computer model that will respond to perturbations in the variables of interest to the policy-maker or analyst. There is always assumed to be a large data base, in addition to the information base, that can be tapped on demand. Finally, there is the assumption that the decision sector is going to make use of the results of the analysis in some "rational" way. Proponents of systems analysis have often gone so far as to suggest that if the decision model suggested by policy analysis is not the way that policies are made in the real world, then our current decisionmaking structure ought to be changed to operate in the more technocratic fashion derived from systems analysis.

The designers and proponents of systems analysis are not fools. They obviously saw such a technique work in a technology development arena, and although Ida Hoos[5] disagrees, many felt that it worked in the defense area. Clearly, as we shall point out, it has had trouble in the rest of the public sector. There are several reasons for this difficulty. In a generic sense, these reasons can be grouped under the heading "the world does not operate as advertised." One way to illustrate this phenomenon is to recount some experiences I have had recently with a series of workshops, all related to improving the information base or techniques for formal analysis.

DIFFICULTIES IN ENERGY-ENVIRONMENT ANALYSIS: SOME EXAMPLES

Several methods might be used to carry out a research program or project on any specific subject. Regardless of which method is chosen, there will be a need at some point in the design to figure out what is known about the subject and where one stands in relation to this knowledge base. These exercises often go under the guise of surveys of the literature or state-of-the-art reviews. They can be carried out in several ways: as library searches, by questionnaire, by interview, or, as we shall discuss—by workshops. In any case, the use of workshops is becoming an important and some say a unique part of any research or analysis function.

The three workshops summarized here were staged in part to provide a consensus of where we now stand on some broad issues of importance to the Department of Energy, and to help provide some direction for future research. The specific workshops were designed to gather together experts from diverse but related fields to address a specific or hard-to-handle question in a discussion mode, rather than the more usual staff model of the bureaucracy.

The conferences were not originally planned as a part of any overall grand scheme. Each was convened to address a specific question of concern in the area of energy and environmental analysis. The subjects chosen were issues not handled in most public policy analyses. The workshops set out both to discover shortcomings and to suggest how present practice could be improved. They were well attended, and the participants generally entered into the problem-solving mode of sessions with good intentions and high spirits. However, the results of the individual conferences were, for a variety of reasons, not as useful as had been hoped. Further, the quality of the workshop proceedings varied considerably, but none resulted in the beginnings of innovative solutions, also for a variety of reasons. This is not to say that the results were not useful, however. Individuals interested in the specific topic areas would find that each workshop resulted in a clear addition to their general knowledge base. In most cases, there was recognition that there were no clear-cut solutions to the problems under discussion. In all cases, the problem areas addressed were more clearly delineated, arguments were updated and verified, and the need for new approaches presented in a clearer fashion. In each case, however, the hoped-for new approaches were not realized. Let me briefly review the purposes of these three workshops.[6]

INTEGRATED ASSESSMENT FOR ENERGY-RELATED ENVIRONMENTAL STANDARDS

The substantial inability to determine systematically and objectively whether any given trade-off leaves us better or worse off in the aggregate—i.e., the lack of any integrated environmental assessment capability—is emerging as a central problem of contemporary environmental policy. An integrated assessment attempts to present the full range of consequences of a given policy action—all the costs and benefits, whether economic or environmental, intended or unintended, prompt or delayed—in order to determine whether the action will make society better or worse off in the aggregate, and by how much. The first workshop's purpose was to review the state-of-the-art of integrated assessment for environmental standards affecting energy technologies, and to draw lessons from the history of applied integrated assessment.

The workshops concluded that no federal agency practices integrated assessment, broadly or consistently, not even in the narrow technical sense of making sure that all factors that might impact on energy technology are considered. When integrated assessment is widened to include the political pressures and time constraints of the top-level administrators and decision-makers, the improbability of its being carried out increases substantially, even though administrators do try to consider a wide range of impacts. Identifying which impacts (and the extent to which attempts should be made to interrelate them) determine synergistic, genuinely integrative effects, is where personal and professional opinions split. Integrated assessment is practiced as an art, however scientific it may be in concept, and the opinions of experts and decisionmakers will determine how it is performed. Integrated assessments won't replace the decisionmaker, but they might help assure—if they could be done well—his less frequent replacement if a so-called "unexpected" result could become anticipated and mitigated.

What constitutes integrated assessment for various agencies at various times differs in practice, and probably in concept. The mission of each determines what impacts must be taken into consideration, or at least which should be given priority. It becomes obvious that each agency must construct its own framework for integrated assessment.

How can a process like integrated assessment be institutionalized to progress beyond the usual federal bureaucratic assessment procedures? The secret of implementing integrated assessment is realizing that it represents a fairly fundamental change in the reward structure of federal agencies. Good managers are presently defined as technically competent, and integrated assessment appears to overtax their competence to make the broad judgments that would be required of them. To change the reward structure of policy and planning with agencies requires a shift in attitude. Most people would agree to a reasonably clearly defined, objective function if the shift were recognized by their superiors—the decisionmakers—and used.

NATIONAL-REGIONAL ENERGY-ENVIRONMENTAL
MODELING CONCEPTS

The purpose of this workshop was to identify and evaluate approaches to regional economic and energy supply, and to demand forecasting best suited to assisting DOE in the assessment of environmental impacts of national energy policies. Specifically, the Office of Environment (OEV) uses models to assess the impacts of technology change, to analyze differential impacts of various energy policies, and to provide an early warning system of possible environmental constraints. Currently, OEV applies both a "top-down" model system to analyze national scenarios and a "bottom-up" assessment conducted from a regional perspective. A central theme of the workshop was to address the problem of how OEV should integrate the so-called top-down and bottom-up approaches.

The participants agreed that there was a need for both top-down and bottom-up approaches, so that various levels of interactions in energy-economic-environmental modeling systems could be adequately represented. Most of the comments, however, were directed toward the development of a new methodology. The participants felt that a core set of related models should be developed that are modular, dynamic, and consistent; they also wanted to see an interindustry accounting framework, interregional linkages, adequate documentation, and an appropriate methodological framework. To improve the quality of the data used in any policy analysis model, they recommended that OEV develop and maintain an integrated system of economic, environmental, and energy accounts coordinated with the statistical agencies that collect the data. An independent group should be established to oversee energy data collection, coordination, and verification. OEV should play a major role in ensuring that the data it needs for policy analysis models are collected and compiled in a suitable way. States and regions should be involved in the assessment process, with the state as the basic geographic unit, and states being encouraged to participate in the siting and disaggregation processes, as well as in the interpretation and evaluation of the impacts.

To improve the design of assessment programs, recommendations were made for improvements in energy and economic scenarios, the cost of environmental standards, and the appropriate time frame for conducting a given policy analysis. Five major themes emerged from the individual working group recommendations. First, the top-down and bottom-up approaches to policy analysis are compatible and can be used in an integrated fashion. Second, the methodology suggested for the integration processes should consist of a core set of linked basic models with other special purpose models for specific assessments. Third, the data and models used in this methodology require review, verification, and validation by outside groups. Fourth, regional and state involvement are necessary in any federal assessment process to enhance credibility and to increase accuracy. Finally, there is a need for a close relationship and communication between the decisionmaker, the model, and the modeler in order to guard against misuse of the model results.

NON-SITE-SPECIFIC ECOLOGICAL ENERGY TECHNOLOGY ASSESSMENT

The reliability of assessments decreases as the spatial scale broadens. Quantification has been achieved for some specific kinds of impacts, but not for the assessment of the ecological impacts of energy activities. The third workshop focused on ecological processes, species populations, and ecosystems to elucidate broad coverage of concerns. To develop an analytical framework, these were addressed in terms of near-term assessments, longer-term assessments (up to 30 years), differing spatial scales, and new methods and data.

Key ecological processes were identified as productivity, cycling of elements, and succession. The important issues in dealing with these processes are long- and short-term changes in productivity, changes in energy flow, changes in soil fertility, effects on adaptability and resiliency of systems, and changes in the rates of timing of biological phenomena. Most assessments of impacts on changes in land use or hydrologic regimes, or by releasing harmful residuals to the air or water, have to be qualitative at this time. Estimates of impacts at larger scales are particularly difficult to make.

Five kinds of species should be considered in an assessment of impact on populations: rare, endangered, keystone (species that play a critical role in the ecosystem), dominant, and indicator. For each kind of species, the important issues relate to habitats, stability and homeostasis, population, survival level, changes leading to secondary effects, distribution and range, and reversibility of impact. For future non-site-specific assessments, collection and assimilation of distributional data is needed, including improved local studies and biological information. For assessments or populations at different spatial scales, a major concern is data reliability.

Two major concerns related to ecosystems are resource and species interactions within and among ecosystems and ecosystem patches, and the "normal" pattern of perturbations or stresses that maintain the ecosystem. Characteristics of ecosystems identified as important in addressing these concerns include regulation of structure, composition, and function; frequency of perturbation; regulation of biochemical cycling; ecosystem interactions; ecosystem resiliency and health; and patch-mosaic properties. Methodology suggestions include use of a three-dimensional "conflict matrix" with different energy technologies on one axis, ecoregions on another, and ecosystem types on the third; identifying the limiting factors in energy/material flows within a system; and tracing the total flow of materials throughout the system. Models for terrestrial systems similar to those already developed for aquatic systems must be developed. Basic research on ecosystem geochemical responses should be expanded. Data bases should be developed that show landscape patterns for a broader area, and methods developed for describing existing patch dynamics at the county level. As many instances as possible of human alteration of perturbation cycles should be documented.

INSIGHTS FOR POLICY ANALYSIS

One might reasonably ask what benefit was gained from these workshops, and whether similar exercises be held in the future. Overall, the experience was disappointing; the results tended to add little to what was already known about the individual workshop themes. Because the amount of effort and organization in setting up the workshops was adequate, and because the participants were generally highly qualified and motivated, we concluded that the questions themselves might have been too fundamental and too difficult to be addressed in this fashion. Since the questions had been considered for a long time by smart people with appropriate backgrounds and yet were still largely unanswered, then putting these people together in one place, we hoped, would spark a symbiotic response--though admittedly the odds were against it.

This somewhat disappointing result does not, however, prove in and of itself that the workshops should not have been held at all. The individual workshops tended to sharpen the problem areas in a useful fashion. Further, it became clear that no simple or short-run solutions existed to the issues posed by the workshop conferees. These, in and of themselves, are useful conclusions and help to focus future research plans. Further, some ancillary research insights were gained for those interested in improving the art of public policy analysis, although these insights were not part of the original design of the workshop organizers.

Looking at each workshop once again, we can suggest at least several results for observers and participants which were not intended:

- The workshop on Integrated Assessment for Energy-Related Environmental Standards was designed, among other things, to investigate the benefits, techniques, and feasibility of looking at environmental impacts in a comprehensive, integrated fashion. As one of the inputs to the discussion, working papers were prepared which reviewed the development of environmental standards and policy in areas ranging from air to water to strip mining.

  The people preparing the papers used secondary sources and had the papers reviewed before presentation. Let's assume that the papers were at least technically adequate. As a part of the workshop design, people were invited who were active (in a policy sense) in the development of all or a portion of the standards or policies addressed in the papers. *These practitioners disagreed not only with ascribed motivation, but even with actual events described in the papers.* It appeared evident that the reasons for the discrepancies were that the actual reasons for decisions or descriptions of actual events *were not available in secondary sources.*

  A recent article by Henry Fairlie in the December 7, 1980, Washington *Post* referred to a similar incident where an academic was giving a paper on happenings in the Nixon Administration. The people in the audience who were in Washington, D.C., at the time did not remember it that way. The paper given was too "orderly" and it force-fit the reality into an unrealistic political theory.

  Checking to see whether such findings would hold for other areas beside the environment would be a subject for some interesting research. For the moment, let me merely note that much of the development and refinement of the techniques used in the analysis of policy issues is done by academicians and researchers who usually must rely on secondary sources for information on the situation and on the institutional and organizational framework in which policies are made. If the understanding they have of the policy milieu comes from incomplete or inaccurate descriptions, how can the techniques they develop and refine be useful to policy a. .lyses? The scientific method requires continual observation and reporting of phenomena and the development of theories from such observations. If the observations are flawed or skewed, the theory developed from them is sure to be. Hence, the models and techniques built from these theories are bound to be inaccurate also. The resulting predictions, based on flawed theory and techniques, may reflect the work of the descriptions, but not reality.

- The primary issue addressed by the workshop in Savannah, entitled National Ecological Assessment Workshop, was how to do non-site-specific assessments which could be used for technology analyses of broad energy and environmental policies. It was attended by several highly qualified ecologists who spent most of the time at the workshops cataloging the issues and building taxonomies for broader-based assessments. It became clear as the workshop progressed that the questions posed by the workshop were somewhat alien to the way these scientists had been trained to think. There was evident discomfort at providing information which was relatively "inaccurate," in that it had not been exhaustively studied in a carefully controlled situation (was not "scientific") or was not site-specific in nature. "Average" coefficients, even for screening purposes, were suspect. Further, there really were no methods or data bases available to carry out such assessments, although some beginnings could be made. *In short, it was clear that nobody present at the workshop appeared to have really thought extensively of questions in this top-down fashion before and their science did not really prepare them for such analyses.* Yet such assessments are certainly needed to carry out public policy analyses. Thus, although the ecologist has provided yeoman service to the environmental community in his inputs to environmental impact statements, his contribution to such wide-reaching issues as acid rain may tend to be anecdotal.

- The third workshop, National-Regional Energy-Environmental Modeling Concepts, was held in Reston, Virginia. The purpose was to look at the competing perceptions of top-down and bottom-up modeling with an eye toward melding the techniques. The workshop had invited participants from both modeling camps who discussed their experiences with their pet techniques. The working sessions then went on to look at questions of cost, feasibility, and other such matters.

In general, the workshop concluded that one method was not better than another, and that clearly both were needed. This was to be accomplished by creating a family of linked models. *What was more interesting, however, was the failure of the participants to recognize or address such questions as why such a family of models hadn't been built already, if built, where it would be housed, and what it would be used for.*

In summary, no definitive conclusion can reasonably be drawn from these workshops. The findings we have noted were secondary and not really a part of the purpose of the workshops as planned. Had such been the purpose, a workshop series might have been designed with this in mind and a series of testable hypotheses presented. Further, none of the findings, even of these individual studies, can be spoken of as anything but suggestive. Even so, these partial and haphazard findings are interesting.

The Integrated Assessment conference suggests that there is serious reason to question the whole basis on which our policy analysis tools are constructed: to the extent that secondary sources are the bases for hypothesis-building about how the public sector works, they are very likely to be incorrect. The modeling conference suggested that when technicians get together, they can agree on what really should be done to put together a first-rate analytic capability, but they fail to adequately address questions of how to go from concepts to reality and why such ideal schemes are not in place today. Finally, the ecology workshop suggested that even when there is a stated need for information from the science community, unless the question is asked in a fashion which will allow them to use information readily available, or unless it is possible to transfer a methodology from another field to organize the information in an acceptable fashion, the science community, even when it wants to help, is often inadequate to the task.

They are pretty gloomy insights. One hopes that reality is not as bad as I have portrayed. Possibly the findings might either have been aberrations because of the questions asked in the workshops, or the result of frustrations of the people invited, or some other factors. Or this present analysis is invalid and overdrawn. As I noted above, the workshops were not designed to test the questions posed in this section, so a charge of drawing specious conclusions from this sample could be valid. On the other hand, I would argue that the impressions gathered from these meetings were shared by several people, suggesting that maybe there is something here after all. Certainly the implications relative to bases of public policy analyses are so important that research in this direction should be initiated. Part of my training as an analyst always tells me to look back once in a while to check the adequacy of the emperor's raiments, and the time has come to do a wardrobe check.

Impedence Mismatches

- What if the sciences look at problems in a fashion that is ill-suited for use in decisionmaking?
- What if there is some evidence that there is a mismatch between theory and reality?

PEOPLE AND PERSPECTIVES

What constitutes public policy analysis, who should carry it out, and how it should be done is not universally agreed upon. One of the sources of such confusion is the technical training and organizational bias of the parties discussing the requirements. The following table, taken from a recent book by Stuart Nagel, illustrates this point.[7]

This table characterizes some selected perspectives of five groups: the scientist, the professional analyst, politician, administrator, and individual. Each of these stylized groups has a legitimate perspective of how the world does (or at least ought to) work. The scientist might approach a policy issue as a question among a very long list of questions which must be addressed in the never-ending search for truth. The analyst sees the policy issue as a challenge to his skills and an opportunity to apply the techniques of his trade. The political, administrative, and individual perspectives are apt to see the issue in terms of advocacy or efficiency, or in terms of its impact on the quality of life. Each of these perspectives are clearly legitimate and each group has developed more or less formal techniques and paradigms for dealing with the world and its issues with such a perspective. Each has its own logic, its own jargon, and, based on the goals of its organization, its own legitimization. Although it might be unlikely that those in one school would agree to the formal logic and techniques used by another (lawyers and statisticians, for example), there is a need to recognize at least that the techniques are proper for the purposes espoused. Let me go into a couple of these descriptions a bit further.

THE SCIENCE AND POLICY ASSESSMENT PARADIGMS

I shall describe the two sectors of science and assessment as polar extremes. The purpose of these descriptions will be to see the extent that they agree or disagree. At the outset I shall make no claim that these descriptions are exhaustive. For our purposes, it is not necessary that they

TABLE 1.1

Type of Policy Analyst	Public Policy Problem	Motivation	Approach	Relevant Training
1. Scientist	Theoretic	Search for theory, regularities, "truth"	Scientific method, objectivity, pure analysics	Basic research mehtods, canons of social science research
2. Professional	Design	Improvement of policy and policymaking	Utilization of knowledge, strategic	Strategic; benefit-cost analysis; queueing, simulation, decision analysis
3. Political	Value maximization	Advocacy of policy position	Rhetoric	Gathering "useful" evidence; "effective" presentation
4. Administrative	Application	Effective and efficient policy implementation	Strategic, managerial	Strategic; same as professional with stress on those talents useful in implementation
5. Personal	Contention	Concern for policy impacts on life	Mixed	Use of many models and techniques from other approaches; sophisticated

be so. More importantly, a broader brush view is required to highlight the major underpinnings of these groups.

Throughout the so-called civilized world, to call one a *scientist* is to speak in honorific terms. Science is a fellowship to which these people belong, which is worldwide and crosses many discipline lines.

Tradition: There has been a fellowship among those who consider themselves scientists which has existed for hundreds of years and across several cultures. Examples and evidence of this tradition (or club, or fraternity) are abundant. One is the international institutes which have been set up around the world and are membered by representatives of all countries, generally regardless of the political postures of the parent country. In fact, it is often proclaimed that science is above politics. Capitalizing on this belief, former President Johnson, for example, approached the previous head of the Ford Foundation, McGeorge Bundy, and encouraged him to create such an international organization which would permit communication of nations (at that time, the United States and the Union of Soviet Socialist Republics) even when the political level was in formal disagreement. The resulting organization was the International Institute for Applied Systems Analysis in Laxenburg, Austria. Numerous other societies and similar specialized organizations exist as well.

Science has its own training grounds, called universities, where it inculcates its disciples with the beliefs of its tradition. In some lights, the teachers or professors in these institutions are priests and the students are the faithful. The purpose of these institutions is often to move the novitiates through the indoctrination process; through various stages the undergraduates become graduate students, receive doctorates, go on to postdoctoral posts, and return to the universities (or their sister institution, the research laboratories) to begin further indoctrination in the priesthood of science, culminating in the full professorship—the office of high priest of science.

There are several other examples of tradition. In addition to a training ground, there is a formalized club or society or lodge which is replicated in country after country. In America, the National Academy of Sciences is such a lodge. This group is supposed to be a collection of the intellectual graybeards of science who sit, not only as an honor society for those who have produced "good science," but as an advisory and oversight body which does quality control and acts as a mediation group.

Scientific method: Every principle-level textbook sets down the basic rules for carrying out a piece of scientific research. The technique is quite common-sensical and the model proceeds by steps that include:

- *Identifying the hypothesis:* This step defines the objective and points the entire investigation to a specific goal.
- *Gathering information relevant to the hypothesis:* This step requires the scientist to acquire definite information which reveals the possible effects of various factors upon the hypothesis. Identification of the relation of one variable to another is thus accomplished.
- *Acquiring preliminary observations of the hypothesis:* This step, using the knowledge gained in the previous step, establishes a tentative solution. It is this hypothesis which will be subsequently proved or disproved by means of "controlled" experimentation.

- *Conducting thorough investigation of current knowledge concerning the hypothesis:* All available pertinent information is examined.
- *Securing additional information from controlled experiments:* In many cases, available and current knowledge about the hypothesis is insufficient to confirm or disprove the tentative solution. Hence, additional data are required, to be obtained by means of controlled experiments.
- *Classifying data obtained and stating tentative solution:* Information pertaining to the problem is sorted and the interpretation of the data is delineated. In some cases, the tentative answer is easy to discern, while in other cases, it is extremely difficult. Inductive and deductive reasoning both come into play in this step.
- *Testing the tentative answer:* This is one of the most important steps in the scientific method. If the investigation has been thorough, the tentative answer should correctly and scientifically identify the hypothesis. The tentative answer, however, should be tested. This consists of actually trying out the answer under prescribed conditions and noting what results are obtained.
- *Making needed adjustments and revising answer:* As a result of previous steps, there will be cases where the tentative answer will require revision. The revised answer should be clearly stated and documented.

These rules are drummed into every budding scientist and are agreed upon as ideals or goals that every research project should use. Of course, it is admitted that the rules are often more honored in the presentation of the research results than in the process of doing the research per se. Further, they are more readily applicable to sciences like physics, which has a subject matter, inanimate and micro items, and less so in areas like zoology and epidemiology.

Peer review: In its purest form, science is able to be practiced by any individual trained in its rigors, regardless of whether the scientist is internationally recognized already or is just beginning his career. In other words, previous recognition or reputation should not be a factor in deciding whether results are accurate or not and should be excluded from any judgment of the merits of the argument. To accomplish this, papers are often referred to the professional journals and circulated without the author being identified.

Another type of peer review consists of reviews of programs of a specific group (or scientist) as opposed to a review of the findings of a specific project. Such reviews are usually done by a collection of recognized scientists who perform similar research. Finally, the design of new science efforts in specific areas is often done by bringing together groups of people under the aegis of organizations such as the National Academy of Sciences. These same groups might do program reviews also.

Peer reviews are made possible by the belief that there is a current body of knowledge agreed upon by all the "cognoscenti" in the field. The purpose of the peer review is to ensure that there is general agreement that the new information is truly an addition to the information base.

Agreed upon knowledge base: In general, within any particular subcategory of science there is a widely recognized and agreed upon core of knowledge, although this argument tends to be less solid as one moves toward the frontiers of knowledge. This body of knowledge is sufficiently well categorized so that students can feel reasonably comfortable in their ability to study the basics of a particular field of science almost anywhere in the world and to transfer to another location to continue their education. At some level, for instance the undergraduate, most people grounded in a science can be expected to have the same information available to them regardless of where it is taught. It is only in graduate school, where specialization and research are larger factors in the education process, that the homogenization of information can be thought of as being less certain.

This consistency in information allows great efficiency in transmitting additions to knowledge as, coupled with the peer review process discussed earlier, the base builds and shifts more or less uniformly everywhere.

Incremental change: The slow, deliberate pace suggested by the above features of science lead directly to the observation that change in what is "known" takes place slowly and incrementally. Seldom is it expected that one scientist (or even a group of scientists) will make a revolutionary breakthrough. Most of these are rewarded by Nobel Prizes in their fields (one or more are so honored a year). Many of the more recent leaps in scientific knowledge have been confirmatory in nature and have come to pass with the aid of impressive additions to the scientist's research kit bag in the form of technical hardware (electron microscopes, computers, and the like). In the main, though, most scientists at the working level zero-in on the same fairly specific items which they study, restudy, and check in order to ensure that their results will be judged additions to the knowledge base—hopefully new and necessarily accurate.

Replication: If the sciences are going to treat the information and the methods used to generate that information with care, then one of the obvious requirements to be placed on the end result is that anyone else trained in the sciences would be able to replicate the experiment.

All of these factors of the science model are related, in the sense that they tend to dehumanize the scientist. Flashes of brilliance are treated with suspicion in fields where almost everyone is very bright, and where care and rigor are important traits for the practitioner. In truth, the real world is not as neat or tidy as these principles suggest. In some fields, as we already noted, the principles would be more or less accurate. In others, less so. But most science managers and those who are responsible for funding research might agree that it would be difficult to fund research which did not at least pay lip service to formal scientific method, and if it were not performed by individuals or groups who belonged to and adhered to the general principles of a recognized scientific discipline. On the other hand, there is an equal consensus that is may be possible to reach results faster under a situation of different priorities by increasing the expenditure levels in an area and shifting the scientific resources being focused on a problem.

In summary, the average scientist is trained by his professor to be conservative. He is trained in formal logic and proceeds to "solve" a problem with the general feeling that he is to know "everything" about a specific issue before he is willing to say anything definitive about it. He expects to be in control of his analysis, from data to technique.

The *analyst,* to take off from where the above description ended, uses almost the reverse of this formal structure. He is given questions that must be answered and specializes in formulating these questions into issues that can be analyzed using existing data and information. (These are to be distinguished from the hypotheses of the scientist which are to be "tested" for correctness.) The analyst's job is to provide the best response to an issue, given available time and resources It is often more of an art than a science, in which the possible is separated from the unguessable in as expeditious a way as possible. To some extent the analyses address only a portion of the questions, and these portions are decided by available information and the situation in which the analysis is being done. In no way can this process be understood as a search for basic knowledge; rather it is a search for alternative responses to questions embedded in the context of the "current situation." In some respects, this type of situation parallels that of the engineer who is expected to do the best he can, given a specific time period and definite resources. As with the science paradigm, let us try and sketch some of the general features of the analysis model.

Tradition: The assessment of issues and policies is a relatively new discipline which has been derived to a large extent from cost-benefit analysis, systems analysis, and operations research. It has only been within the past two decades that professional training and societies relating to the assessment discipline have been formally organized and recognized. Since the issues with which the analyst must deal are closely tied to political and upper management decisionmaking, they are constantly changing in character and importance. The result is a lack of a universal knowledge base in specific areas which can be expanded as in science. Instead, methodology is the only common element in the assessment discipline. Often the limits of analysis and assessment are not recognized; the users frequently expect too much.

Methodology: The goal of the analyst is not "truth" per se, but a "good" analysis. The approach used in assessment is to break issues into their component parts for further examination. In doing so, the alternatives for resolving the issues are studied, and where possible the quantification of the issues' elements may be attempted. Often, data and information initially obtained by others (e.g., scientists) are used in the analysis. Some research, however, may be required to gain insights and to establish relationships not obvious in the assessment of a complex issue. In the assessment discipline, problems addressed are generally considered ill-defined and not well bounded. Much of the effort is often centered around merely delineating the issue in a way that enables some usable results to be obtained from the information at hand.

Timing: The policy analyst normally operates under a restrictive tyranny of time. The analyst refers to the situation in which "the policy window is open," meaning that the analyst is intellectually in favor of carrying out long-range research, thereby improving the quality of data bases and methods. The realities of life, however, often do not allow such a course of action. On issues worthy of attack, a policy decision will be made whether or not an analyst completes an analysis. An obvious and immutable rule for an effective policy group is that an analysis must be ready before the final decision has to be made.

Consequently, complex issues with little time for examination may get analyses whose reliability is open to question. Even so, these may be the best that could be performed under the circumstances. If an analysis is periodically revised because the policy issue resurfaces or similar issues come to the fore, or because a mandate requires periodic assessment (i.e., an annual report), analytical tools can be expected to lead to more reliable results, allow shorter turnaround time, and yield more comprehensive and sophisticated analyses.

The realities of public policy analysis mean that analysts must constantly deal with "brushfire" issues. The actual day-to-day job of the professional policy analyst consists of responding to crises—real or imagined—that are important to a policymaker. The response to most such crises are "pick and shovel" jobs, and often require little more than a telephone call or two to verify the situation, gather data, and then to prepare the informative paper or response. The highly sophisticated, technically demanding, event-shaping analyses so often discussed in the literature usually arise only a few times each year. But they appear often enough to challenge the more creative analysts who inhabit effective public policy shops.

Resources: The setting of national welfare eligibility criteria can hardly be expected to be analyzed with the same resources and fervor as the question of a revised budget for a minor government unit. Although this comparison is extreme, it does remind us that most public decisions could be considered as policy or as providing the basis for policy formulation. More sophisticated and complex methodologies and analyses are required for the more difficult policy decisions. The matching of issues and resources is often a difficult task, even for those experienced in analysis. Preliminary screening and consideration of analytical alternatives are usually examined before significant resources are devoted to an analysis.

Just as little time may be available for an analysis, so too the resources to carry it out are often characteristically limited. It might be hypothesized that the government should allocate resource levels that are appropriate to the value of the policy decision at hand. This could mean that millions of taxpayer dollars would be spent for, a public policy that would result in billions of dollars of expenditures. The vagaries of the political process, however, often make it difficult to allocate adequate resources to many such proposed policies. Spending large sums of money on every proposed policy that might potentially have sizable economic or social impact causes the further quandary of trying to guess which place to put these large resources. Obviously, all policies will not come to pass. Spending sizable sums on all of them means a very large budget expenditure, most of it on policies which will not see implementation. Further, the size of the staff required to manage such a budget and still do reasonable policy analysis is beyond the level of effort presently considered reasonable in most parts of the public sector.

Personnel: Probably the rarest commodity in analysis is talent—the talent to perform sophisticated, balanced, insightful analyses under extreme pressures and usually in a short time. Good analysts get to the heart of an issue quickly. Because of familiarity with general issues, they can relate a current issue to others in the policy stream at that moment. In addition to their technical skills and political sense, analysts rely to some extent on their share of luck, given the uncertainties of the political process. Whatever comprises the elusive components of (analytical) talent, policy analysts are difficult to find, to train, and to keep sufficiently challenged for long periods of time.

In the average policy shop, where the tasks are numerous and characteristically of high priority with short time fuses, there is usually an imbalance of jobs to be done and people to do them. In addition to the number of tasks that are assigned, a complicating factor is the variety of approaches required to dispense with the broad set of tasks that are covered in a policy shop over a course of time. A query may be handled by the analyst spending an hour writing a letter, another by a team of three or four analysts working full-time for several weeks. Generally there is no way to predict how many tasks or what level of effort will be required for analysis, both type and quantity, until an issue is presented and the policy climate in which it resides is examined.

Policy shops sometimes require the assistance of outside consultants to smooth out the surges of demand for information and analyses. Ideally, the policy staff continues to provide the basic analytical capability for addressing policy issues so that the general policy analysis expertise remains in-house. The credibility of a policy shop breaks down when it seems that the policy staff has contracted out much of its analysis. When the policy issue under discussion is particularly sensitive, having an analysis done by outside consultants becomes especially sensitive. If the in-house staff is not fully knowledgeable of the details of the analysis, then it may become necessary for the decisionmaker to invite others into the deliberations. The very least of the ramifications of being backed into such a corner is an increase in risk to his/her own political career. More importantly, the Congress, more and more in recent years, has taken a dim view toward the use of consultants for such purposes, insisting that policy analysis be done using existing in-house manpower.

Quality: Maintaining objectivity in the course of doing an analysis is a constant problem for policy staff. Ideally, civil servants approach their work with a high degree of objectivity, since they are expected to be impartial with respect to the public they serve. Therefore, public sector analysts attempt to be objective in the empirical aspects of their work, fully expecting that the decisionmaker, usually politically appointed, will factor into the decision the necessary political and other inputs. But objectivity for an organization person is often a subjective concept, as Rufus Miles and others have so aptly stated. Miles's Law states, "Where you stand depends on where you sit." It is his contention that no person can totally rise above his institutional perspectives and responsibilities when asked to perform in a statesmanlike fashion. This layering of perception as to what is "objective," "realistic," "possible," and so forth changes with the people involved, the situation, and the issue. Combined with the usual paucity of information, it is what makes policy analysis the art it is.

Clients: At least the form and often the content of a policy analysis is influenced greatly by the known or anticipated desires and demands of the decisionmaker for whom it is being prepared. This may have many manifestations. When the recipient perceives himself to be an expert in a partic-

ular area, analysts preparing policy papers for him sometimes find their
responsibilities changed from merely performing an analysis to participating in a professional environment which makes the use of the "appropriate" assumptions and recognition of the "proper" alternatives as important as the results themselves. In short, the form serves to be emphasized
as much as or more than the substance. Although such a situation might
result in better policy analyses being performed, it might just as easily
result in more elegance in the form of the analysis, which is not always
commensurate with the importance of the ultimate decision. Indeed,
elegance is a luxury analysts can ill afford in the time-pressured policy
area.

At the other extreme, there is the policymaker who is not familiar with
the technical aspects of the professional area in which the decisions are
required to be made. In these circumstances, policy papers have to be
made more detailed and sometimes more tutorial.

Then there is the decisionmaker who cares little for analysis and tends
to use policy analysts as general staff, including the job of post hoc
justification of preconceived policy decisions. Lastly, we should mention
the decisionmaker who has a tendency to "satisfice," to require sufficient
analysis to render a decision that is "good enough" for the momentary
situation. All of these stereotypical types are found in policy positions,
and all cause a policy shop to assume a particular presentation style when
briefing them on analysis results.

COMMUNICATIONS

Communication is fundamental in the policy-making process, yet it is
most apt to be relatively neglected as an important part in the staff
presentation of the analysis to the policymaker, who then must communicate the results to peers, superiors, and the public. Because, as we just
said, policymakers have different levels of training and skills and differ
widely in personality and motivation, they differ also in how they would
like information presented to them.

Policymaker and staff usually settle on the mode for presentation of
analytical results during the design phase of an analysis. The quality,
depth, and type of each analysis will depend on the specific mode of basic
communication (memo, letter, white paper, and so on). The policy staff
leadership or person responsible for presenting an analysis to a decisionmaker must have a clear understanding of what the analysis is about, the
approach and methods used, the quality of the data bases, and the realities
of the political climate in which the decision must be made. During the
presentation, questions and feedback from the decisionmaker should be

answered directly in the context of the analysis performed. Ideally, the decisionmaker will have been involved in the analysis throughout its performance. As we shall note here, this is usually not the case, so that many analyses are only seen at the policy level when first asked for and when being briefed as a finished product. Consequently, the written form of the presentation of the analyses has to be heavily augmented by the verbal presentation (with attendant visuals), and by the open give-and-take questioning and responding of the analyst and policymaker.

In summary, it is clear that the two groups, the analysts and the scientists, have very different backgrounds and responses to their respective agendas. Given these differences, there is no reason to suppose that the information being developed in the science area is available to or is understood by those in the analysis field. At the same time, there is also no reason to suppose that the scientist would necessarily understand what information, or even what *form* of information, is required by the analyst. The discussion presented above addresses the manner in which each of these professions really looks at the job they have to do. Some scientists would look upon analysts as intellectually inferior, doing slapdash work. On the other hand, the ivory-tower fable is well-known as the counter-pejorative slur. What I have tried to show is that these perceptions are a function of the professions and are as apt to act as barriers to effective communication and decisionmaking as any other difference in language or attitude might.

There are other areas in which mismatches could occur. One of the most common is between the perspective of those who develop or improve or teach analytic techniques and that of those who use them. Frequently, the nonuser groups come up with techniques which are conceptually appealing but impossible to implement. Or perhaps their arguments are couched in normative terms. The user group, responding to different audiences and pressures, often finds such techniques too elegant or unrealistic for operations. We shall return to this theme again and again from several perspectives, but will elaborate on the mismatch aspect here.

REALITY VERSUS THEORY

There are several possible examples of situations where the analyst might like to present or study a subject in a fashion which, for one reason or another, is inappropriate for real-world application. The example chosen here is the current interest in risk analysis. But similar technique-driven examples are possible and will be addressed in later chapters. We shall also return to the subject of risk analysis in more detail and from a different perspective.

ANALYST'S POSITION

There is a clearly recognizable school of thought which holds that some information is better than no information at all.[8] There are other researchers, however, who would maintain that if the state-of-the-art of such fields as risk analysis, particularly when applied to the area of energy-environment trade-offs, is not sufficiently mature to speak definitively about the mortality and morbidity impacts of a policy, then it is an open question whether anything should be said at all. In short, a little knowledge may very well be a dangerous thing.

Control standards were set to produce a level of environmental pollution, especially in the air media, that minimized public health dangers. This was done by pulling together all of the information available about the health effects of some six pollutants, and then setting the threshold for each at a level which was deemed to be politically feasible and scientifically reasonable. Because of the way the law was written, there was no discussion of whether a variable standard could or should be set or whether, in making the decision, it would be possible to construct a damage function which relates pollution load to morbidity/mortality levels. As a matter of fact, few such damage functions exist,[9] and even these are the subject of considerable controversy.

The technique of determining pollution generated by a process or a combination of processes is really straightforward. A given amount of physical (or economic) activity is measured or postulated. This activity is expected to produce a certain amount of useful product and generate a given amount of waste (pollution). Some percentage of this waste may be captured (controlled) before it reaches the environment; the rest is released. The released amount provides an exposure level of the surrounding population and environment. These exposures are often reported using such measures as population-at-risk. This exposure measure is then related by a damage function to allow translation to mortality/morbidity figures. As an analyst moves from the beginning of the procedure described above to the end, he deals with less and less certainty as to actual relationships and quality of data. In fact, at the tail end of this process, there is some question as to whether the information generated is of any statistical value at all. Here, then, is a proverbial case of producing heat without light.

BASIC ASSUMPTIONS

One of the most widely used definitions of risk incorporates the notion of probability of an event occurring and the magnitude of the event. Risk is then characterized by the shape of the probability distribution of an occurrence plus the amount of damages associated with each specific occurrence. The exact functional form for the risk equation can be quite varied, but the most frequently used form is to assume that risk equals probability of occurrence times expected damage; or overstated, risk is equivalent to the mathematical expectation of damage. This assumption is made because it is more easily handled than more complicated (though perhaps more accurate) mathematical forms. Most importantly, perhaps, is that it has the implied assumption of risk neutrality on the part of the assessed agents. This means that those to whom the damage may occur are indifferent between positive and negative outcomes with the same expected values. However, public reactions to risky situations have frequently been of the type that demonstrates that this is an invalid assumption.

Questions of the correct functional form for the risk equation aside, there are still major problems in developing probability and damage estimates. These problems are associated with both data requirements and the logic of estimate derivations. Sometimes estimates of probability can be objectively derived, but more often they must be subjectively determined. Objective probability distributions are developed from data generated in experiments or "real-life" phenomena. Rigorous rules for data acceptability and manipulation have been developed by statisticians. Those rules require certain conditions to hold for a random sample or for selection of a control group. Frequently these rigorous rules cannot be met in analysis performed for government decisionmaking. Perhaps the most prevalent problem is lack of an adequate sample size or the nonexistence of a comparable situation to be monitored. Much of DOE analysis involves considerations of emerging technologies for which commercial size facilities have not been constructed. No observations therefore exist! In other cases the sample sizes are very low. The smaller sample sizes have increased degrees of freedom (i.e., unknown relationships) which reduce their applicability and their credence, causing the relationship between statistical correlation and actual causality to become strained in many of these cases.

When rigorous rules for data cannot be met, some have recommended subjectively determining probability distributions. Survey research techniques are used to assess an "expert's" judgment concerning the probability of an event occurring. The argument for such a technique is that with no or little objective information, an expert's opinion is better than nothing. This has intuitive appeal, but several problems limit its application. Expert judgment should not be viewed as an accurate reflection of an absolute probability distribution. At best, it is opinion on relative probability that could prove useful. In other words, if an expert says the probability of a nuclear accident is .9, we should take little confidence in that judgment. If, however, he says an accident of a certain magnitude is twice as likely as another event, then the judgment is more credible--whether it is correct or not.

A second difficulty with use of experts concerns aggregation or comparison of expert probability distributions. One need look no further than the nuclear debate to find an example of experts of goodwill with very diverse but legitimate opinions. How are their opinions to be compared or combined? Certain techniques like Delphi[10] aid in the combinatorial process, but the sophistication inherent in the technique can strain the system's ability to communicate the user's meaning to decisionmakers or the public. Further, there is even some question as to the legitimacy of the technique among the professional community. Only in specific, limited circumstances does such a technique prove useful and credible.

The other major weakness in using risk analysis involves data problems for estimating damage. Basically, what is required is an estimate of people's willingness to pay to preclude an event's occurrence. In those cases where the activity being purchased is also traded in markets, one's confidence in the estimate may be adequate. If, however, as is usually the case, there is not an analogous market transaction, then analytical techniques must be used which estimate value as if the activity were traded in markets. Less confidence can be given in such cases, since the observations are synthetic. Data problems, in addition to fundamental structural questions, arise with such techniques. An example of the latter is the meaning of value estimates about things not usually purchased; for instance, the value of another day of rain.

Finally, we ask: how good are the estimates or even the guesses as to the form of a statistical function when the extrapolations are based on a handful or less of data points? There are actual cases where the expected level (say 50,000) is caveated as having a level of variation that could be as low as 0 (no effect) or as high as 200,000 (4 times the expected effect). These numbers are associated with predicted increases in premature deaths. The public policy maker must decide a strategy after being told that the decision made may have no impact or might shorten the lives of a number of citizens greater than one-half the population of Wyoming; the policymaker might have some misgivings as to the utility of such analyses.

In addition to the types of problems with risk analysis articulated above, there are perspective problems. Introducing stochastic analysis into policymaking implicitly implies a changed perspective about how outcomes of actions are to be judged. Culturally, we have tended to judge people on performance (outcomes). But in stochastic analysis, it is clear that an act may quite rationally be expected to result in an adverse outcome. Hence, the implied criterion for evaluating decisionmakers is the way they make the decision, not the outcome. This may be a change of perspective too difficult for the public to accept.

WHY LOOK AT RISK AT ALL?

It is clear that little can be done, given the data sources, about health effects of economic activities on human populations. A recent thought-provoking paper questions the whole paradigm which has evolved and which has as its root the reduction of risk for the lowest level possible.[11] In summary, it says an attempt to spend greater and greater amounts of the Gross National Product to reduce the level of risk in society (because risk prevention is assumed to be nonproductive in an economic sense) will mean that there will be fewer resources available for anything else. This practice is, in the long run, counterproductive. Our society is the safest society (relatively speaking) in recorded history. We are relatively safe because we are so rich. These riches allow us to produce more of everything, which permits surpluses, redundancy, diversity, and in the ecologist's terms, greater resiliency. The presence of resiliency in the system permits adaptation to adversity and thereby results in a safe society.

I personally find the argument compelling. Added to the thesis of this work, that the state-of-the-art of risk analysis is so primitive as to actually result in a disservice when its results are introduced into the emotionally sensitive world of political policy, there is some question as to why there is any interest in pursuing questions of risk at all. One part of the answer is a standard scientific one; it is studied because it is there. But the question continues to be of a more immediate and practical nature: how does one bring the issue of risk into the policy arena? How does one move from the relatively straightforward question of risk and a single policy area to the trade-off questions posed by relative risks of competing policies across policy arenas?

The challenge exists. It remains for those who propose risk analysis not only to improve their art, but to convince the public and the policymaker that talking in terms of people killed, maimed, or incapacitated really adds to the decision process; a clear case of where theory and technique clash with political reality. Let us go on to some other questions.

Decision Realities

- What if there is a perception of decisionmaking capability which is considerably more comprehensive and much more in-depth than is really possible?
- What if the types of decisions to be made are fundamentally different than the analysts and technique-builders realize?

- What if very little of the decisionmaking process is in any way "strategic"?

One of the features of systems analysis at which I have heard policy-makers and their staffs laugh the loudest is the popular impression of how the policy formulation process works. There seem to be several myths surrounding the process. For example, there is a feeling that the analyst merely has to query the decisionmaker for what is to be done, then do the requisite analysis to make clear what the best choice should be, and the decisionmaker will follow the advice. After all, most workdays for political level appointees consist of a full day of meetings, and many of these require them to make one or more decisions. In the vast majority of the cases the decisionmaker has no previously held opinion, so most of the time he will trust the judgment of a principal advisor.

Another myth is an assumption that the so-called decisionmaker is operating much like a monarch, with considerable power at his disposal. In fact, not only information restrictions (and the lack of time and resources to improve the information), but realities of politics, positions relative to other goals, and other situational and climatic factors may set limits to the possible decision space.

Still another myth seems to be a carry-over of the child's misconception that all decisions made by "big people" are important. In reality, of course, this is not the case. Clearly, every decision made by the policy level is not destined for national attention either. In fact, for most, the number of such significant cases that they lead or to which they have an input is likely to be less than half a dozen during their career. For some, none ever reach this proportion. Most decisions are small, incremental, and rely heavily on inputs from past decisions on similar topics.

The term "strategic" is not one which is as universally understood as one might imagine. It is clearly different depending on where one is doing the strategic planning or analysis. A hierarchy starting with the world and progressing through the United States, the Executive Branch, the Department of Energy, the Assistant Secretary for the Environment, the Office of Environmental Assessments, the Technology Assessments Division, and the Renewable Resources Branch would clearly result in the production of a different strategic level plan. In fact, to some extent the nesting just presented allows the strategic level plans of one group to become a part of the tactical level plans of another.

A quote from a recent symposium of Assistant Secretaries makes the point:

The brand of rational, all-encompassing strategic planning that most academics tend to discuss when they consider the generic problems of policy making and the policy process is not what the assistant secretary is concerned with. Most of the assistant secretaries who participated in the FEI symposium made it very clear that they are involved in day-to-day crises and, consequently, they have very little time to think about—let alone deal with—the "big picture." On the day-to-day level, the tangibles drive out the intangibles of the policy making process; most assistant secretaries deal with short-term needs rather than long-term needs or strategic analyses.[12]

For our purposes, the delicate semantic argument as to what is strategic and what is tactical can be left to those who get their jollies building and filling taxonomies. What we can say, though, is that it is clear that some form of strategic planning goes on at all levels, and that there is nothing special about such a practice. Further, the grandiose nature of such cognition suggested by the term (probably coming from the popularized discussion of the military generals doing strategic plans) falls far short of the mundane day-to-day practice of public sector management.

Reference to the long-range plans produced in the public sector would quickly show that as a group, they are written very generally and are really not useful as operational documents at all. Such documents are found in both the private and public sectors. They are the annual reports of the corporations, public documents which are not really taken seriously by the line troops who have to run the system, and that are seen (and usually produced) as sales rather than operational pieces.

In summary, the very sophisticated tools developed for use in strategic decisions are not needed or appropriate for the majority of decisions that must be made in the policy arena. If there is a belief that formalism will of necessity improve the quality of decisions, then it will have to be demonstrated that this information fits the needs, constraints, and requirements of the using decisionmaker, not just the design rules of a model or technique developer.

The "Decisionmaker"

- What if the decisions made by the policymakers are logical and analytical already, but that they require other assumptions and givens than the system analysis proposes? Further, are they apt to be compartmentalized?
- What if there is really no "big" policymaker, if everything (when placed in perspective) is not much of a change?
- What happens if "decisionmakers" really do not "make" decisions, but merely ratify them? If true, who really makes decisions?

- What has happened to real-world decisionmaking since analytically trained decisionmakers (or advisors) have been in place? Has decisionmaking become more "rational"?

The role of the decisionmaker in the public sector is surrounded by folklore. At times it appears that the tales are actually believed both by those who observe the practices from outside the system, and unfortunately, by some who are active in the policy roles. Professionals who are concerned that decisions should be more analytical are convinced that they understand enough about how decisions are made to want more rigorous inputs, based on the belief that such structure would improve the ultimate product. The more radical of these proponents wish substantial replacement of the present-day method of policymaking by computer-based models. But such models have the benefit, regardless of how complex, of being able to be explicitly specified, and decisions can be tested and modified time after time until some desired end is realized. The real problem comes to the fore when one realizes that somebody has to make explicit what a "desired end" might be. The more such an outcome can be stated exactly and the more the requirements for getting these are known, the more likely that formal models can help. Optimization models is a branch of modelling which is designed specifically to accomplish this end.

There is clearly a limit to the amount of definition which can be done for most public policy issues. In many instances there is a need to get input in terms of the desires of the voters. Often this input varies by such factors as location, age, sex, race, time, and so forth. An opinion poll could be used to gather such information, but it would have to be running at the time and cover such a variety of issues that, even if some way could be technically devised to carried it out, it would be so time-consuming and onerous to the public that it would surely fail. The alternative to such madness is a form of representation where individuals are put in (and removed from) decisionmaking positions to make policy and choices in the name of the rest of society. These individuals are expected to balance alternatives and make trade-offs among competing opportunities to secure the maximum possible public benefit. It is their knowledge of the populace, buttressed by analysis and situational factors, which permits a relatively smoothly functioning decision process.

But is it rational? Clearly, on a day-to-day basis, with situations changing and with current and proposed decisions impacting on each other, the knowledge, skill, and judgment of individuals is all that can really be pragmatically depended upon to balance the myriad of factors necessary. No computer-based system in use today or envisioned in the near future would come even close to handling the information load. Added to this, the difficulty of validating, maintaining, and applying a formal system makes the alternative hopeless. The logic used by lawyers, musicians, and poets is different from that of the mathematician, but it is no less formal. Good politicians, who are generally agreed to be doing a successful job in the service of the public, also operate with a logic that permits their repeated success. The fact that the decisions made cannot be put on a computer or reduced to a series of equations does not, in and of itself, demonstrate that the decisions made were not the "best" ones, or that using formal computer models would have made them better. The mere fact that the decisions made satisfied enough of the constituency to allow the decisionmaker to make more policy attests to his success in factoring the relevant factors (quantifiable and qualitative) into the decision process.

One final point should be made here. With all the input required to make a good decision, and with the range of decisions which have to be made each day, the only way such a process could work over time is for individuals to handle each decision more or less in a vacuum or behind separate partitions. This doesn't mean that there is no awareness of the actual or potential cross-impacts of decisions, but merely that some will become background to others while a specific issue is being addressed.

The political appointee soon learns the lesson of President Eisenhower. President Truman commented before he left the White House in 1952 concerning Eisenhower as President:[13]

> He'll sit here . . . and he'll say, "Do this! Do that!" *And nothing will happen.* Poor Ike—it won't be a bit like the Army. He'll find it very frustrating.

Nobody seems to have enough power to make a decision that makes a real difference. Because, as Commoner put it, everything is related to everything else; everybody seems to have to be advised before any decision is made. Energy policy is related to economic policy, to environmental policy, to international policy, to labor policy, to health policy, to transportation policy, and many more. Each policy area has a differing constituency and agenda. Each sees the other as subservient to its goals, and indeed, may see other policies as competitive. This means that for decisions which may have a broad impact, several groups may have interest, and may further feel that they legitimately have some say over the results.

To gain some control over the candidate decision, the scope of the decision, even if it seems to fall in one general area, becomes harder and harder. Looking at energy, many of the pieces that appeared in the popular press and professional journals were concerned with global strategies for reducing our dependence on foreign oil. But it is clear that nobody had enough power to unilaterally implement the policies suggested in these pieces. To the extent that all the projects had to be implemented at once, no implementation strategy exists to create a synergistic effect from their multiple adoption—hence no such analysis was ever presented. The comprehensive, big picture strategy tools used solution situations that nobody could bring about, while the less exciting, but necessary, step-by-step means to carry out the programs that would accomplish the suggested goals were sluffed over. Strategies suggest that everything will change dramatically and at once. In fact, it is not so much that everything is incremental by choice; it is just that the whole panoply of decisions that have to be made, when looked at from a national or global perspective or when reoriented in time from the immediate and routine to a different and longer-range perspective, resets the policy structure to a much broader context, and we consequently find its ability to make decisions to be relatively small in comparison to the job to be done.

It would be frightening to think of a society where all the decisions being made in the public sector would be so significant that each would be considered "major." Such a situation would suggest a highly unstable, wartime or revolutionary system, and one which was not destined to be around long. Functioning systems by definition are relatively stable and only require a minimum of mid-course correction from time to time. Although any one of the numerous decisions might appear monumental to those involved, it is certain that such decisions are, in the scheme of things, almost pro forma. To the extent that relatively few of the decisions being made are significant, the rest of the admittedly busy days at the policy level must be taken up with decisions which are not so earth-shattering.

The myth of the policymaker constantly involved in making one strategic decision after another leads easily into an allied myth, that of the existence of "the" decisionmaker.

Another pitfall associated with implementation is the 'myth' that there is a unique decisionmaker. Analyses are ordinarily designed and carried out, although perhaps not always deliberately, as if they were to assist a solitary decisionmaker who had full authority over acceptance and implementation.[14]

How often have you heard the comment that a study was being done or a technique perfected for a "decisionmaker"? To those who participate actively in policy analyses at the federal level, there is some question as to whether the monarchical or powerful individual paradigm is operable. Even in situations where it could be, if such power were exercised too often, it would cost an organization dearly in terms of morale. In truth, most policymakers are in control of large staffs who make a career of performing analyses. These people and others also manage contracts of people who perform analysis or do background studies. This very large amount of analysis effort filters its way (or at least part of it) to the full-time staff which has the responsibility of formulating issues for a final decision. It is hard to believe that the members of this large, formalized structure would like a policymaker who consistently ignored their input or habitually "shot from the hip." Let's look at how a typical issue might normally be handled by a policy analysis group.

Although a policy issue can originate almost anywhere—in the news media, from public interest groups, business, the Congress, the courts, or elsewhere in the Executive Branch—I want to focus on that type of policy issue which begins with or is specified by an Assistant Secretary and is passed down to the troops for analysis. Let us assume that the requirements pass through a normal chain of command to an individual analyst who is two to five levels down in the management chain from the Assistant Secretary. The request for analysis is received and several things take place. The analyst might do the job himself, farm it out to a consultant, or both. In any case, a process begins which defines the scope of the issue to be analyzed (including whatever guidance is received from the management levels above the analyst); an information base is sought, and a method for analysis is chosen. The detailed analysis will be done within the confines of the resources and information available and the skill of the analyst/consultant(s). In the end, an issue, option, or decision paper is produced which may or may not be exactly what the person seeking help with the issue hoped for. The paper begins its way up the chain of command and may or may not be modified and altered depending upon several organizational, personality, and situational factors. By the time it gets to the level which requires it to make a decision, there is usually little time left before the decision has to be made, and the policymaker has little choice but to ratify the results of the analysis or to somehow refute the findings altogether.

Because of the recognition, the Assistant Secretary symposium referred to earlier suggested that structures be set up to ensure that the information they need is forthcoming by making their guidance available to the analysts.

And yet, frequently, policy is being made around us and even much below us. In fact, we may sit up there thinking that we are making policy, while the policy is being made by a GS-15 or a GS-13. So really, an assistant secretary has to develop a structure to assure that he will receive the type of input he needs to have in order for him to make policy.[15]

In addition to the time constraint which does not allow a decision-maker to require a redoing of a particular piece of analysis, it is reasonable to assume that not all persons in the policy position will be technically qualified in all aspects of the area over which they have jurisdiction. Consequently, the details have to be handled by someone who is so qualified. In an attempt to overcome this deficiency, before an actual decision is made the principal may be briefed to the level it takes to enable a thoughtful choice among the proposed policy alternatives. To the extent that time pressures or lack of interest (or capability) intrude, these briefings may or may not take place. It is not inconceivable that there could be a technical knowledge gap so extensive that no practical amount of briefings are possible. Further, the principal may, because of personal reasons, choose not to be totally informed about specific policy issues, instead letting the decisions really be made a level or two below and merely ratifying them. (Lord Nelson sometimes put his telescope up to his blind eye.) The test of correctness in terms of whether the actions suggested were appropriate then becomes one of seeing if the policy options survive the levels above the nominal decisionmaker if there is a need for higher level ratification, and/or in the public arena if the options are to go into immediate implementation. If the options survive these tests, then the policy analysis (and the analyst) will be trusted the next time. If not, alternate forms of analytic support will be sought or possibly ignored altogether.

This latter course of action is especially difficult for the appointed policymaker when most of the policy support comes from the Civil Service. Compared to the private sector, there are relatively limited choices open to political appointees who want to switch a significant percentage of the people working for them. Civil Service regulations make wholesale personnel shifts as difficult as mass hirings.

> I cannot emphasize enough that although the term decisionmaker is often used in a way that visions of Zeus or Solomon are produced, these people are humans. They bring to the job a whole series of factors tied up with this humanness, their personality, biases, skills, knowledge, and the like. At the same time, these people have or affect a considerable value structure. Some of these are tied to the political structure that got them the position, others to the organization they serve and manage, and some to the values they hold. Included in these are ideological and policy values that shape their perspective of the public interest they have sworn to serve.[16]

In sum, the institutionalized process of the public sector bureaucracy, plus the personality and situational realities of the decisionmaker's job, make it apparent that there is little basis to the myth that individuals who accept political appointee positions have any real opportunity to gain sufficient control over their own environment to have sustained or significant policy presence. This reality (which clearly has been disproved in certain specific cases) is not normally perceived by those who take the political appointee positions, nor by the constituencies who fight to get them there. It is enlightening for one to talk to a sampling of these people both before and after they have served in office. Although most experience the feeling of power, few know real influence, and almost none to the level that they thought they needed or expected to have.

Finally, we shall turn to a set of questions which examines another dimension of reality. Since the late Fifties and early Sixties, there have been more and more people who are trained in the fields of operations research, systems analysis, and allied areas filling the ranks of the Civil Service. In fact, it is difficult to imagine how one could get a job today in a policy analysis shop without demonstrating some skill in one or more of these disciplines. Further, the members of the Senior Executive Service of the Civil Service, who have the ultimate responsibility for these analyses, are also normally trained in these analytic skills and are aware of what techniques are available and when they should be applied. In general, at all levels of the policy analysis chain, from the civil service manager to the analyst to the consultants who support them, there is increasing awareness of and facility with sophisticated analytic techniques. The question is:

Given this ability and sensitivity on the part of the professionals, has decisionmaking become any more "rational"? The answer is: Probably not.

The reasons for this are several. In the first place, the essence of policy analysis is that a decision has to be made which is out of the ordinary. Policy means a new problem or a deviation from the presently institutionalized way of doing things. Often, this feature of policy means that information is not apt to be readily available to perform a technically adequate analysis. It may also be the case that several of the things which are candidates for analysis are not amenable to empirical treatment.

One of the features of analysis which is often forgotten is that competent analysts who are in a particular position for a long time gain experience which often allows them to estimate or interpolate a response to a question without the necessity of going through a detailed or sophisticated problem-solving exercise. Very often these "back of the envelope" calculations are all that is required and, for some issues, all that is available. In such instances, there is some question as to whether the quick and dirty analysis buttressed by experience and ability is any better than the information produced by those not so well trained in analytic techniques but rich in practical experience (say, some politicians). In the end, however, it is certain that few if any significant decisions can be said to be solely the product of an analytic exercise—even with wall-to-wall trained analysts as participants. Possibly the fact that they have the training has made them aware of the weaknesses which have reduced the reliance on such techniques. On the other hand, experience has to be supported by analysis. This work is an attempt to find how this balance of practical experience and common sense can be melded with formal, analytical techniques.

The Underlying Rationale

Following is a series of questions which might be thought of as relating to primal assumptions as to how the decision system operates.

- What if partial versus comprehensive, incremental versus holistic, are the wrong perspectives for policy questions?
- What if the tools and techniques being developed are not really aimed at real decisionmakers?
- What if "some information" is not always better than "none at all"?

There has been a running battle, exacerbated by the environmental movement of the early Seventies and the "General Plan" thrust of the Sixties, between those who do and those who do not feel that in order to make responsible decisions, one has to take everything into account. The ecologist's web-of-life concept and the tale of the loss of a horseshoe nail leading to the loss of a kingdom are constant reminders of how decisions may be disabled when placed in a context, and that this context should be as broad as possible. On the other hand, there are those who take the directly opposite perspective. It is better to know a lot about a little than a little about a lot is the logic behind this school of thought. It is probably better, however, to know a lot about a lot. Unfortunately, scientific study and training is so structured that it is more natural for an individual or a team to zero-in on particular topics. Further, there is little call to handle global questions at the federal policy level. In fact, such perspectives are usually assigned to undergraduate or survey courses—hardly the domain of the aspiring professional.

Those who decide to specialize in comprehensive analysis are apt to be less respected than others in their discipline fields. Only a few very good scientists have been able to transcend a single discipline successfully, as attempts to do so are treated with the strictest sanctions. Both physical and life scientists are trained, as we have discussed earlier, in the so-called scientific method, which among other things requires problems to be attacked from the bottom up. Subjects are decomposed to the smallest possible units and then studied intensively. Wherever feasible, several case studies are carried out by different researchers. After these investigations are complete, one is permitted to integrate across the findings of these numerous individual studies to create a general theory. To proceed in any other fashion is to invite the affirmation that one has spun a theory out of whole cloth.

The logic that supports the physical sciences is not easily transferable to the social or policy sciences. The physical sciences already have hypothetical general or natural laws that seem to govern our existence and describe the universe. The partial-analysis technique of science is used to explicitly demonstrate a fact that fits nicely into a mosaic already understood. It is only when one of the partial studies concludes something that does not map onto the general hypotheses of the sciences that the partial studies begin to cause the assumed general-system paradigm (a natural law) to change. In order to systematically carry out this type of analysis, physical scientists have imposed great rigor on their experimental methods, allowing them to replicate and completely document the results. Thus it is possible for them to explain their findings to any of their colleagues throughout the world, and thereby to multiply the scientific effort, since they may avoid starting as if no one else were in the field.

Although the above description is idealized, the social and policy sciences have nothing resembling this model. Rather than speak of the model of the social and policy fields of science, it might be more accurate to call much of the work of these fields as "structured opinion." Because no one can prove himself correct and because few theoretical or descriptive works appear to hold true for very long or for all cases, there is much pious talk of legitimate duplication of effort or attempts to refute earlier work. There must be at least a dozen or more econometric models of the national economy that are essentially the same, for example, but supporters of each stress the superiority of their system over the others. Each talks of the need to improve their own work. Seldom are serious suggestions made to conform the efforts and phase some of them out. Some of our social scientists have apparently chosen not to follow the research rules (scientific methods) of their colleagues in the physical and life sciences. They seem to have selected paradigms instead that make them resemble the automotive, soap, or cigarette industries where emphasis is on market control through real or imagined product differentiation.

HOLISTIC AND COMPREHENSIVE

The existence of holism comes to the fore when one attempts to measure that elusive notion, often gestured toward by the politicians, of the Quality of Life (QOL). A recent book by Baumol and Oates, titled *Economics, Environmental Policy and the Quality of Life,*[17] suggests that we, as a nation, devise a new super measure of welfare called the Quality of Life—though they admit some measurement problems. This suggestion ignores the considerable experience already gained in trying to develop such a measure. There has been considerable effort directed toward an integrated measure cutting across all economic, social, and environmental concerns, and capable of considering the overall QOL of a group of people in a specific locale. It was an outgrowth of other indicator efforts such as economic, environmental, and social ones that are presently done in a partial, segmented fashion. There is predictably little agreement on how to carry out this objective of integrating these independent efforts though, and no general consensus is being established on either the need for such a measure or the importance to policy formulation if it appeared.

Probably the most frequently asked question is how one can measure something thought to be so totally dependent on personal values. If the QOL is different for each individual, how does one develop one which purports to represent everyone? Quantifying QOL generates numerous other questions. What should be included in the measure? What relationship should it have to other indicators? How can it be used in the decision process? Further, there is the fear that once a QOL measure is devised, it will be used to manipulate rather than to measure performance. This latter point has real significance in a nation like ours where states and localities are very jealous of their own prerogatives. There is considerable reluctance on the part of many to be driven toward some national norm or average, thereby losing their own identity. Care would have to be taken to ensure those who hold such perspectives that the QOL measures would be used to permit greater movement of our people to and from areas that they wanted because of the relative partial indicators. This would mean that an area which had relatively little in the way of economic opportunities but significant environmental attractiveness would not be forced to change because of some relative national standing, but that the information would be available to those who wanted to use it.

Realistically, the fears of those who oppose homogenization are apt to be well-founded. Congressional lawmakers, regulators, and those who dole our federal funds are always looking for measures and indices they can use to trigger or guide these programs. A readily available QOL set of indicators would be too tempting to leave alone. Depending on the size and number of programs and policies tied to the measure, there would likely be a force exerted toward sameness or minimal performance levels.

During the Seventies, the Environmental Protection Agency funded two studies that attempted to develop a QOL measure.[18] The Midwest Research Institute (MRI) tried to quantify a QOL measure at the metropolitan level from secondary source data. A profile of indicators was developed to show the relative level of living in various metropolitan areas of the country. Stanford Research Institute attempted to look at QOL in terms of thresholds—the setting of a series of limits to different QOL phenomena involving either natural processes or policy pronouncements. The exercise was related conceptually to the carrying capacity concept to be discussed in the last chapter. Deviation from these limits could then be used to measure the part that our social system prevents or induces.

Even if there were considerable interest at present in comprehensive indicators, and even if the technical problems were surmountable, the politics of their development and application would probably be considerable, particularly since no recognized national application is on the horizon. Moreover, the actual publication of QOL results can be expected potentially to incite strong reactions on the part of many individuals and groups. This could cause political difficulty for the agency responsible for perfecting and updating the measures. Witness the reaction after the publication of the MRI study. That report published a set of indicator scores of the QOL on various "standard metropolitan statistical areas" (SMSAs) across the country. Letters from members of Congress, governors, mayors, and citizens flowed into the EPA. Even those in areas which had a high QOL index were often displeased, for they did not wish to encourage immigration. The study engendered considerable political heat even though its results appeared to compare favorably with other independent studies. Its unpopularity seemed to stem from the fact that it was a federal study which purported to measure the performance (and satisfaction or happiness) of local communities.

There is a long way to go from these pioneering efforts to really useful policy results, and numerous serious institutional and technical difficulties remain.

(1) Picking factors that comprise a QOL index has been found to be a controversial process, and may turn out to be an exercise in circular reasoning. Our culture (like all cultures) sets up the standards for us to determine what is right or sufficient. Although these factors are ingrained in each of us, they are not trained explicitly everywhere in the culture, and some diversity occurs. Ethnic, regional, and religious differences are among the more obvious reasons for variation. This means that the factors that comprise QOL are not exactly the same throughout the country.

(2) Even if the factors could be agreed upon, the objective measures for calculating the value of many of the parameters are not available and surrogates have to be found. The amount of error introduced by the use of these surrogates is usually unknown.

(3) The step from measuring the value of one of these QOL factors to any other one is complete guesswork. There are no objective standards for applying the necessary weights. Surveys and other forms of cross-sectional analyses are the only gauges presently available. In addition to technical difficulties, the search for weights runs into cultural difficulties similar to those found in developing the factors themselves.

(4) Even if the above noted technical problems could be overcome, the resulting parameters would be all but meaningless. Some form of

relative scale must be derived so that those using the indices would have some guide as to what the different values mean. A ranking or popularity contest does not really help.

(5) Finally, there is no way to demonstrate causality between the value of an index and a given policy choice before or after the policy is implemented. Consequently, to the extent there is change in any indicator over time, there is no way to demonstrate causality, and so it is a poor policy tool.

Again, the collection of the data to provide the indices is likely to be an annually expensive chore. Expense, scientific uncertainty, and fear over the outcome tend to provide resistance to a comprehensive indicator ever coming to pass. It is somewhat confusing why there is such fear of using relative measures of the QOL variety. The hostility engendered by the results of the MRI study works against improvement, although it is certain that the results themselves will not be the thing attacked, but rather the methodology ("the numbers are no good"). Possibly nobody wants to know the results.

It is the constant call for the implementation of unrealistic conceptual schemes that appear logically elegant but are empirically impossible to implement which makes up the bulk of the current discrepancies between the practitioners and the proponents of analytic techniques. As we shall see in the upcoming sections, there are often considerable gaps between the ideal concepts of policy analysis and what it is possible to do.

LITTLE VERSUS ALL

The incremental versus holistic school of decisionmaking debate is similar, in that the holistic tries to relate everything to everything else, once again calling for a context. The incremental suggests that decisions come to pass a little bit at a time, and that the corresponding analysis should be similarly passed. These notions, as others in the chapter, will be discussed in more detail in later chapters.

In general, these squabbles are not germane to day-to-day policy investigations, although they occupy much of the literature that purports to study the policy process. These terms are descriptive of ideal processes developed for descriptive or pedagogical purposes and have little meaning to the practitioners. Policies are analyzed as completely (or holistically) as necessary, given the available resources. The scope of the analysis is a function, usually, of the interests of those who are in power or of those who introduced the policy question, rather than of some ideal construct.

The area of interest often is centered around the most recent political concerns of the agency or office in which the analysis is being conducted. For example, environment/energy policy which was done, say, two years ago would be most concerned with the criteria for air pollutants. Today, such an analysis would not be complete without mention at least of CO_2 and acid rain impacts. New concerns, new emphasis, new variables for analysis.

If the decisionmaker is defined to be the political appointee (or alternatively, the elected representative), then the objective functions of social welfare described in so many conceptual models are not necessarily ones that would best serve their goals. As just mentioned, the politically important variable of the moment could be almost anything. The only certainty is that whatever it is currently, it will be a part of a specific policy model only accidentally. If the model isn't designed to address that variable in the sense, say, of optimizing its value, then there is likely to be hell to pay to get the model reoriented. It certainly is unlikely that it could be done in the normal time available for most policy questions. Consequently, a model redesign might be in order—conceivably one of significant proportions.

More to the point, the personal desires or goals of the political appointee or representative are certain to include that of remaining in office or keeping out of trouble. At the same time, it is not really believable that a politician would make explicit the desire to ensure that his/her every action, if it did not enhance the potential for survival, at least did not make it worse (if such desires were really present). A formal model with voting impact as the objective function would be hard for the public to swallow in a system such as ours. In the same vein, although there is little evidence that policies are set on the basis of any form of optimal solution, there is some suggestion that almost any strategy is likely to be adopted as long as it is at least able to accomplish a set of requirements, and as long as it does not get the principal in trouble or engender needless risk.

Formal models might better be used to serve the analysis level in performing assessments where there is more time, and where the aims of the study are not so directly tied to the immediate goals of the policy level. In such cases, the models could be modified when needed or could be used to help gain insights into areas which are apt to be useful in later policy analyses. Remember, we have already said that the experience of the policy analyst is a very important ingredient in the analysis process, and the richer this experience, the better the resulting policy is apt to be.

Finally, let us address the question of whether all available information ought to be used in policy analysis. It is really hard to argue with such a concept at first blush. Certainly, the decisionmaker should not have information withheld deliberately which may fundamentally alter the decision made. On the other hand, there is some question as to whether one ought to rush ideas into the policy arena before they are validated. There are examples in every field of information based on one study (or worse, one concept) which resulted in bad policy. One example is the famous Coleman Report.

In 1966, James S. Coleman published a study titled *Equality of Educational Opportunity*.[19] The study investigated the linkage between educational policy and achievement levels of students. Until the time of this study, several factors such as size of class, per pupil expenditure, physical plant, quality of curriculum, and other such matters were thought to be the prime determinants of learning quality. The report showed that the then-held beliefs on education and learning quality were inaccurate, and that only peer group and family influences really mattered. The data and the study were used by the U.S. Civil Rights Commission as an underpinning to its desire to justify the busing of black children to predominantly white schools. This policy of trying to bring ghetto children into contact with a better educated peer group resulted in an attempt to racially balance schools. The story of busing per se is well known. It certainly was controversial.

In 1979, Coleman reversed his study and recanted his findings. That school desegregation improved the quality of education for black children was found to be false for all but the better black students. Of course, the proponents of desegregation implied that the purpose of desegregation was really not pedagogical at all but to fulfill an American commitment to a just society. Busing was largely an unnecessary, possibly even worse, policy.

Another example, which we have discussed above and will discuss again later in the section on risk, is that of health-related environmental policies. To the extent that health statistics on the impact of specific pollutants are accurate, there is no question that they should be included in an analysis. But if these data are so uncertain that the measured errors are little more than influential "guestimates," then there is some reason for caution. If the stages of analysis move from an estimate of the amount of residuals produced from various sources to estimates of, say, populations-at-risk, and then to estimates of morbidity or mortality, then the transformations at each stage should be dependent on data of sufficient quality such that the resulting findings can be considered information. If they are not, then one might question why the analysis would proceed from one stage to the next. If the information generated in, say, the health statistics is flawed, the emotional response evoked by using these data may be counter-productive to that which results from the use of the population-at-risk figures. We shall return to this example later.

Concluding Remarks

This chapter has suggested that for a decade or two, we have tried hard to bring the concepts of systems analyses into the public policy arena. The implementation of these principles across a number of arenas and as applied to a number of issues has resulted in attempts to rigorously structure the decisions process along a set of clearly defined lines. The chapter also tried to look at a few of the underlying assumptions of this approach and to see whether these assumptions (posed in the form of questions) are valid when looked at in the light of recent experience. Does the theory match the reality?

The first set of questions concerned which of these assumptions were incorrect. The section suggested that indeed there is some reason to assume that the underpinnings were false or not really demonstrable and that the whole field may have been based on less than fully demonstrated premises. It was further suggested that the professionals who set up the state-of-the-art of the theory are not likely to have access to the real information as to how a policy was developed.

The next set of questions concerned the difference between the policy world and how others might perceive that it is or ought to be. This section found that different technical, scientific disciplines look at topics so differently that it is possible for considerable misunderstanding. Further, those who develop the structure on which systems and policy analyses are based do so with such formalism that there is little relation to reality. It becomes a normative rather than a descriptive exercise.

Another set of questions turned to the existence, power, and concerns of the person identified in the literature as the "decisionmaker." The message was that decisions are not made in the public sector as neatly as the technician might think or hope. Further, that the personality and styles introduced by the wide variety of policymakers and their staffs is such that the monarchical model supposed by the designer of systems analysis is flawed indeed.

Finally, there was a series of questions which develop around some of the basic "truths" underpinning the systems analysis model. Questions such as comprehensive versus partial analyses, as well as those surrounding the use of formal tasks per se, or even ones which look at all the evidence, suggest that experience does not bear out the preconception of the policy or systems analyst schools, and that reality is much more straightforward and simplistic than the theory suggested. In the end, there is some question whether the information gathered on the basis of what may have been false premises and hypotheses adds or detracts from the policy formulation process.

These questions are obviously only a sampling of what could be asked about the use of sophisticated techniques in the policy field and the application of systems analysis and its derivatives. The comments made on several of these techniques may be terse in spots, but it is anticipated that the points will be amplified to the degree necessary in the ensuing chapters. We shall continue throughout the book to question the technical and conceptual underpinnings of the use of formal analytic techniques in policy analyses, admittedly spending most time on documenting failures. It has been over a decade since these ideas were brought forth, and the time has come to present a critical appraisal from the practitioner's perspective.

NOTES

1. I shall use the terms policy analysis, systems analysis, and operations research interchangeably, since I believe that the need for formalism and analytic techniques is similar in all, as is the underlying system structure and response.

2. Joseph F. Coates, "What is a Public Policy Issue?" *Judgements and Decision in Public Policy Formulation,* AAAS Selected Symposium 1 (1978): 34-69.

3. David Halberstam, *The Best and the Brightest* (New York: Random House, 1973).

4. A similar and related set of statements was put forth in "Expect the Unexpected: An Adoptive Approach to Environmental Management, Executive Report 1," IIASA, Laxemburg, Austria, 1979:

- Assessment should include all conceivable results of a proposed program.
- Each new assessment is unique.
- Comprehensive surveys are necessary to assessment.
- Any good scientific study relating to the problem helps to solve it.

• Systems analysis will choose the best alternative.

5. Ida Hoos, *Systems Analysis in Public Policy: A Critique* (Berkeley, CA: University of California Press, 1972).

6. See also "A Summary and Report on Four National Environmental Workshops," DOE/EV-0098, U.S. Department of Energy, July 1980.

7. Stuart D. Nagel, "Improving Policy Analysis," in B. Bordes and M. Dubuch (eds.) *Motives and Methods of Policy Analysis* (Beverly Hills, CA: Sage, 1980).

8. Such arguments are based on the presumption that the scientist is politically indifferent and unbiased. The Gori article referred to below not only questions this point, but suggests that in areas like carcinogen research, the information itself is flawed and incomplete.

9. L. B. Lave and E. P. Seskin, *Air Pollution and Human Health* (Baltimore, MD: Johns Hopkins University Press, 1977). L. D. Hamilton, S. C. Morris, and K. M. Novak, *Data Book for the Quantification of Health Effects from Coal Energy Systems* (Brookhaven National Laboratory, 1979).

10. We shall discuss Delphi in greater detail in Chapter 3.

11. A. Wildavsky, "Richer is Safer: Risk Assessment in the Large." Part of a proposal to the National Science Foundation, July 1979.

12. Peter Woll, *American Bureaucracy* (New York: W. W. Norton, 1963), p. 142. Original citation in Richard E. Neustadt, *Presidential Power* (New York: John Wiley, 1960), p. 9.

13. Op cit., #13, pps. 1-46.

14. Op cit., #13, pps. 1-46.

15. Op cit., #13, pps. 1-46.

16. Op cit., #13, pps. 1-46.

17. William T. Baumol and Wallace E. Oates, *Economics, Environmental Policy and the Quality of Life* (Englewood Cliffs, NJ: Prentice-Hall, 1979).

18. Peter W. House, *The Quest for Completeness* (Lexington, MA: Lexington Books, 1976).

19. James S. Coleman, *Equality of Educational Opportunity* (Washington, DC: U.S. Government Printing Office, 1966).

CHAPTER 2

ANALYSIS AS A FORMAL PROCESS

Formalism and Policy Analysis

Decisionmakers usually feel comfortable with rigorous analysis—but not all decisionmakers. Large bureaucracies in the private sector have operations research groups and other analysis teams as a captive part of their own organizations. These groups are habitually called upon to provide input to major business decisions from scheduling to acquisitions. The skills required to staff such shops are routinely taught in business administration schools and are practiced so ubiquitously that both the analyst and the manager are likely to be grounded in similar disciplines. Consequently, they are able to communicate with each other with relative ease.

The defense sector also makes extensive use of all forms of systems analysis. People trained at the various military academies are taught to use sophisticated techniques for problems ranging from ordering supplies to gaming a wartime situation. Again, there is the likelihood that the analyst and the officer are both well versed technically. Both feel comfortable using sophisticated methodologies, and both would expect them to be used in decision analyses.

The world of hardware and concretions populated by the engineer also makes extensive use of analytic methods to plan and implement various projects. These projects range all the way from designing office complexes to putting together whole cities. Again, the engineer is taught to use these techniques naturally. In this case, however, the client may or may not be versed in the analytic methods used. Rather, the engineer is hired as an expert, and under this guise may not have to explain the method, only the result of his analysis.

The federal nondefense public sector has come late to this formal assessment/analysis field and has transferred or borrowed several techniques from the three decisionmaking groups noted above. The essence of each of these borrowed techniques is a rigor which permits them to be taught, used, and replicated for each potential application. After more than a decade of developing these formal principles, they have been reduced to a few generalized rules. Quade, in his landmark book on *Systems Analysis*,[1] probably summarizes these stages as well as anyone. I have relied heavily on his work in the next sections.

Quade approaches analysis as a scientist would. He pictures the world of public policy decisionmaking as one where there is a decisionmaker with a discrete, definable problem which can be articulated to an analyst. His elements of analysis begin with:

- Objectives: In this stage, there is the requirement to understand exactly what issue is being addressed, and to clearly ascertain what it is that the decisionmaker wants to do about it.
- Alternatives: A search is then made to determine the options or means available to address this issue, keeping in mind the goal of the decisionmaker. This stage requires a testing of the possible alternatives and a decision as to whether these options are viable.
- Impacts: Analyses are performed to test the consequences of the various options or alternatives. Care is taken to specify these impacts in as many ways as possible, looking for secondary or unintended results.
- Criteria: After all of the impact analyses are performed for all of the potential options, decision rules have to be formulated to rank the options, in order to present the results to the decisionmaker in a manner that suggests which of the options best addresses the original issue in terms of his/her objectives.
- Model: All these bits of information are then combined in a model and used to predict in an empirical fashion the array of consequences.

Quade goes on to produce and discuss a series of diagrams to illustrate various aspects of systems analysis. They talk to the concept of policy or systems analysis as iterative processes. As noted earlier, this picture of the analysis process is probably more accurate when used to describe activities that are part of the research world rather than the world of policy.

Unfortunately, there is normally never enough time or resources to take a leisurely look at any given policy issue. More importantly, there is some genuine policy-level resistance to continuing to study and restudy an issue, particularly after there has been a stance taken and a policy or set of policies adopted. Continual studies under these conditions might possibly show the way toward a better solution than the policy already adopted. But in the normal course of events, such a resolution clearly cannot be politically beneficial for the policymaker who has just taken a public stand in favor of another position. Any studies that are suggested as part of the policy pronouncement are characteristically scheduled to yield results well downstream, where mid-course corrections in the original policy would be less apt to be politically embarrassing. Characteristically, if there is a strong feeling that not enough is presently known to make final decisions, and that more research and analysis is really necessary (and most people would agree that this was the case), then the preferred policy might be to suggest deferring a decision until more is known. The required research could be deliberately designed so that scheduled outputs and the resultant fine-tuning of an implementation strategy would occur well past the present crisis. Given this understanding of the reality of the research/ analysis situation, let us look at how a rigorous iterative system would operate in an ideal world, and use this description as a springboard toward an understanding of where such a system fits (or doesn't) into the policy formulation process.

The system to be described here is similar to the one mentioned above, where a problem or issue is identified through a series of symptoms which somebody says require mitigation. Because they impact a specific group or area and can't be handled adequately or quickly enough by private sector means, some level (or levels) of government is called upon for assistance. The issue is then studied so that it can be clearly articulated, and so that its specifications can be agreed to by both the analyst and the decision-maker. Once some agreement is reached on exactly what problem is yielding the undesirable symptoms, then there has to be some clear agreement as to what the objectives will be for the public (and the private) sector in shifting the system to clear up these symptoms. This normally can be done in a variety of ways, and each way should have its impacts specified. In the beginning, there should be a tendency to err on the side of too much information rather than too little. Later, analysis will pare down the set of alternatives. At the same time, formal criteria should be developed so that each of these alternatives can be tested in the same fashion and the results compared. The criteria selected for effectiveness therefore become important, and tests will have to be made to assure that each of the potential alternatives truly can be judged by the same vector of criteria.

Having set up the background for the analysis, the analyst then goes on to begin a collection of the data and information that will be required to actually perform the study. Care will be taken to ensure that the quality of the data is commensurate with the rest of the study information. At the same time, the system to be studied is modeled. The requisite characteristics of the total system are specified, and all of the components are integrated into a model that specifies their interrelationships. The model and the collected data are validated in terms of a reference case before any of the proposed policy alternatives are tested.

The policy options are then run in the model and the different impacts arranged for comparative purposes. The impacts are presented, to the extent possible, so that the costs and benefits are commensurable. They are then interpreted, evaluated, and ranked so that those at the policy level are able to choose an alternative. According to these diagrams, the lessons learned in performing one round of analysis become the basis for further analysis. We shall demonstrate later in this chapter how such an iterative procedure could result in considerably improved information for decisions. As we have already noted, though, most policy analysts don't have the leisure to perform such iterative assessments.

All the while this extremely complex decision process is going on, the traditional proponents of formal analysis methods picture a situation where there is exceedingly close interaction between the analyst and the person or persons who will have to make the ultimate analysis. This relationship is seen as important because the political milieu of the decisionmaker must be woven into the evaluation process. It is clearly importance to get the political perspective on such facets as: When and how did the issue arise? What are the "acceptable" solutions? To whom? Will any solutions be apt to engender political enemies? Will anyone be likely to implement a mitigation strategy? These and dozens of other questions are apt to come to mind; unfortunately, however, no formal decision analysis process designed to date is able to take them into consideration fully and explicitly.

The Decisionmaker as Omniscient Being

Let us take a set of ideal or idealized statements (or questions) and use them as a template with which to measure reality. This is by no means a complete set, nor is it meant to be the basis for any analyses. Rather, if one is going to use a technique to analyze a system, and that technique is designed from a rigorous scientific or engineering basis, then some assumptions (first principles) have to be made about the system being analyzed in order to use a mathematically based technique. The issue raised by this set of questions is not whether any single one of these is right or wrong, but whether it is more or less necessary for each "requirement" to be true before one can use a formal analytic method.

- The decisionmaker has total authority to implement whatever goals or strategies are desired.
- The decisionmaker knows what his/her goals are and can identify them in an explicit and quantifiable fashion.
- All parties to the decision have the same technical training (or an understanding of each other's) and the same perception of the world.
- The analysis to be carried out is understood by both the analyst and the decisionmaker, and both agree that the information to be produced is all that is really required for the decision.

POLICIES AND GOALS

There are plenty of rules, regulations, procedures, and the like in the federal civilian establishment. These requirements are normally all that is necessary for a government (or nation) to operate in routine times when there is one directive or another available to cover most situations. To some extent, it is only when the situation is unique, when there is a crisis or a politically derived desire to change the status quo, that there is any need for a decisionmaker at all. This considerable superstructure of agreed-upon procedures under which the various parts of the nation operate is a normal and somewhat comforting situation for the culture as a whole. It means that it is possible for us to change our leaders periodically and that the system will continue to function while the new decisionmakers learn the workings of the structure. It means that policies which turn out to be a mistake do not, in the normal course of events, bring the whole system to a grinding halt. It also means that few decisions are apt to be so earth-shattering that they have fundamental impact on the system.

In addition to the systemic rigidity of our large, operating establishment, further rigidity is provided by the organizational form of a functioning bureaucracy. Max Weber,[2] in his classic work on bureaucracy, describes this form as:

- a continuous organization of official functions bound by rules;
- a specific sphere of competence;
- the organization of offices according to the principle of hierarchy;
- the rules which regulate the conduct of an office being technical rules or norms;
- it being a matter of principle that the members of the administrative staff should be completely separated from ownership of the means of production or administration;

- in order to enhance this organizational freedom, the resources of the organization having to be free of any outside control and the positions not being monopolized by any incumbent; and
- administrative acts, decisions, and rules formulated and recorded.

In addition to the rest of the features of this organizational form, the bureaucracy survives because, among others of its characteristics, it is segmented. That is, it is broken into its component parts so that there can be a division of labor and lots of specialization. It is the haven of the subject matter expert and it is tailor-made for the technician. In fact, it is likely that our whole modern society would have been impossible without this organizational innovation.

Because the existence of a bureaucratic form means that each part of the federal government will be cellular in nature, with loosely tied relations with other components or cells, the policy leader who has management control usually has control over only a very few of these cells. When the decisionmaker wants to make a change which is wholly within the cells under this control, the odds of success are high. On the other hand, when the policy would result in considerable change in other cells, or when action is required on the part of other cells to affect a result, the use of mere positional power by the leader to affect a decision has to give way to such things as coercion, bargaining, or cooperation. These approaches are obviously considerably weaker than absolute authority. To this end, in a society as complex as ours, it is difficult to envision many policies of any significance which would not require policymakers and their bureaucracies from several areas to participate in their implementation. Given this segmentation of duties and responsibilities, and the considerable heritage of rules and regulations already in place that may actually act as boundary conditions in the decision process, there is some real limit on the effective authority of a single person to make a decision and put it into action.

There are probably few, if any, people who attain a policy-level position in the public sector who come to the job with a complete agenda that they want to accomplish. Surely, each of them comes with a perspective as to how they expect to look at issues under their purview. Many will have a few broad goals, and still others some specific ones they want to attain. But to a large extent, the issues they will have to face will be ones generated from situations over which they have little control. These policy issues will more than likely bring to the fore decisions or requests for staff guidance on subjects and in areas which were of little concern or knowledge before the appointee accepted the position. In short, the goals specification requirement that is so important to the technically oriented analyst who requires them to operate a model is not really consciously known by the policymaker for the full range of issues that will inevitably surface during his tenure. In fact, for some number of these issues, there will be a desire to minimize the conflict and risk associated with being involved with a policy. This risk reduction becomes a sort of negative goal, as opposed to the positive one of attempting to accomplish something.

As with most human goals, their expression is apt to be vague. In the analyst's sense, they are most apt to have a known sign, but no clear magnitude. Analysts tend to ask questions such as: "How badly do you really want this?" Or, "In relation to all the other goals you have and stances you are taking, how important is this particular issue?" Such questions assume almost nonhuman consistency in terms of all one's goals and objectives, and a care to detail that would be remarkable. For even the most empirically oriented individual who has thought about and planned several phases of his life, the best he could probably do would be to ordinally rank his full set of goals. Even this unlikely (but impressive) circumstance would be of limited use to the analyst.

COMMUNICATION

One of the most serious problems in any system is the failure of the parts to communicate and interact with each other. In interpersonal relations, if the parties are experiencing what might be called sender/receiver mismatches, at best the desired outcome of a combined effort will not come to pass. At the extreme of total noncommunication, we can conjure up all kinds of disasters.

Theoretically, the more technical a field is, the easier it is for those who are practitioners to communicate with one another. A highly specialized language, a kind of shorthand grows up which permits rapid and precise transfers of information. Yet the very features of this shorthand which make it so useful for those who are members of the group can also make it unintelligible for those who are not trained in the field. The shorthand then has a tendency to turn into gibberish.

Communication can't be a one-way street. Even people who are well trained in a technical field may from time to time have problems talking to someone else trained in a different field, even when discussing a related field. For example, several years ago, Washington, D.C. was introduced to the message of a book titled *Limits to Growth*.[3] This message was controversial and based largely on the results of a single computer model. Among the many responses to this work was the formation of a White

House Task Force on the use of models. Each department or agency was asked to send representatives to discuss how the public sector uses or should use models and, as an ancillary question, what utility might flow from the model and modeling used in the Club of Rome book. The meeting was so chaotic that it was almost comical. Although most were conversant with the jargon of modeling, few of the representatives could talk to each other in a meaningful way. Even within a field as narrow as model use, the shorthand developed by the users made the conversation around the table a replay of the Tower of Babel. In the end, it became necessary to write a handbook, *A Guide to Models,*[4] to act as an aid to translating all professional and agency shorthands. Ultimately, some ten thousand of these books were distributed and the work was reprinted as a textbook.

Even assuming that there is communication on a technical level between the decision and analytic people, there still has to be agreement that the work actually performed fulfills the original information need and does respond to the issue. Because there are numerous issues, large and small, most of which will require some analysis attention, the frequency with which the analyst will be able to check back with the policymaker client is largely a function of how significant the issue is to the client. Situations have a tendency to change during the course of any study. The sources of change could be anywhere. A change of emphasis could shift a policy option or analysis method. Or, the amount of available information could be more or less than anticipated. Changing conditions may mean that the enthusiasm with which the results are received could wane, or in some cases, the client could have forgotten the original purpose of the assessment and be expecting something quite different. In terms of the analyst's situation, there is a tendency to go where the data takes him, and to produce as responsive a piece as possible. In the end, however, the report produced may not be what was anticipated by anyone, even by those who were present at the start of the effort when the analysis was agreed upon. When there is little or no communication from the start of the analysis to the final report, an unanticipated result could be somewhat disconcerting to the policy level, which is obviously quite possible.

A more important aspect of this finished product, as we found with the original expectations situation, is not so much the surprise aspect, but the question of whether the results are useful when they do surface. Properly made analyses can sometimes be assumed to yield surprises in terms of the results, and yet are not a problem in and of themselves. The difficulty comes about when the analysis is deficient, for whatever reason, in the sense that it does not address the issue in sufficient detail (or with sufficient accuracy) to give the policy level the information it needs to make a decision. In such cases there is seldom enough time to redo or expand the analysis, and consequently the policymaker is left with the necessity of falling back on his best judgment (without analytic support) to effect a decision. This is exactly the result that the technocratic community wanted to avoid! In summary, it is necessary for the policy-maker and the analyst to keep each other informed as much as is feasible or possible. At the very least, this communication should be done in those instances where either party anticipates a major change in issue definition not know by the other (e.g., data availability, political shifts, and so forth). The rule in operation is an extension of the one which calls for "no surprises" to the leadership level.

Finally, there is an implicit expectation that there is perfect communication between and among systems. This requirement refers not only to the relationship of one subsystem to another, but of one group of people to another. A few examples should suffice to illustrate.

All formal models are designed to run in a milieu which is referred to by the technician as "background." By this term, the analyst means that the variables not modeled are assumed to work as they always have or to remain constant. This is an assumption made by every analysis group throughout the private and public sectors, even though each of these groups is making and implementing policies which change the direction of their future development on a more or less routine basis. In addition to this, there are impacts of decisions of one group on another which will fundamentally change the direction of the other's growth. For example, the decision on the part of the American automotive industry to use the catalytic converter to control automotive emissions meant a great deal to the platinum industry. It suddenly had a surge in the demand for its product (an integral part of the converter) that was outside the industry's control or planning. Similar examples exist elsewhere: coal policy on transportation policy, environmental regulations on energy policy, safety standards on housing policy, and so forth. For all kinds of reasons, though, these continued perturbations of all groups on the postulated general system and on specific parts of the system are generally ignored by the analyst. From a pragmatic point of view, there is little else that can be done. In a technical sense, the practice may not be so bad, depending on how much effect one believes any series of short-term modifications in present policy to have on a system the size of our national economy.

But this technical discrepancy is only a part of the problem. Similar communication difficulties occur on the human level. In theory, the policy and technical levels should be in communication with each other so that the impacts of one proposed policy are considered in the discussion of another. At best, such an information procedure may bring to the attention of those involved in policymaking and analysis things which are first-order impacts but that will be unlikely to be useful for considering less obvious or secondary impacts.

In an attempt to look at a broader range of potential impacts, the federal government has instituted several "impact" statements which have as their purpose the specification of a broad spectrum of impacts of a given decision. Some feel that given the ambiguous nature of our transportation and communication networks and other features of our economy, that not only are decisions in one area apt to have impacts on others, but to have them more rapidly than has historically been the case. To attempt to at least make it possible for the decision level to be cognizant of these impacts, formal documents are required. Many feel that the documents have little real impact, however. Here are some examples:

FEDERAL PLANNING AND THE DECISION PROCEDURES

Federal agency procedures for program planning and decisionmaking include numerous opportunities for interagency coordination. Through relevant laws, executive orders, and agency policies, the opportunity (indeed, often the requirement) exists for federal agencies to assess the potential implications and impacts of proposed federal initiatives on existing federal policies and programs.

The impacts include broad economic considerations as well as other important factors, such as environment, natural resource management, and urban development. Ideally, these assessment mechanisms should be an opportunity and an incentive for federal agencies to prepare integrated analyses of the impacts of proposed policy and planning decisions. The weight which any individual agency will give to integrated analysis in an individual case cannot, of course, be determined in advance, but the mechanisms are in place. Their effectiveness is up to the agencies and the administration.

Following are some examples of federal efforts to improve the decision-making process by providing for integrated analysis of the impacts of potential decisions: Environmental Impact Statements; Regulatory Analyses and Review Programs; and Urban and Community Impact Analyses. The National Environmental Policy Act (NEPA) requires all federal agencies whose decisions or actions affect the human environment in a significant manner to evaluate the impacts of such actions in advance and to integrate such evaluations into the agencies' decisionmaking processes. The Environmental Impact Statement (EIS) documents these evaluations and requires considerable interagency cooperation. The Regulatory Analysis Review Group (RARG) is an interagency committee responsible for analyses of major new regulations. The RARG has as members the principal economic and regulatory agencies of the Executive Branch. One of its principal actions was to require an economic impact statement. The Community Conservation Guidance is an effort to avoid unnecessary duplication and waste in urban and energy policy. The mechanism the Guidance provides to accomplish this goal is the Urban and Community Impact Assessment (UCIA).

ENVIRONMENTAL IMPACT STATEMENTS
(THE NATIONAL ENVIRONMENTAL POLICY ACT)

The National Environmental Policy Act (NEPA) is a very clear example of a mechanism for the interagency review and coordination of federal decisionmaking. It requires all agencies to consider potential environmental impacts in their decisionmaking processes. In addition, it requires all agencies to develop procedures to ensure that environmental consequences are considered early in the decisionmaking process, not after a large expenditure of funds has already altered the benefit-cost balance of proceeding with the project.

There are numerous types of agency activities which are subject to the NEPA requirements. In essence, some form of analysis must be performed on all major federal agencies which could significantly affect the quality of the human environment. The EIS, the principal formal document through which this is accomplished, is a thorough analysis which estimates the magnitude, direction, and duration of the likely, significant impacts of a proposed action and alternatives. Under the new CEQ guidelines, the EIS is directed to be short, concise, well-written, and helpful to the generally nontechnical decisionmakers. Technical analyses and data are an important part of the EIS but generally are not in the body of the text. Such material should be available through reference, or, if appropriate, in appendices of the EIS.

REGULATORY ANALYSES AND REVIEW PROGRAMS

Efforts and programs designed to review and coordinate government regulations and programs thus far have largely fallen under the executive office of the president. One of the first substantial efforts in establishing a mechanism to assess the impacts of regulations was the Economic Impact Statement Program started in the middle 1970s. This earlier program required federal agencies to prepare inflation impact statements on major new regulations. The criticism was that the program tended to analyze the impact of regulations after they were developed instead of attempting to bring impact assessment into the regulatory decisionmaking process.

In 1978, the Carter Administration implemented the more ambitious "Improving Government Regulations Program." This program attempted to institute mechanisms that would insure that the impacts of proposed regulations were ascertained and alternatives considered in advance. It also called for the evaluation and adjustment of existing regulatory programs to maximize their effectiveness while minimizing their burdensome impacts. Through Executive Order 12044 (later extended to April 30, 1981, by Executive Order 12221) and other actions, President Carter attempted to ensure that regulations would be cost-effective.

INTERNAL AGENCY REGULATORY ANALYSIS

Executive Order 12044 specifically requires each federal agency to review existing regulations and to develop a program for analyzing major new regulations which have major economic consequences. Major economic consequences are defined as having either an annual effect of $100 million or more on the economy or leading to major increases in costs or prices for individual industries, levels of government, or geographic regions. Each agency is required to submit its procedures for these reviews of existing regulations, as well as analyses for major new regulations, to the Office of Management and Budget. Although the agencies are encouraged to "tailor" procedures to meet particular needs, they must follow certain guidelines called for in the Executive Order. Thus the analyses must contain:

- a brief description of the problem that requires action by the federal government;
- a description of the major alternatives (alternative regulations and stringency levels, alternative timing, and alternative methods of ensuring compliance) being considered by the agency to deal with the problem;
- a comparative analysis of the direct and indirect economic effects of each of the alternatives; and
- a detailed explanation of the reasons why one alternative should be chosen over the others.

URBAN AND COMMUNITY IMPACT ANALYSIS

On November 26, 1979, the White House issued the Community Conservation Guidance. It provides implementing procedures for an aspect of several of the Carter Administration's policy initiatives, including urban policy, energy policy, and targeting of federal assistance. The primary objective was to encourage, through appropriate federal, state, and local action, the targeting of limited resources on the redevelopment and/or development of older commercial areas by the private sector.

This Guidance grew out of the need for a process through which state and local officials could request that federal policies and practices be reviewed to determine whether they might cause an erosion of existing community resources and investments. It is important that federal policies, grants, and decisions not have unintended effects of eroding existing commercial centers, whether they be located in center cities, the suburbs, or rural areas.

The Guidance reads in part:

> To improve the Administration's ability to encourage, through appropriate Federal action, the development and/or redevelopment of healthy older commercial areas, the President's Interagency Coordinating Council (IACC) encourages closer cooperation with respect to Federal programs directed at helping neutralize older commercial areas. The IACC oversees the following agency activities:
>
> - simplify current guidelines governing economic and community development assistance programs in order to improve their responsiveness to locally defined needs; and
> - facilitate strategic use of economic and community development programs in order to build public/private partnerships directed at older commercial area revitalization.

When a UCIA demonstrated that significant negative consequences would result from the pending federal action, the federal agency responsible for the action had to consider modifications to the proposed action. The President's Interagency Coordinating Council (IACC) facilitated closer cooperation with respect to federal programs directed at helping revitalize older commercial communities. The IACC was to oversee the Community Conservation Guidances and four Executive Orders issued by the President in 1978 dealing with urban policy.

Each of these formal assessment requirements is only a step in the direction of increasing the information base of the decision process. It is unclear whether this information is taken seriously or if it is even really communicated to the decisionmaker. At least, though, there is some real attempt to formally assure that some of the more important impacts are looked at and that they surface for consideration.

Resource Questions and Techniques

- There is a complete and validated information base known and used by everyone.
- The model to be used in an analysis is truly representative of the system being studied.
- There are adequate resources (including time) to carry out the necessary analyses.
- There is perfect communication throughout and between systems.

There is an implicit assumption made when one talks about performing a policy analysis that the information and resources exist to perform the task. In fact, there is no reason to believe that this will always, or even ever, be the case. One of the very first things which a responsible analyst has to do is pull together existing information in the form of data bases and other sources. These source documents are more or less adequate depending upon several factors, including the historical popularity of the policy question or the accidental overlapping of the policy question and ongoing research in the science community. If a piece of analysis is called for in a general area when lots of recent or earlier research and analysis was carried out, there is likely to be a data base available which is more extensive than an analyst would find if the policy issue were a fairly new one. In addition to the data and information available from the extant analyses and assessments, the analyst depends on information to be found in the scientist's research community. If the policy issue happens to be in an area where there has been recent and considerable research effort, there is obviously more potential information for an analysis than might be so otherwise. Irrespective of the surrounding situation though, one of the fundamental assumptions made about policy analysis is that enough data and information exist to do an assessment.

Regardless of whether this is true or not, the most difficult technical questions might not occur with the existence of the raw data per se, but with calibrating the data sources so that they can be used with each other. There must also be at least a general agreement among knowledgeable people that the data to be used are the "best" available. Data are collected for many reasons and the assumptions made in the collection process are very specific. For example, an electric utility might be based on such things as 3 percent sulfur coal and a unit that produces about 500 megawatts. If one wanted to combine the available information on the unit with, say, that of one burning 1 percent sulfur coal in a 1000 megawatt plant to try and look at the environmental impacts of a power plant siting, there might be problems. Whole series of other plant configuration data would have to be normalized before one would be able to make use of, say, two data sources on the 500 and 1000 MW plants. Careful inspection would have to be done to ensure the users that the data synthesized for a particular assessment could rightly be used in the fashion envisioned.

Finally, a large number of the areas where policy is required are so highly controversial that there is clear evidence of an adversarial process at work. Once two or more adversarial groups engage in battle over a domain or an issue, each will put little trust in anything the other says. In fact, the adversarial strategy requires polarization of perspectives which may or may not be driven to agreement through debate and confrontation in the public arena. If each group develops its own information sources, the policy analyst has a real problem in establishing universal credibility as he tries to ascertain which information base (or what combination of bases) will be used in his assessment, because by definition they are in conflict.

THE ANALYTIC MODEL

The mere existence of a question and a usable data base are only a part of the requirement. Quade, as noted above, specifies the use of a model to integrate inputs in a dynamic form to permit "what if" excursions. The models which might be used in an analysis would (because of resource constraints) likely already be in existence. In addition to all of the questions and problems noted above, these models would have to be truly representative of the system under study. This requirement breaks down into two questions: One, is the model representative of the system it was originally designed to address? And two, is the model useful for handling the policy question under review? The first of these questions is one that takes up a great deal of professional time in the modeling community—the attempt to validate a formal computer model. The rationale underlying the quest for model validation can be found in a variety of fields, such as the natural and physical sciences, engineering, and statistics. The use of validation techniques, simply stated, is the process of matching a known distribution of data with findings obtained in some fashion or other.

One of the uses of the concept of validation is to take a model which is a faithful replication of reality and then use it as an experimental device, i.e., to be the centerpiece in a series of "what if" exercises. It is the use of such logic in areas where the underlying natural law is unknown that is at the base of our concern. Let us touch on two aspects of this use of validation.

First, let us assume that the model we are going to validate is one which concerns an institutional, organizational, or social structure. As such, there are likely to be a number of times over the period being used to build and validate the model where the situation described can be said to be reactive to an event or series of events. The greater the number of variables being modeled, the more likely it is that this will be the case.

For example, an economic model would have to take into consideration factors which would normally be exogenous to the system being modeled, but whose happening would affect all events after its time. Often such events are called turning points; World War II and the OPEC embargo are two obvious examples. A model which was calibrated to truly mimic these happenings would be one which was a simulation of a series of events which were (it could be argued) *absolutely unique*—a situation dramatically opposed to the natural law hypotheses from which validation grew in the sciences. As such, the use of such a model to test "what if" hypotheses is open to serious question, particularly if there is no opportunity for the model to act behaviorally to situational changes. Small perturbations in noncritical areas for very near-term forecasts might have some credibility, but any more aggressive tests would be wanting.

The second use of model validation is to provide a basis for forecasting the future. Many of the problems alluded to above apply here also. Rather than become too involved in a detailed argument on this point, let me simply lay out a few flat assertions. In the first place, the only utility that validation has in the forecasting field is to test whether the model is performing as it was designed to. Although this is not a useless exercise, it is a far cry from claiming that its validation gives it any prophetic capability. Further, regardless of how well validated a model is in terms of aping the past, one still has no idea how useful the model is to forecast the future—unless the future is expected to be almost exactly like the past. Since no human-related phenomena have really conformed to any such repetitive cycle, especially not in recent decades, the feature of formal validation adds little to forecasting. Again, to lighten the sting, let me admit that knowing that the model operates as advertised means only that in the hands of competent analysts, the impacts of varying certain variables can be explained to others in terms of what would have happened had such changes occurred in a society much like the one we are all familiar with, given extrapolated changes in all other variables. Again, it's a useful input to decisionmaking but a far cry from a crystal ball.

A model with many variables can cause statistical problems of uncertainty, suggesting a situation where the results contain so many compounding errors that the output of a given model run is apt to be in the region of "noise."[5] (Noise is a term used to indicate that the information is a prediction too fine for the accuracy of the model; say, a change of 5 percent in a model with a known error of 10 percent.)[6] In reality, little can or has been done about this presumption of corresponding errors; however, it still remains to be shown that it is at all possible to specify individual errors before worrying about the potential for making them additive. Regardless of whether or not one agrees with the philosophical proposition that validation is impossible on the basis of logic alone, sheer size would limit the capability. To even begin to get a very large model down to a size where existing statistical tools can come into play is a design problem which has not yet been solved.

Probably the best form of validation can be found in the judgment of the analysts who use the forecasts. Recently, I heard this concept referred to as the "laugh test." A qualified analyst looks at the output of a run to see if he finds the results amusing. Such a test would only exclude those runs which, after the scrutiny of a thoughtful analyst, are found to be impossible or ludicrous or both.

The aspects we have described thus far suggest a bleak and discouraging future for the complete validation of models. In fact, it might almost appear expedient to abandon attempts at validation and look only at the usefulness of models for aiding the policymaker. Numerous compelling arguments that support modeling have appeared in the literature, so even if we are unable to validate them, we shall not present an apology for their use here. Instead, like a good modeler would, we shall extrapolate some present trends in such use.

Computers are coming into application in more and more sectors of our society. As experience increases and technology improves, the time cannot be far distant when the impact of computers will bring about societal changes as great as those from the Industrial Revolution. Computers are remarkable for their ability to store and organize large amounts of information. It is inevitable that such data will be used to project into the future assumptions based on our present state of knowledge. After all, it is in this manner that the human mind traditionally makes decisions, and certainly mankind will tend to use a tool which extends our own mental processes in similar fashion. The real question, therefore, is not whether we should place confidence in such devices, but how effective they are when compared to other available tools.

Now we view the problem of validity from a different perspective. Models should be tested not against reality but against alternative methods for measuring reality (mental models) and their successors. Research along this line has not yet been done, and will be difficult to carry out. The case can be made that the standard validation tests that some would require of models are significantly more rigorous than those we require of alternatives, or of the policymaker himself. In the latter case, decisions are subjected only to ex post facto validation when the policymaker or his/her organization must suffer the consequences of invalid projections.

In both cases, using either the mental model or the computer model to help make policy, a concerted effort on the part of the policymaker to act as if the models were true tends to yield cases of "self-fulfilling prophecy." The introduction of such purposeful behavior in the midst of any attempt to validate either the mental or the computer model scientifically makes for serious difficulties. The fact remains, however, that the computer model is normally the only one required to prove its credibility in any rigorous fashion before it is used to guide policymaking.

The second point is almost never addressed. Even if a model is considered to be "valid" in a technical sense, there is no reason to believe that using it for purposes other than what it was built for would yield valid results. More to the point, it is unlikely that any given model will be exactly suited to handle any given policy issue unless it was designed to do so. Consequently, there has to be some kind of modification of the model for each new study. These modifications often require significant redesign of the system, because the assumptions built into the original model may not be appropriate under the new circumstances—even if the original model was. We shall return to the issue of validation from a more technical perspective in Chapter 3, as this feature of model use and design is important in the policy area.

TIME AND POLICYMAKERS

Because policymakers are important people, conventional wisdom holds that resources will be made available to study any given issue they want. This may be true as a generalization, but it is not always the case. When a considerable number of issues are bunched together within a short time period, resources will likely not be forthcoming and analysis trade-offs have to be made. Most often the scarcest resource turns out to be time.

This resource is not one easily stretched. To some extent, the time constraint problem can be softened by bringing more in-house manpower or consultant resources to bear on the issue. However, the old saw that nine men impregnating a single woman will not bring out a term baby in one month highlights the limitations of this strategy. At some stage, the addition of technicians turns the problem of helping with the specific issue into a management quagmire.

The time constraint is often exacerbated by an additional factor. Under the pressure to prepare a policy position, time constraints are sometimes made worse by public or media interest. Such conditions allow for extreme fluidity and shifts in the policy perspective, and make change seem almost constant to the analyst. The analyst who expected to use very formal analytic methods is clearly doomed to considerable frustration when there appears to be almost no time to set up, run, and then check the models. There is no formal, professionally recognized methodology for deciding that a piece of work is "good enough." The tests are ones of the battlefield rather than the operations rooms, and are binary in nature; for in the policy adversarial situation, the analysis helped to win or lose the issue, as far as the policymaker is concerned, is likely to be one that helped him win a position, regardless of whether it was technically elegant or not. This latter factor has severe moralistic overtones and has a lot to do with the difference between real-world and ideal policy analysis as it is taught—the latter often being normative in nature.

FORMULATING POLICY ON COMPLEX ISSUES:
PROBLEMS WITH FORMAL TECHNIQUES

The formulation of national energy policies involves consideration of a highly complex and much debated set of issues, most of which are politically charged.[7] The complexity stems from many factors, ranging from disagreement on the nature of the energy crisis (or even whether there are crises) to considerable disagreement on ways to rectify the situation. Recently, the Iranian oil export cutback and gasoline shortages have once again highlighted the United States' domestic oil shortage issue. The Three Mile Island nuclear incident,[8] along with debates on the Clean Air Act Amendments,[9] and on the potential for increased use of coal, illustrate the difficulties encountered when technological alternatives to the extensive use of oil are brought forth. To determine how such alternatives might be examined and priorities established for development and deployment of new energy systems, a small portion of the overall energy policy debate is addressed; namely, the "cost" of energy in environmental and, to a lesser extent, economic terms. These complex trade-offs should be made in a defensible, analytical manner. Regardless of what methods and knowledge are available, such trade-offs and prioritization are constantly being made, and more specificity in our nation's energy futures is called for daily by the public.

COMPARISON OF ENVIRONMENTAL IMPACTS

The market penetration of any one of a number of promising energy technologies can be limited by stringent environmental constraints, depending upon the pollutant or medium doing the constraining. For example, a total coal strategy could result in considerably more air pollution than a total nuclear strategy; a total nuclear strategy could result in more incidents of exposure to ionizing radiation than a total solar energy strategy, and so forth.

Each major energy technology tends to have such unique environmental, health, and safety impacts that comprehensive, formal intertechnology comparisons are very difficult, if not totally impractical. The problem of comparisons of environmental impacts of energy technologies is compounded by a general lack of data on such things as the health effects of energy-related pollutants. Present day concerns about nuclear energy systems center around radioactive waste management, public safety, and effects of low-level radiation. For coal-based systems, only a few of the many known pollutants have been definitively and quantitatively linked to health effects. Even for an area where health standards exist, e.g., total suspended particulates, the most recent analyses indicate that the fine particulates, which are not specifically regulated and for which pollution controls are less effective, may prove to be the more serious health hazard.

Recently, it has become even more popular to discuss environmental regulations as being one of the most significant barriers to energy development, and conversely, energy development as having the potential for producing significant damage to the health and safety of humans, and to ecosystems themselves. It might be argued, therefore, that any policy which produced energy at the least risk to the environment would be, per se, preferable. This book will not further muddy this swirling stream of controversy by introducing still another opinion; instead, I suggest that the very attempt to analytically demonstrate the superiority of one technology over another, given the state of our knowledge, may actually exacerbate the choice problem. This is not to say that trained analysts might not use such information as that available to provide insights to the debate, but that the limited information available and the lack of a commonly accepted calculus make the use of sophisticated analytic techniques unreliable and the guidance they offer potentially misleading.

To demonstrate this assertion, I reviewed a number of studies that have purported to measure energy/environmental trade-offs. Not all of the studies comparing the environmental impacts of energy technologies or those which suggest the role of environmental considerations in policy-making have been presented in the following section. The studies examined represent a sampling of the better-known efforts that provide a representative picture of recent attempts in comparing impacts of energy technologies.[10]

In general, none of the studies is a universally acceptable assessment of the environmental impacts of the various energy systems. In the first instance, the fact that each energy system tends to have a unique set of impacts makes their comparison difficult. At present, as we noted above, there is no well-developed, widely accepted calculus for handling this complex trade-off problem. Other reasons for questioning the findings of these studies include:

- failure of analysts to consider one or more of the factors that are crucial in formulating public policy in these areas, e.g., security of energy supply or market readiness;
- lack of sufficient empirical data to substantiate the models employed, e.g., there is insufficient supporting data for realistic implementation of cost-benefit techniques;
- poor integration of national goals, such as energy independence or security, into the quantitative objective functions required to implement most of the decision models;
- failure of analysts to consider distributional problems;
- failure of most assessments to be totally objective—either through personal bias or variation in the quality of the data used; and
- failure to account for the effects of environmental regulations generally or as specifically applied in particular situations.

PRACTICAL CONSIDERATIONS OF POLICYMAKING

There are specific advantages and limitations of a variety of quantitative techniques for comparing the impacts of different energy technologies. But quantitative models in general have some inherent problems when their results are used to formulate policies in the public sector. In the next several pages, we will discuss the generic deficiencies associated with the practical application of the types of analytic techniques discussed above.

Our concerns are generic, not with data availability or the application of a specific model to analyze a given issue; the model and its results are assumed generally to reflect the best that can be done with available information. Nor are we concerned with inappropriate conclusions that result from an oversimplification of analytical process. Problems of this nature relate generally to the quantitative analytical techniques, and will be discussed in the next chapter in more detail. Rather, we are concerned with broader problems related to the mismatch between the analytical design and the way the results are used in a practical sense.

The major concern is that there is probably no way to design and implement an energy/environment/economic paradigm which adequately allows trade-offs to be made between real-world energy, environmental, and economic considerations. Certainly, such a paradigm can be conceptualized. When displayed in a matrix format to portray the essential elements of a major policy issue, however, a number of cells will always be vacant. The vacant cells have little to do with the complexity of the technical process, the availability of technical data, or the appropriateness of data. In this instance, the vacant cells show us the points where quantitatively undefinable processes become dominant; for example, cultural habits, societal choice, and institutional relationships and politics.

The well-bounded decision world in which most of the analytical methods originate is, unfortunately, different from that of the public policy world. The paradigms used in the private sector are not necessarily useful for the general welfare issues of the public sector. The "bottom line," seemingly so clear in the private sector, is less obvious in the public sector. Although one can legitimately argue about the relative importance of the profit motive in private sector decisions, profit is still a necessary, if not sufficient condition in most such decisions. No such clear-cut, objective function exists for the public sector. Consequently, techniques which incorporate concepts tied to the profit motive (e.g., rate of return, value of labor, costs of money) do not usually transfer well into the public policy arena. This brings us back to the inclusion of incommensurables in comparative analysis. Public policy operates in a highly complex, not always fully rational world, and it must give equal weight to a number of factors that are not easily obtained, either objectively or from quantitative analysis.

THE INCOMMENSURABLES

If we combine analytic and political models, short-term and longer-term needs in the energy area, we cannot predict the ultimate success of the effort. It is clear that difficulties have arisen in collectively determining energy goals and assessment methods over the past several years. To some extent, these difficulties were expected, and to some extent they were a result of organizational structures. Consider the political barriers to quantification and in-depth analysis in general, without saying which are most germane to the energy situation. All of them are relevant to the question of using the results of comparative analysis to formulate energy policies that incorporate new energy technologies.

Not now. Quantitative analysis generally, and modeling specifically, often concentrate on the future. Survival for a politician means concentration on issues of the present. This vital tie to the present does not preclude concern for the future, but altruism and public service aside, issues arising beyond his next reelection date are often of minor interest to a politician. He can spend time on a national long-range issue only if it is in vogue and can be used to gain short-term support, or if it is part of his own value structure.

Not a winner. There are few notable examples of success in the use of planning and analysis in public decisionmaking. This does not mean that there have not been any—only that proper planning, analysis, and implementation avoid troublesome situations; success defuses notoriety. (Planning for emergency situations or popular national goals are exceptions.) Successful fire, rescue, and police actions are usually well covered by the press. Yet such actions can be routinely successful only through effective functional decisionmaking, although individual performers usually get the credit. The United States lunar exploration program is one of a few shining examples of good visible public decisionmaking; NASA planning techniques were held up as models to all other federal agencies for several years. NASA, however, had advantages that most other agencies lacked: a concise goal (a man on the moon by 1970); almost unanimous public support; almost no budget constraints; and little need for interagency coordination. Most other federal issues have far less than unanimous public support and lack, to one degree or another, the rest of these advantages. Even a successfully planned and executed set of programs such as that resulting in our network of interstate highways will often have enough vocal detractors to make the programs appear to be less than a complete success. A politician cannot always afford to be associated with a concept having such a questionable chance of payoff.

Bad poker. From the policy perspective, one of the greatest fears of comprehensive decisionmaking analysis is that it will work, and in working, will cause an early tipping of one's hand. In general, the politician's experience (backed by scientific conflict theories) concludes that the probability of success in launching an initiative is increased by keeping it relatively quiet until it is in place and tested. The more people that know about it, and the more who have the ability to comment or sign-off on it, the greater its odds of dying on the drawing board as the victim of the ever present nay-sayers.

Clear-cut decision objectives not only means other groups can survey the early progress of a project, but it also means each group must rationalize its project goals (and expected impacts) with those of other projects sponsored by other groups. Seldom does such a coordination exercise result in the proposed policy getting more resources or in having resources shifted to do more work. In general, new initiatives give up resources to more developed, less speculative efforts, even if the eventual promise of the former appears greater. As a result, being candid about the future comprehensive benefits or impacts of a project often puts the project at risk despite little assurance that future costs or benefits will occur.

Out on a limb. Likewise, legislative constraints and bureaucratic inertia make a policymaker reluctant to embrace a decisionmaking exercise that would result in his shifting resources among programs, unless such a shift did not require outside approval. The risk of deemphasizing one area to increase another is that the decrease may be accepted and the increase resisted, again resulting in a budget reduction—not a happy result for the policymaker.

Incompetent bureaucrats. The average policymaker works with the average bureaucrat every day, each often having conflicting goals. The stereotypical image of the bureaucrat does not induce great faith in his ability to carry out large-scale analysis efforts. Even if the politician thinks otherwise, he may be reluctant to convince a constituency that believes in the incompetent bureaucratic stereotype, especially if he is a policymaker who promoted such a stereotype in gaining or retaining is office.

Uncomfortable thoughts. Decisionmaking requires thinking about the future and about subject matter outside one's area of expertise. Since one is most knowledgeable about past events in one's own field, only bold, liberal thinkers will adopt comprehensive analysis voluntarily.

Can't afford it. Any kind of decisionmaking, even simple coordination, takes time, money, and effort. Since almost all policymakers feel they have insufficient staff to carry out immediate demands, why should they embrace a decisionmaking effort voluntarily, knowing that payoff may be years away? That the real world confronts difficulties with decisionmaking and futuristic thinking does not mean that all exercises in looking to the future are willing to deal with these same difficulties.

Doesn't have all the answers. Because quantitative techniques, by their very nature, must operate as closed systems, they can never supply all the answers the policymaker needs. Since their partial answers are often incompatible with the other, nonquantitative solutions, they may be ignored. The above situations lead some to dismiss the quantitative side entirely, and others to throw up their hands and exclaim that the nature of our system precludes good decisionmaking. Neither is true.

The fact that a decision cannot be fully quantified does not mean that we cannot make a decision or a good decision. The desire to make energy and environmental trade-offs is generally described in an exceptionally broad fashion. Political and administrative problems discussed above make the development and use of comprehensive or combined models very difficult. This does not, however, mean that quantitative analysis has no place in the decision process. For me, such a situation merely indicates a need to redefine the trade-off techniques. The quantitative framework, and the drivers within that framework, which frequently described a closed system to policy analysts, must instead be viewed as a subset of a larger political process. One must take into consideration the political assumptions and public perceptions which are the front-end drivers of our policy system, and which determine the eventual decision. Then one can put quantitative analysis into the proper perspective. This would require that models be used for backup data and information to show the potential feasibility, popularity, or success of a particular decision. Used in this manner, any one or a combination of several quantitative techniques may well be appropriate. To be appropriate, however, they must operate at a microlevel by providing the policymaker with the detailed information that will allow him to put the nonquantitative aspects of a decision into a context.

Unfortunately, the problems discussed above are seldom discussed openly and seldom remembered in the heat of daily operations. The neatly reasoned and structured process portrayed in textbooks characteristically does not exist, while forces often not articulated are equally or more important to the establishment of policy than any rigorous, formal, highly quantitative or empirical analysis. The mismatch between theory and practice, however, is not unique to policy analysis.

There are several ways one might go about doing a policy analysis, but the one most frequently seen in the adversarial world of public politics is a form of impact analysis. That is, if such a policy is adopted, how will it impact my program or interests? This parochial perspective leads one to view all decisions in terms that are most meaningful to the subject area; e.g., money, jobs, air pollution, exports, or number of students. Many times, the attempt to relate policies to the variable of most interest to the decisionmaker makes it hard to use these results in other analyses, exacerbating further the problem of information transference.

Given the complexity in formulating national energy policy, the variety of variables that should be examined, the lack of data on environmental impacts, the uncertainties in the existing data, and the many public interests, how then does one address the issue of environmental trade-offs between energy alternatives? This issue is explored in the remainder of the section, focusing on three general questions:

- How have complex trade-off analyses been carried out in the past?
- What methodologies are currently available for performing such trade-off analyses?
- How can trade-offs of energy, economic, and environmental issues be improved?

We shall also present a couple of reviews as a sample of the current literature, as it was this effort which helped spark the analyses. These reviews will of necessity be brief, and will only give the reader a general idea of what is the whole piece. Further, only a partial critique is done of the study in terms of such factors as data consistency, accuracy, and utility. Where possible, the analyses will be related back to the ideal structure presented in this section.

We will then move from the actual attempts presented above to a more generalized discussion of the various techniques and conceptualizations proposed to handle trading off such variables as energy, economics, and environment. Again, a critique is given of each of these, primarily from the perspective of their utility today in real-world policy issues. No intent is implied as to their utility as useful approaches for some energy analyses.

Finally, we will summarize the principal limitations of current analyses and methods and suggest several ways to handle the problems of comparing energy technology alternatives for decisions on national energy policy that must be consummated in the next few years.

A PROCESS FOR TRADE-OFF ANALYSES

The process shown in Figure 2.1 is offered to order our thinking for judging the completeness of the environmental assessments (called "the

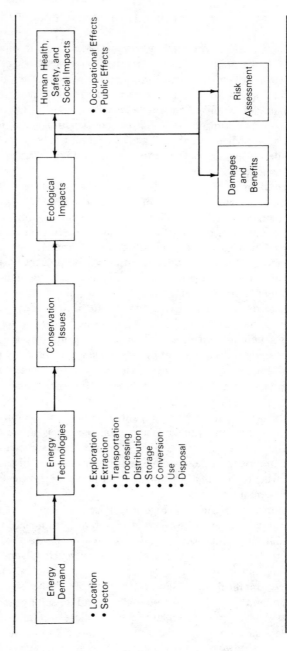

Figure 2.1 "Ideal" taxonomy of energy-environment issues

81

ideal" in the next section). A complete analysis should take into consideration all of the items presented in Figure 2.1. The process begins with an agreed upon scenario that estimates the amount of energy required by a specified technology at specific locations in the nation. The agreed-upon mix of technologies would then be analyzed over the total fuel cycle (including secondary impacts induced by construction) and for those impacts unique to each geographical location. The site-specific impacts are then used to derive average coefficients for environmental impacts which are regionally sensitive.

Environmental impacts will ideally include consideration of such factors as habitat conservation and other ecological effects, as well as accidents and human morbidity and mortality effects due to illness. Finally, this raw impact data will be used to derive damage estimates, the benefits of avoiding the damage, and intertechnology risk estimates.

Unquestionably, the use of quantification in the process portrayed in Figure 2.1 is difficult and one not likely to be fully developed in the near future. The level of understanding we have as a society of those significant energy-related environmental impacts that might occur in any given situation is rather primitive. Even in particular areas where we have better understanding, there is still great debate over the interpretation of the data. In many analyses, the description of the energy technology processes themselves are highly aggregated, not differentiated by process, not colocated geographically, and some are skipped altogether. Often the only environmental effects that are studied in depth involve health and occupational impacts, with little attention paid to ecological systems. For all intents and purposes, the full environmental picture is not considered, thereby making most energy trade-off studies weak and somewhat biased. The methods employed in these studies do not represent all of the possible methods by which one might compare alternative energy technologies. Conceptually, several more exist.

The taxonomy presented in Figure 2.1 is made up of two major portions. The lefthand side is designed to represent questions of where the pollution loading is taking place, when it is apt to occur (and what else is occurring at the same time and place), and how much is generated. To accomplish this, questions of energy demand (and conservation) are addressed by geographical locations and by sector of the economy. To supply this demand, the energy technologies are addressed by stages of the fuel cycle, so that at any particular time and place one knows the full supply and demand picture for energy-pollution-related changes against a backdrop of complete system environmental growth or change.

The second portion of the figure represents the translation of environmental coefficients into total impact values. The coefficients are specific for location, time, sector, and stage of the fuel cycle. Clearly, these requirements for a full assessment of any single technology make the study very complex, resource-using, and time-consuming. To do several such studies for each fuel or technology type, although desirable, would be difficult indeed.

No refutation is implied as to the value of analysis per se in this section. However, the line is drawn at several points:

- Data ought to be presented in analyses only if the analyst is fairly certain of their causality, value, sign, and so forth. Highly speculative relationships, values, and the like, or ones which are known to be very incomplete, have no place in a policy analysis, although they may be useful in a longer-range, properly formulated research or assessment piece.
- At least, a taxonomy of effects and impacts may be all that is able to be presented in a trade-off analysis, and in areas where emotional impact is indirectly present in the nature of the subject matter, great care ought to be exercised not to present unreliable findings, regardless of how well documented.
- When the analyst is stretching hard to come up with enough information to say something meaningful about a specific trade-off situation, it is fruitless to suggest very sophisticated techniques that rely on a richness of data to enable stochastic and distributive measures to be applied to the findings.

In addition to these three general desires or limits placed on anyone who is trained in a professional fashion are the realities introduced by the political/bureaucratic system. We have discussed these realities throughout this work. The following sections will give the reader a flavor of how failing to adhere to these general principals produces a very wide variety of study results impossible to use in a comparative sense, even if each one were individually accurate.

A COUPLE OF RECENT STUDIES

Over the past few years, but recently appearing with greater frequency, a number of studies purport to show the relative environmental acceptability of one energy technology in contrast to others. Because the studies themselves are more or less unique, in the sense that they are not clear examples of methodologies developed by a particular school, it is difficult if not impossible to categorize them. Most of the authors search for a common unit or attribute that allows an analyst to compare technologies. For several studies, the analytical basis consists of estimates of morbidity and mortality per unit of energy production. In general, the individual authors are honest enough to admit that their data are sparse. Depending upon such factors as relative data availability and ingenuity, however, the authors go on to quantify the risks associated with different stages of each energy technology fuel cycle. From this, estimates are made of "costs" and impacts of energy production. In contrast, a more revealing study would be one that estimates the total "cost" of an energy technology cycle on ecological systems and human health for all subtechnology and all phases of the fuel cycle. No study I am aware of even approximates this ideal. A review of two exemplary recent studies follows.

HEALTH EFFECTS OF ENERGY PRODUCTION AND CONVERSION

A study by Comar and Sagan, published in the *Annual Review of Energy,* estimates the health effects caused by energy technologies to a risk value. The study delineates a series of shortcomings of earlier analyses, including the fact that synergistic or additive effects among various pollutants have not been considered, health effects have usually been expressed in terms of single factors such as number of either premature deaths or serious disabilities, and finally, there has been a tendency to ignore the limitation of using risk estimates which monetize impacts in terms of abatement costs.

The authors describe damage functions in terms of exposure from low to high levels of pollutants and the effects of such exposures, ranging from no effect, undetectable effects with low probability, undetectable effects with high probability, clinical symptoms, and ultimate death. The low probability, little-effect area distinguished between threshold and non-threshold agents. For the former, there are levels of pollution below which no effects have been detected. From this the authors assert that it is relatively easy to set pollution standards for nonthreshold agents which have harm associated with any level above zero.

The concept of risk employed in this study is discussed in terms of the probability of death caused by energy-related pollutants. The effects of various forms of energy production are appraised in terms of their impact on the general population, although the authors recognize the relative risk of death to highly age-specific populations as a part of their calculations. Their results are therefore presented by age cohort.

TABLE 2.1   Methodological Steps for Integrated Assessment of
             Coal-Based Energy Technologies

(1)   Identify Issues, Alternatives, Policy Options
(2)   Review Past and Ongoing Related Research
(3)   Identify and Select Coal Processing and Utilization Alternatives
(4)   Identify and Describe External Future Changes
(5)   Develop Systematic Procedure for Relating Elements
(6)   Develop Baseline Futures
(7)   Identify and Describe Decisionmaking Procedure and Parties of Interest
(8)   Perform a Series of Sensitivity Analyses
(9)   Identify "Important" Alternative Futures
(10) Identify and Describe Impacts of External Changes on Model
(11) Identify Potential Impacts
(12) Evaluate Impacts of Alternative Futures
(13) Conclusions and Recommendations (Alternatives Strategies)

Information from various sources is used to generate a comparative analysis of the health effects, in terms of premature deaths and occupational injuries, associated with the operation of a 1000 MW powerplant. The results are presented in terms of ranges bounded by high and low values for each stage of the coal, oil, natural gas, and nuclear fuel cycles (Tables 2.1 and 2.2).

Finally, the authors convert the health effects data to estimates of risk. The information presented not only is age-specific and technology-specific, but relates the estimates of impacts from energy technologies to normal risks of death from any and all causes for the same age groups. The final conclusions of the study are that occupational deaths from the use of coal are considerably greater than for the other technologies. Premature deaths are also likely to be larger from the use of coal and oil than from natural gas or nuclear fuel.

Critique. Introduction of risk estimates for comparing different energy fuel cycles adds a dimension to the issue of technology trade-offs. In this specific study, however, the damage functions employed come under question because the calculation of final risk is not actually presented and documented. Although not explicitly stated by the authors, it appears that the health effects data are translated to deaths and injuries per unit of output and then to risk of death per year. The risk table is portrayed in discrete values by age cohort, but the health effects table presents results with large ranges of uncertainty. As with most studies of this nature, the effects of long-term, low-level exposures to powerplant emissions are not adequately addressed. Sorting out such effects from similar impacts caused

TABLE 2.2   Research Tasks to be Applied in the Conduct of an
             Integrated Assessment of Coal-Based Energy Technologies

1. Review, evaluation, and update of pertinent coal and coal-related previous and
    ongoing research
2. Definition of problem areas and identification of issues related to coal-based
    technologies
3. Selection and prioritization of technologies and supply systems to be assessed
4. Selection and prioritization of end uses to be assessed
5. Identification and description of social and energy alternative scenarios which
    will influence energy demand and coal-based technology choices
6. Identification of configurations of technologies, supply systems, and end uses to
    be assessed
7. Description of the existing biophysical and socioeconomic environment at
    appropriate local, regional, and national levels
8. Interactions that may occur between the technologies and supply systems and
    the biophysical and socioeconomic factors
9. Refinement of existing energy-demand projections for appropriate regional and
    national levels
10. Development of alternative scenarios for various technological mixes and the
    rates, levels, and timing of development
11. Identification and description of relevant legislation, regulations, and decision-
    making processes and involvement of the parties of interest
12. Identification of significant attributes in the process model (sensitivity analysis)
13. Assessment and comparison of the biophysical, socioeconomic, and energy
    impacts of each composite scenario ("important" alternative futures)
14. Aggregation of local, regional, and national impacts
15. Assessment and comparison of the long-range cumulative impacts of coal-energy
    technology depliyment
16. Identification and analysis of the csocial, economic, biophysical, political, legal,
    institutional, and technological constraints and alternative strategies for policy
    implementation ot avoid or mitigate undesirable impacts
17. Communication of the study results to EPA policymakers and other users and
    audiences

by other sources of pollution, such as smoking, vehicle emissions, and
natural sources, is very difficult. The information presented is in the form
of coefficients and so is really only an input into the taxonomy we
presented at the end of the first section.

RISK OF ENERGY PRODUCTION:
ATOMIC ENERGY CONTROL BOARD, CANADA

Recently, a study by Inhaber,[11] sponsored by the Atomic Energy
Control Board of Canada, considered eleven technological ways to gener-

ate electricity or equivalent energy: coal, oil, natural gas, nuclear, hydropower, solar thermal heating, methanol, wind, solar photovoltaics, solar space heating, and ocean thermal. These were chosen, not on the basis of being an exhaustive set of energy technologies, but because the authors felt the necessary data for the analysis were reasonably available.

Inhaber considered two types of risk for the analysis, catastrophic and noncatastrophic, the latter consisting primarily of risk to human health from industrial and occupational sources or from pollution effects. These risks were quantified for each fuel cycle from extraction to energy end use using a variety of data sources and assumptions about the current state of technological development. Seven sources of risk were considered, corresponding to seven defined stages of each fuel cycle: material and fuel production; component fabrication; plant construction; operation and maintenance; public health risk; transportation; and waste disposition and deactivation.

Three major types of data sources were used: statistics on (1) health effects due to pollutants, (2) industrial damage and disease statistics, and (3) materials and labor used for energy systems. By calculating or estimating a risk value in terms of mortality or morbidity to each stage of the cycles, Inhaber concluded that nonconventional energy systems can have substantial risk to human health. For coal and oil, most of the risk is associated with electricity production or end use (air pollution); for natural gas, nuclear, and ocean thermal, it is due to materials acquisition; and for wind, solar thermal electric, and solar photovoltaics, the risk is a function of the backup systems required (assumed to be coal).

The total man-days lost per megawatt-year net energy output over the lifetime of each energy system were also determined. Natural gas and nuclear were noted to have the lowest values, and most of the nonconventional technologies had values similar to coal and oil. The high values for the nonconventional energy sources were a function of the large amount of construction materials required, the risks associated with the required backup energy, and those associated with storage of the energy produced.

Critique. The comparison of eleven different methods for generating energy is a significant contribution to the literature in terms of risk analysis. A major problem I encountered, however, was that in order to make the relevant estimates for the health effects, results from a larger number of studies that were designed for other purposes had to be used. Normalization of values to one common unit for comparison purposes necessarily resulted in one sense of "apples being added to oranges." As with other such studies, this analysis does not go beyond the coefficient stage of data presentation.

There seem to be four general criticisms that the Inhaber analysis is open to: (1) the data were interpreted in a fashion not intended from the perspective of the original source of the data; (2) insufficient data are available on specific technologies, and the analysis is based on tenuous assumptions used to cover data gaps; (3) errors have been made deliberately or inadvertantly in assembling or presenting the data to justify the author's bias; and (4) the comparative technique chosen yields a static analysis without allowance for future technological development.

Although Inhaber's approach clearly captures a relatively large number of cross-technology comparisons, modifications might be in order in two areas. First, making the approach more dynamic over time would allow his results to be more useful. The study does not take into consideration the mix of technologies and the health effects of shifting this mix by specific geographical region or energy supply/demand circumstances. Such logic would require an analyst to discuss health effects in terms of ambient conditions in which a populace resides. It is not possible to capture different regional pollutant background levels in a static, technology-by-technology presentation. Second, a static analysis tends to lose the secondary impacts of future decisions to select one mix of energy technologies over another. The resources and economic activity which are required to establish and maintain one technological mix of energy systems or another, to lead to more or less energy of various forms and more or less pollution and occupational risks, depends upon the mix chosen.

LIMITATIONS

The investigation of these studies (and others)[12] makes it clear that the theoretical structure outstrips the capability for carrying out the actual assessments. In fact, in this area of environmental trade-offs, when health and safety risks are the principal impact variables, the inability to have confidence in the data means that the adage of a little information being better than none at all is replaced by a little knowledge being a dangerous thing. To be more explicit, the high levels of uncertainty in health-related statistics add a dimension of exaggeration to pollution or safety information which does not help the decisionmaker in the sense of shedding light on the problem. For example, a recent study done by Brookhaven National Laboratory as a part of the National Coal Utilization Assessments translated the air emissions data calculated on the basis of industrial and utility combustion into long- and short-range transport of pollutants. These data were then used to compute the expected health effects of the study scenario.

In 1985, between 7,600 and 122,00 excess deaths were forecast and in 1990, between 8,600 and 140,000 over a base of 7,500-120,000 in 1995. Ignoring the inflammatory nature of the term "excess deaths" for the moment, the significant fact is that when the confidence limit is extended to 95 percent (two standard deviations) in 1985, the number of excess deaths is estimated to be from 0 to 250,000.[13] These numbers, assuming that one can give some credence to them at face value, provide a range so great that it is unclear what a decisionmaker should do. Such data are so primitive that it is questionable whether they can truly be considered "information." Truly, can it be held that the steps from pollution emitted, to population-at-risk, to estimates of mortality, really add to the caliber of the decision, if the data deteriorates as rapidly from each of these steps to the next as experience suggests?

We are assuming that the studies which attempt to trade off energy, and environment are not normative in nature. Let us be explicit about what is meant here. It is right and proper for an analyst to continually strive to introduce the best analytical process that can be brought to bear on an issue. In this sense, he can talk of one technique as being the "right" one to use in a particular situation. It is not the place of an analyst, though, to prejudge the outcome of an analysis by proselytizing a specific technology at the expense of others. Although the latter is extreme, the former often gets out of hand when proponents of a technique go so far as to condemn a decision process in favor of their own pet theory or technique regardless of the practicality of actually carrying out the assessment. Normative analysis which sets out to teach the policymakers how they "ought" to make decisions comes dangerously close to the prejudgment flaw. In short, the proper function of the analyst is to aid the decision process by making available the best information that can be brought to bear in a timely fashion, and in as objective a fashion as possible.

CONCEPTUAL METHODOLOGIES

Despite progress in understanding environmental effects, there is still considerable uncertainty about possible physical, biological, and social consequences of large-scale energy projects. Even when potential consequences are known, the likelihood of their occurrence is not. Decisions on major energy projects, however, cannot always be delayed until enough data and understanding are available to absolutely and unequivocally assure that the related environmental impacts are acceptable. Such decisions will be made and decisionmakers will select methods and analyses to help make those decisions. In the previous section, we examined a couple of attempts to compare the environmental impacts of promising energy technologies in order to provide some rational basis for proceeding with the deployment of one technology rather than another. These attempts were flawed for several reasons, including use of inadequate data on environmental effects, plus analytical methods that were found wanting.

In this section we shall examine an assortment of methodologies that might be used for comparing technologies. Some of these methods were employed in the studies surveyed above. But before proceeding with a glimpse of these methodologies, a few general comments on the use of methods and models are in order. In the methods and models reviewed herein, attempts have been made to empirically determine the relevant variables, collect the data, and test the model. A major problem involves the quality of the data used, since frequently the specific data called for in the original design cannot be found, or the expense to collect it is prohibitive. Consequently, analysts tend to modify certain model paradigms to be able to use available information. Such models frequently become "data driven," reflecting only the information available and not the information that might more properly have been used if one were to address the issue at hand adequately.

On the other hand, some extremely complex and quantitative methods focus on how decisions *ought* to be made (ignoring how decisions actually are made). Their supporters suggest that if the prescribed techniques were followed, good decisions naturally would result. The major difficulty with such a normative approach is that it does not reflect actuality; it defines reality to be consistent with the model or the modeler's conceptual design. Just as models that do not capture the critical facts about a technology will likely not pass muster before the scientific community, those that ignore significant political realities of a situation will be rejected by decisionmakers. As such, normative models, techniques, and analyses are often seen as intrusions onto the turf that decisionmakers see as their own.

Even if data problems do not exist and models or techniques seem to reflect reality, additional difficulties may arise over the relative importance of the variables in the model in terms of the decision at hand. Consider, for example, the problems of placing a value on human life. Despite resistance to thinking about life in economic terms, individuals by their actions actually do place finite values on their lives. Decisions about installing safety features, buying life insurance, or accepting a more hazardous job for extra salary all carry implicit judgments about the value placed on life. Likewise, assigning measures of relative importance to the various impact categories is normative, based on the attitudes, beliefs, and opinions of the decisionmaker. There are several ways that one could go about grouping the methodologies which follow; for example, some are more or less "objective" than others or require more or less quantification; some methods add or make explicit the concept of uncertainty; some allow input of undocumented human opinion or judgment. No one taxonomy is to be preferred, per se. All the approaches attempt to assess energy technologies in a comparative fashion using factors such as environment or economics as indicators of preference. In all these approaches, some degree of human judgment is necessary to guide the analysis. Knowledge of the psychology involved in such judgments causes concern, since people (including experts forced to go beyond available data and to rely on intuitions) have difficulty in comprehending complex and uncertain information and making valid inferences from such information. Each method has some serious flaws that have become evident in actual use.

DELPHI TECHNIQUE

The Delphi Technique is an attempt to solve the problem of incomplete data in conducting trade-off analysis.[14] The approach requires analysts to be exposed to views and opinions of experts and to one another through a program of sequential questions, with feedback concerning consensus and conflict. It attempts to improve the traditional panel or committee approach to issue assessment by formulating or estimating collectively the most likely value, issue, or weight.

The method (and its several variants) is designed with the idea of obtaining iterative evaluations of a question in a fashion that imputes weights from a range of experts without undue influence from a dominant personality. To eliminate assertive personality or peer pressure, participants are often physically isolated, with group consensus learned only through written documentation provided by the analyst. The method attempts to distill the combined technical judgments from a group of experts, and reduces the importance of stated opinions, biases, and personality dominance within the assessment system that might alter the decision process.

Critique. Although Delphi is widely accepted as a legitimate attempt to fill in an important gap by providing empirical data to the decisionmaker, the very novelty of the technique allows for several criticisms: (1) the experts chosen can be biased merely by the fact that they are experts (the technique works best when the experts represent one specialty rather than different disciplines, preferences, or other interests); (2) it frequently takes a significant amount of time to carry out a study; (3) because the technique allows the issue to be "enriched" by the participants adding additional subissues and questions to the original list, the number of items that each participant has to consider often grows to unwieldy lengths; (4) there is no real guarantee that after the exercise is complete that the results will have any validity or are better than a completely subjective evaluation of the same issue; and (5) the cost of the analysis of a major issue is not apt to be small in terms of either time or money.

HEALTH EFFECTS ASSESSMENTS

The most common comparative technique used to measure the environmental costs of emerging energy technologies in the articles previously surveyed is health effects assessment.[15] Although the techniques used to determine health effects vary slightly, and the data sources and means of data manipulation are considerable, the general methodology employed is conceptually similar:

(1) The energy technologies are segmented into the phases of the total fuel cycle: exploration, extraction, refining and processing, transportation, generation, and waste disposal.

(2) Health effects types are categorized in terms of such items as occupational and public health, accidents, chronic diseases, and fatalities.

(3) Values are then assigned to each type of health effects for each phase of the fuel cycle for each technology. These values are generally in the form of coefficients, sometimes with ranges reflecting the certainty of the data.

(4) The relative amount of each fuel used is mapped onto this coefficient data base by scenario, and health effects estimates by technology are generated.

(5) More sophisticated techniques go a step further to translate these estimates into risk or damage values. Others combine the health impacts with those of ecological insults such as acid rain, increasing carbon dioxide concentrations, and water use.

Critique. This technique is appealing to those concerned with ultimate environmental impacts of energy development. We have already discussed some problems above, but will review them here again. If results can be obtained reliably and presented in a fashion that is widely agreed upon, this method could be useful in decisionmaking. Unfortunately, obtaining adequate cause and effect data which are specific for each phase of a fuel cycle is not yet possible. Not nearly enough research and analysis has been performed. Instead, inferences are made of the relationship between laboratory tests under controlled conditions on animals and the effects on humans of real-life conditions. The techniques used are expensive, time-consuming, and often of debatable relevance to real-world situations. On the other hand, the statistical studies of population reactions to exposures or insults are equally problematic due to the fact that there is no way to say for certain that the effect noted is caused by the specific pollutant being studied.

More importantly from the decisionmaking perspective,[16] this methodology focuses only on human health effects. Even if accurately measured, such effects are only a part of the overall environmental picture. Health effects assessment focuses on populations at risk and ignores the potential ecological impacts of energy technology development. Translating health effects estimates into units that can be explicitly compared with similar types of economic and energy parameters is an exercise for which methods and criteria are not yet available in a readily acceptable form.

NET ENERGY ANALYSIS

Net energy analysis is a method that examines the total energy required by an energy technology to realize a given amount of useful energy.[17] The energy components considered include those of the total fuel cycle and of the energy lost in ecosystems that have been altered or destroyed. Total energy (necessary to generate useful energy for human purposes) is estimated for each alternative. Technologies can then be compared on the basis of net energy generated.

The conceptual methodology is straightforward. Its proponents want a total energy balance calculated which includes all of the energy expended, directly and indirectly, in the production of a given unit of energy for end use. The amount of energy used in the production of the end use energy is subtracted from the delivered amount, yielding a "net" energy balance. This fundamentally is the net energy approach, although the concept could be extended to include other realistic effects like environmental damage caused by operation of the generator. The estimated energy content of such damage would be subtracted in the calculation of the net energy produced, to yield an even lower net energy.

Critique. The attraction of this technique is that it offers an absolute standard of value. Activities are assessed in terms of a ratio measure that is stable in the changing circumstances of the real world. The amount of energy embodied in particular units of capital and labor is a physical relationship. Technical change, which is a socioeconomic phenomena, may alter the nature of an item before its production; but once produced, it is essentially given in terms of energy content. However, at any point in time, the state of knowledge, capital stock, or labor force composition may not permit expeditious switching to alternative fuel sources. Assessing public policy alternatives requires the consideration of categories of energy supplied instead of merely energy content in a physical sense.

This procedure also misrepresents the decisionmaking process, which ideally allows direct human action toward collective goals. National energy policies in general try to alter the allocation of resources to achieve an acceptable balance in supply and demand for the public. Judging the impacts of energy policy on the environment only on the basis of energy utilized is too restrictive. Net energy has additional weaknesses. It fails, for example, to illuminate or aid in the assessment of impact from government policies or regulations. Also, net energy analysis does not adequately contribute to the sequential and adaptive aspects of decisionmaking. No mechanism exists in the process for dividing the analysis into sequential steps, nor for taking into account possible future adjustments due to newly acquired information.

BENEFIT-COST ANALYSIS

The benefit-cost approach is based on a method of assessing the value of the gains to all gainers and the value of the losses to all losers. These are taken to be the willingness to pay for the activity or not to have the activity, respectively. If gains (benefits) exceed losses (costs), then the project is worthwhile in the absence of a budget constraint. Where there is a budget constraint, the funds are allocated among all projects so that benefit less cost is greatest from all projects.

Estimating all types of benefits and costs is difficult. Monitoring gains and losses is complicated because of commensurability problems, e.g., comparing the losses of scenic vistas and flora and fauna to gains in conservation. This problem also becomes more complicated because of equity considerations. For example, an impact from an energy technology can be a benefit to some individuals, while a disbenefit or cost to others. An arid area that is stripmined and then seeded with nonindigenous plants may appear more aesthetically pleasing or economically preferable to some, although not an improvement for those with strong preferences for the original desert environments.

Two procedures are useful for overcoming these deficiencies. The first is observation of market prices. This is best where benefits are directly monetized in the marketplace. A hydroelectric facility, for example, will generate at least one output (electricity) which is bought and sold. Thus, data from extant facilities can be used in the development of benefits estimates. Second, most environmental resources are not exchanged in markets, and therefore benefits are not directly observable and monetized. In such cases, surrogates are often used, providing an indirect method for expressing benefits. Types of surrogates range from partial measures of total benefits to parameters that attempt to encompass total benefits. An example of the former would be travel cost measures. A hydroelectric facility's value to society could be the reduction in recreational costs to boaters, such as travel costs to more distant boating sites.

In this regard, development models that attempt to optimize consumer behavior are examples of trying to account fully for the benefits of energy activities. In such cases, non-market-related environmental impacts may be treated as constraints upon the surrogates or benefit estimates obtained from the model. There are a variety of such models, and there is a common thread in their use of estimation of benefits by inputting values to nonmarket activities from observed market behavior.

Critique. Benefit-cost is not a sequential decisionmaking process. It assumes that the benefits and costs are relatively independent. This is a simplification of the real world, since a decision on the desirability of a project may affect the benefits and costs accruing from future development projects. Benefit-cost analysis also does not adequately handle the problem of uncertainty. While some aspects of uncertainty associated with the probability of certain events occurring can be incorporated, this approach has not traditionally handled the problem of uncertainty about future preferences.

In essence, benefit-cost analysis has been used as a data reduction procedure that attempts to quantitatively express political and social policies in economic terms. Through its use, public policy formulation becomes an exercise primarily of economy and efficiency, without due consideration of the broader goals of social equity and public welfare. Cost-benefit analysis has been classified as a decision framework which excludes all political, social, and institutional considerations, as well as all nonquantifiable variables. In practice, substantial items that might be thought of as benefits have proven to be nonquantifiable.

To those on the receiving end of public decisionmaking, the value in using this approach depends heavily on the approach of the political official involved. If a benefit-cost analysis is incomprehensible, its value for policy formulation is lost. If, on the other hand, the political official works too closely with the analysts, then the analytical results may tend to be biased in favor of the official's predetermined disposition.

DECISION ANALYSIS UNDER UNCERTAINTY

This technique incorporates the concept of uncertainty in the most comprehensive fashion of all the other methods discussed here. All aspects of a decision analysis are treated stochastically, and it incorporates subjective, as well as objective, probabilities. The subjective aspects are aggregated measures of individual probability distributions.

In theory, individuals have opinions about the likelihood of various future events occurring, given certain assumptions about related circumstances. This is true irrespective of the existence of data that would be useful for generating objective probabilities. For example, even though slurry backfilling has never been attempted in commercial oil shale in situ retorts, individuals do hold opinions about the likelihood of this method's success. Recent work suggests that knowledgeable individuals may be induced through an interviewing process to reveal their subjective probability distributions.[19]

Since decision analysis is a relatively new technique, a brief description of its more important characteristics may clarify its comparison to the ideal. A distinguishing feature of decision analysis is the use of a ranking function. In benefit-cost analysis, the attempt is to assess alternatives on the basis of "the people's" preferences. Within decision analysis, the assessment is made based upon the preferences of the decisionmaker, who is assessed for his/her values, and the impacts are ranked according to weights derived from these values. Of course, when the decisionmaker is used to generate the ranking function, one does not preserve the value judgments associated with, say, benefit-cost analysis.

The most important advantage alleged for decision analysis is in its treatment of risk and uncertainty. Uncertainty about future goals and the state of the world presents problems for decisionmakers. Possible outcomes of actions may have considerable policy significance, but they may be unlikely to occur. Actions may have associated risks of irreversible damage. Conventional techniques inadequately assess such cases, since they are neither sequential nor adaptive. Decision analysis offers the capability to acquire information and alter the choice of alternatives as an integral part of its methodology. It uses the decision tree framework to break up the problem into partial alternatives. In doing so, it explicitly structures the issue so as to include an evaluation of the benefits of further information acquisition.

Critique. The desire to treat uncertainty with analytic precision is a laudatory goal not likely to be realized in the near future, particularly with the information base presently at hand. Its ranking function and the use of subjective probabilities may make it difficult to convince decisionmakers of the utility of its design. Additionally, obtaining access to the decision-maker for the purpose of assessing preferences is, in most cases, difficult or impossible. The attempt to recognize the uncertainty in human decision-making by the use of probabilities is a step toward analytic elegance, and may have some validity in the better defined world of business; it has yet to earn its spurs in the public policy world, however.

INDICATORS [20]

Another major methodological approach for comparing energy technologies is what we choose to call indicators analysis. This is actually a quite broad category whose most formalized embodiment is to be found in the area of social analysis. The formal work is associated with various sorts of policy analysis presently performed in the government social welfare programs. In the case of social indicator systems, formal structures are developed for aggregation into a single or very small set of goals or indicators. In certain types of conventional indicator analysis often carried out by government analysts, a descriptive model is used to generate indicators which are considered critical for a particular decision. Those indicators may not adequately represent social welfare directly, but are usually believed to be indirect measures. For example, a model that predicts pollutant residual levels might be used, because it is well known that certain types of residuals have health impacts. The model outputs do not provide direct predictions of health impacts, but rather are utilized to produce intermediate indicators, i.e., residuals. An analyst then uses the intermediate indicators to produce a formal analysis of health impacts based on residuals data.

Critique. In terms of our original criteria, an indicators system has a number of difficulties. No formalized procedure for dealing with risk and uncertainty is incorporated into this methodology. This means that it is not at present sequential and adaptive, although it might be made so with further thought to the design. The implications of not being sequential and adaptive have been developed in other parts of this section. It should also be noted that in practice, it will almost inevitably have commensurability problems. The development of connectives will be difficult at the higher levels of the hierarchy. In most cases, the quantification of the hierarchy will stop well short of the most general social goal. Therefore, if an indicators system is used to compare the impacts of various energy technologies, the problem of examining the trade-off issue with incommensurable units becomes one of the major shortcomings of this method.

Just as no single discipline can adequately address all aspects of an energy-technology trade-off issue, no one of the approaches discussed above provides a sufficient basis for determining what levels of environmental protection and safety are acceptable to the general public. In attempting to resolve the problems inherent in these methods, each new approach engenders problems of its own. Therefore, a number of other approaches that attempt to utilize an integrated or combined approach to comparative analysis are examined.

AN INTEGRATED ASSESSMENT

An example of a combined approach is a study plan developed by Battelle Memorial Institute.[21] Although not unique in form, this study was an attempt at an integrated assessment of coal-based technologies and serves well for illustrative purposes. The study framework is outlined in Table 2.1. To turn this conceptual plan into more useful output, specific research tasks given in Table 2.2 are performed.

This approach is relatively ambitious, certainly comprehensive, but it has many of the problems of the more limited methods discussed earlier, especially in terms of the capability for quantifying subjective values. The complexity of this method, although intellectually appealing as the way things "ought" to be done, tends to force required tasks to be completed in a time frame likely to be too late for most short-term policy decisions. Its value would be enhanced for those persistent, longer-term issues for which analysts are provided more time for research.

TECHNOLOGY EVALUATIONS [22]

Energy technologies being developed by DOE to meet the objectives of the National Energy Plan must satisfy a set of "specifications" or requirements imposed by environmental standards mandated under national environmental policies and legislation. In this sense, national environmental policies place boundary conditions on the implementation of all other national policies, including energy policy. Environmental acceptability and safeguards for public health and safety are therefore designed into the technology before it is commercialized. To provide a check on this development, Office of Environment (EV) scientists prepare Environmental Readiness Documents (ERDs) for each technology at critical decision points.

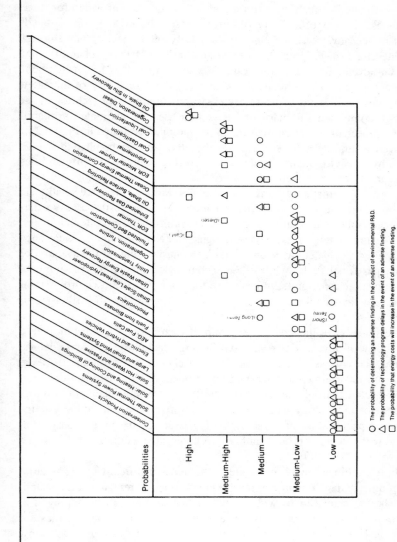

Figure 2.2 Cross-technology comparisons

99

The ERDs themselves do not contain direct intertechnology comparisons but provide information to be used in such comparisons. In each ERD, estimated probabilities (on a scale of 0.1-0.9) are provided for three outcomes: (1) the probability of further research and development will result in an "adverse finding" as to the ability of the technology to meet existing and projected environmental standards; (2) the probability that such an adverse finding would result in significant delays in development and deployment of the technology; and (3) the probability of increased energy cost as a result of necessary environmental control technology. A recently completed summary of ERDs that used the estimated probabilities as a mechanism for comparing 24 technologies is shown in Figure 2.2.

Seven technologies have been judged to have low probability of significant adverse environmental findings, and correspondingly low probabilities of program delays or increased energy costs. These technologies are categorized as "minimal constraint" technologies. Most of these are small-scale systems operating from decentralized locations close to the user, so that large-scale environmental impacts are minimized. Several technologies, such as wind systems, solar passive designs, and electric vehicles, were once widely used in this country but were deemphasized due to the availability of cheaper fossil fuels. While these technologies appear to face minimal environmental constraints, in each case there are significant environmental concerns which require careful design and management with further monitoring and analysis.

The ERDs have judged a large group of technologies to have moderate probability of adverse environmental findings, technology program delays, or increased cost as a result of environmental controls. Although there are significant environmental uncertainties associated with these technologies, it is expected that adherence to standards and use of available or developing control technology will satisfactorily control and mitigate any detrimental impacts. Most of these technologies are in the predemonstration stage, with demonstration and environmental readiness likely to be achieved by 1980-1990.

Six technologies have been judged to have significant environmental constraints that will require extensive environmental research and development before they can be widely used or before they can be deployed in environmentally sensitive areas. Except for hydrothermal power, they are based on fossil fuels. None of the technologies are new, and in fact, most are already in use in one or more locales. Their relatively large scale and their use of new processes, chemicals, or materials are the chief cause of concern.

From the standpoint of comparing technologies, the ERD's summary is indicative, but certainly not conclusive. The ERDs which were summarized represent collective informed judgments, but they were prepared separately with no attempt to "calibrate" judgments for intertechnology comparisons. The cross-cutting look at technologies provided by the summary, however, allows the reader to form some opinions as to the relative significance and intractability of environmental problems potentially associated with individual energy technologies. On the other hand, the grouping of technologies into categories of low, medium, and significant impact does accomplish a rough sort of indirect comparison of classes of technologies; however, there is no attempt made to judge whether the technologies in these categories are more or less acceptable from an environmental standpoint. It merely states that to deploy them in an environmentally acceptable way, relatively more or less would have to be done to mitigate their efforts.

Further, the ERDs do not address many major energy technologies that have already penetrated the marketplace. Examples are nuclear technologies and conventional coal combustion. Omissions of this magnitude clearly make the document less useful than others reviewed here in carrying out a comprehensive comparison of on-line and proposed energy systems in terms of environmental acceptability.

This methodology falls far short of the ideal presented in the first section. It limits itself to a mixed qualitative/quantitative discussion of each technology and, because it is subjective, requires careful interpretation when the individual technology assessments are combined to provide a rudimentary cross-technology comparison.

METHODOLOGIES REVIEWED

Clearly, there is a bias suggested in this section against a number of the formal methods presently preferred for use by policy analysts. The conclusions or assertions I have made about any one of these (or all of them) are not meant to be a ringing denunciation of the method per se. Such is clearly beyond the scope of this chapter, and clearly not enough evidence has been offered to support such hypotheses. The main message I offer here is that there are no clearly defined methodologies widely recognized by the professional community that can be used in their conceptual sense in the real world of policy analyses. This is not due to a flaw in the logic of the original conceptualization, but to an inadequate information base or to the fact that some of the needed data do not lend themselves readily to quantification.

WHERE DO WE GO FROM HERE?

Most formal analytic methods are, at present, wanting. Given this, how can the nation make rational policy choices, encourage safe technologies, and avoid dangerous ones? How can we make energy policy decisions so that damage to human well-being and to ecosystem integrity is minimized?

The first point to recognize is that the failure of analysis does not lead inevitably to the failure of decisionmaking. There are ways of making policy choices other than by basing them primarily on formal, empirical prospective analyses. Decisions that follow the latter method can be considered as an example of the "analytic paradigm" at work. This analytic paradigm, however, is not the way living organisms generally guide their behavior. The reason is simple. This approach cannot work when the future is a mystery and when the understanding of key relationships, even in the present, is poor. Such a state of ignorance and uncertainty describes our present policy situation in energy and environment.

Simon and others have described an alternative to the analytic paradigm. Steinbrunner has termed it the "cybernetic paradigm." Its basic principles evolved in the natural world as responses to complexity, ignorance, uncertainty, incommensurability, and risk.

In contrasting cybernetic notions with the analytic paradigm, we find that the specific propositions used to define the latter in application to the complex policy problem have all been disputed. The analytic assumption of value integration is rejected. It is replaced with a somewhat vaguely specified conception which posits minimally articulated, preservative values, and which does not yield a coherent preference ordering for alternative states of the world under trade-off conditions. The major theme is that the decision process is organized around the problem of controlling inherent uncertainty by means of highly focused attention and highly programmed response. The decision maker in this view does not engage in alternative outcome calculations or in updated probability assessments. The learning process is not casual but, rather, instrumental. At the level of collective decisions the paradigm posits a process in which decisions are fragmented into small segments and the segments treated sequentially. The process is dominated by established procedure.[23]

Another way to describe this approach is by the psychological term "compartmentalization." In the human thought process, rationality is often achieved by segmenting decisions into compartments and operating on these decisions using rules and sets of values developed specifically for each narrow situation. How can this model of decisionmaking be used in dealing with the issue of energy and the environment? In fact, its basic structure is already in place. This is the regulatory process created by recent federal legislation.

The method chosen for this regulatory process by public decision-makers relies upon standards. These standards are based on considerations of absolute and relative levels of public health and welfare. Pollution was regulated at one time by relating emissions to ambient conditions. Other and more recent standards have gone in a number of additional directions: (1) reducing pollution levels to the lowest possible emission level; (2) protecting endangered species and recreational areas; and (3) limiting human intrusion into delicate ecosystems. In all such cases, regulatory limits were formulated with an eye toward providing an upper bound on human activity in specific "compartments." In some cases, a limit was carefully set with the best information available. An attempt was made to monitor performance against this standard. Examples are the ambient or primary air standards set under the Clean Air Act.[24] In other cases, the limit is a strict prohibition against any intrusion; examples are the Endangered Species Act[25] or prohibitions against certain commercial activities on coasts, wetlands, and some rivers.

Under this approach, human health and safety, and ecological systems (e.g., endangered species, forests, and coastal zones) are protected, one at a time, from an agent of harm. Let us assume that the standards are fully derived from the best available medical and scientific information, and that they are enforced. We can conclude that, as far as we are able to know, the environment is protected. If an energy technology can meet the standards, it is thus not a threat to the environment. Different technologies, however, require different costs to meet a particular standard. Then, the choice between technologies can be made on economic grounds, with environment not being a negotiable issue. If environmental standards are to be met regardless, the relative environmental impacts of various energy technologies simply are not relevant.

There is a deficiency with a system of environmental protection of this nature if it were built solely on present practice. There are also key roles for analysis. The deficiency is the lack of a strong mechanism to provide adaptive feedback or instrumental learning, the results of which would be completely monitored. Any synergistic effects with agents regulated under other standards would be carefully noted. New basic research, both clinical and epidemiological, would be performed. Formal analysis would then be used to recommend changes in the standard based on this new information. In fact, analysis would be invaluable in such a situation—it is in standard-setting where it works best. That is, there are clear bounds on the inputs to the problem; the objective of decisionmaking is narrow and tightly focused, and one issue is taken at a time.

It is obvious that analysis still has other important roles to play under the compartmental, decomposed approach suggested for decisions on energy and environment. Analysis is used to help select the areas in which to set standards, to determine thresholds of impact, and to help set the standards. Analysis is used in incorporating new information into revised standards. It *must* be used to estimate whether all the environmental standards would be met under particular energy scenarios. Analysis cannot properly be used, however, to decide which energy technologies are the safest overall, and thus which are most deserving of support and encouragement. If we try to bring analysis out of its proper supporting role, trouble will occur. The nation will be basing its future on false premises.

There is clearly a feeling on the part of some who are concerned with environmental protection that one technology is to be preferred over another. Indeed, one gets a flavor of these preferences just in reading some of the analyses reviewed. I believe that such analyses, intended as adversarial pieces, serve no good purpose. If indeed there are adequate laws and regulations to protect human health and welfare, and if these laws are enforced for each technology, should the environmentalist care which energy technology is chosen? [25] They can all be made equally benign. A fruitful path for those who engage in such adversarial activities would be to ensure that each technology is made so benign in itself, rather than to try and figure out a defensible way to measure the impacts of one in terms of another.

Summary

This chapter has been concerned with the procedure of and need for formal, analytic methods in the formulation of policy issues. It began with a discussion of the basic conceptual underpinnings of systems or policy analyses and laid out the various stages of such analyses and the information needed to do the analysis. Although much of the discussion is centered around the use of models and other formal techniques (we shall discuss models in some detail in the next chapter), it becomes clear that one of the most important components of this process is the decisionmaker.

We went on to look at the attitudes of an ideal decisionmaker for the rigorous process of policy analysis. The ideal is supposed to be both omniscient and omnipotent. In fact, he is neither. He is expected to know his goals and to have the necessary means and authority to achieve them. Often he lacks both. Further, because communication is so important, he is expected to have the same shared technical experience and training as the analysts, and to agree with them on what and how the analyses should be done. In practice, this seldom happens.

The next several sections were a look at the veracity of these assumptions, both through case studies and other assessments of the issues. It becomes clear that although considerable lip service may be posed for formalism, there is reason to believe that other factors are important to the policy formulation process. Much time is spent demonstrating that the technical training of a policymaker colors his world and helps to define how that world is perceived and defined.

The stated intent of the last section was to survey the potential for analytically comparing the various energy technologies in terms of their relative impact on the environment. As noted earlier, there is no stance assumed as to whether it is a proper thing to analyze energy issues from such a myopic perspective. Indeed, we deliberately expanded the trade-off analyses to include cost (economic) perspectives in some instances because the various environmental regulations recognize cost as a factor under certain conditions.

The second section skimmed through a couple of studies, all of which purported in one way or another to measure the environmental impacts of one technology as compared to another. We began with a so-called "ideal" taxonomy which could be used to produce a more or less complete environmental assessment of an energy technology. If one is going to take on the ambitious goals of cross-technology impact assessment, such studies ought to address themselves to each of the areas listed. Because of one reason or another, none of the studies surveyed compared favorably to the ideal. In general, the principal deficiency we found was in the area of data quality. There seems to be a pervasive feeling that the data available to perform energy-environment impact were fairly primitive and that the results that could be honestly drawn were fairly tentative.

Having noted the rather disappointing findings of the studies surveyed, attention was then turned to an investigation of many of the most common methodologies used in public analyses and assessments. Again, I made no attempt to be exhaustive because I simply wanted to see if any of the techniques could reasonably be expected to produce analytically defensible environment, energy, and economic trade-offs. Again, the findings were largely negative. This is not to say that none of these methods are useful in performing analyses in other areas, but merely that given the state of the information base in the areas in question, they cannot be expected to perform well.

Finally, I suggested that all is not lost. I stated that comparisons of energy, economics, and environment were done, but usually only on a single technology, a specific issue, or on technologies of a similar type (all solar, for example). I closed by suggesting that the desire to do energy analyses with environmental protection as the objective function may not be necessary. This is the case because environmental protection is guaranteed in many areas, most particularly in the areas of human health and safety. It is on this point that one might investigate the reasons for doing such cross-technology trade-offs. There is clearly a feeling on the part of some who are concerned with environmental protection that one technology is preferred over another, and indeed, one gets a flavor of these preferences in reading some of the analyses of the type presented in the second section. Another perspective is that such adversarial analyses are not necessary if indeed there are adequate laws and regulations to protect human health and welfare. If these laws are enforced for each technology, should the environmentalist care which energy technology is chosen if, indeed, they can all be made equally benign? My suggestion is that a more fruitful path for those who engage in adversarial activities in energy-environment matters would be to ensure that each technology is made benign in and of itself, rather than to try to devise defensible ways to measure its impacts in terms of the others.

NOTES

1. E. S. Quade, *Analysis for Public Decisions* (New York: American Elsevier, 1975).

2. Etzioni Amitai, *Modern Organizations* (Englewood Cliffs, NJ: Prentice-Hall, 1964).

3. D. H. Meadows, D. L. Randers, Jr., and W. W. Behrens, III, *The Limits to Growth* (New York: Si gnet Books, 1972).

4. U.S. EPA, *A Guide to Models in Governmental Planning and Operations* (Washington, D.C.: ORD/EPA, 1974).

5. W. Alonso, "Predicting Best with Imperfect Data," *American Institute of Planners Journal* (July 1968): 248-252.

6. W. Alonso, "Predicting Best with Imperfect Data," *American Institute of Planners Journal* (July 1968): 248-252.

7. In contradistincion to the belief that these very formal, sophisticated techniques are able to produce useful and reliable policy alternatives, I have chosen to cite liberally from a recent study done by the Department of Energy.

8. "Nuclear Power: Can We Do Without It?" *National Journal* 17 (April 1979).

9. Clean Air Act Amendments of 1977 (P.L. 95-95, August 7, 1977).

10. See *Comparing Energy Technology Alternatives From An Environmental Perspective* (DOE/EV-0109, January 1981) for a more complete review. This section was drawn from this piece.

11. Hubert Inhaber, "Risks with Energy from Conventional and Nonconventional Sources," *Science* 203 (February 1979).

12. P. W. House, J. A. Coleman, R. D. Shull, R. Matheny, J. C. Hock, "Comparing Energy Technology Alternatives from an Environmental Perspective," Office of Technology Impacts, U.S. Department of Energy, December 1979.

13. "An Assessment of National Consequences of Increased Coal Utilization," Office of Technology Impacts, U.S. Department of Energy, February 1979.

14. L. L. Philipson et al., *Investigation of the Feasibility of the Delphi Technique for Estimating Risk Analysis Parameters* (Washington, DC: U.S. Government Printing Office, 1974).

15. Nuclear Regulatory Commission, *Reactor Safety Study—An Assessment of Accident Risks in U.S. Commercial Nuclear Power Plants* ("Rasmussen Report," in several volumes), October 1975. See also "Health Evaluation of Energy-Generating Sources," *Journal of the American Medical Association* 240 (November 1978): 2, 192-193, 195; and C. L. Comar and L. A. Sagan, "Health Effects of Energy Production and Conversion," *Annual Review of Energy* 1 (1976): 581-600.

16. Hubert Inhaber, "Risks with Energy from Conventional and Nonconventional Sources," *Science* 203 (February 1979).

17. David A. Huettner, "Net Energy Analysis: An Economic Assessment," *Science* 192 (April 1976); Gregg Marland, Alfred M. Petty, and David B. Reister, "Net Energy Analysis of In Situ Oil Shale Processing," *Energy* 3: 31-41.

18. Richard Layard (ed.) *Cost-Benefit Analysis* (New York: Penguin, 1974). See also E. J. Mishan, *Cost-Benefit Analysis* (New York: Praeger, 1976); and Henry Peskin and Eugene P. Seskin, *Cost-Benefit Analysis and Water Pollution Policy* (Washington, DC: The Urban Institute, 1975).

19. H. Raiffa, *Decision Analysis: Introductory Lectures on Choices Under Uncertainty* (New York: Addison-Wesley, 1968). See also B. Fischhoff, "Informed Consent in Societal Risk-Benefit Decisions," in Proceedings of the Society for General Systems Research, 22nd Annual Meeting, 1978.

20. Geoffrey H. Moore, "The Analysis of Economic Indicators," *Scientific American* 232 (January 1975). See also M. E. Olsen, M. G. Curry, M. R. Greene, B. D. Melber, and P. J. Merwin, "A Social Impact Assessment and Management Methodology Using Social Indicators and Planning Strategies," Pacific Northwest Laboratory; and Robert P. Pikul, Charles Risselle, and Martha Lilienthal, "Development of Environmental Indices, Outdoor Recreational Resources and Land Use Shift," in William Thomas (ed.) *Indicators of Environmental Quality* (New York: Plenum, 1972).

21. Battelle Memorial Institute and the University of Michigan, *First Year Report for the Coal Technology Assessment (CTA) Program,* prepared for the U.S. Environmental Protection Agency.

22. More than twenty Environmental Readiness Documents (ERDs) have been or are being prepared in the Office of Environmental Assessments for the Assistant Secretary for Environment, U.S. Department of Energy. We will discuss these in more detail in Chapter 4 in a section devoted to this planning process.

23. J. D. Steinbrunner, *The Cybernetic Theory of Decision* (Princeton, NJ: Princeton University Press, 1974), pp. 86-87.

24. Clean Air Act Amendments of 1977 (P.L. 95-95), August 7, 1977.

25. Endangered Species Act of 1973 (P.L. 93-205), as amended.

26. There is an interesting question raised about what might occur if health risks were explicitly introduced into the decision process. If people began to discuss mortality and morbidity in trade-off terms, would these issues become sufficiently important to transcend the questions of cost? What would happen to economics as the underpinning of our society? What does it mean to have a society based on risk avoidance?

CHAPTER 3

MODELS IN THE POLICY PROCESS

The Use of Models

In the previous chapter I discussed the use of formal analysis as the core of modern policy science. These techniques are varied, but at the core of the class of research or assessment I have grouped under the heading of systems or policy analysis is the use of a model in one form or another. Not only is a model necessary for the performance of such analysis per se, but its very existence is the cornerstone of the technique and the "correct" method of performing the task. The emphasis in this chapter will be on the technical capabilities of models, and on their utility and validity. Although the formulation of any policy analysis may entail the use of a model, the discussion in this chapter will be most concerned with models already in existence and consequently being used for repetitive policy analyses, or that are being modified to address a new issue. Second, I want to look at models which are developed as part of a major policy debate of sufficient importance and requiring analysis over a long enough time period so as to move the model used beyond the trivial level.

Quade, in a single sentence, offers the best and most popular argument for the use of models:

> An explicit model, scientific or otherwise, however, introduces structure and terminology to a problem and provides a means for breaking a complicated decision into smaller tasks than can be handled one at a time [Quade, 1975: 48].

The belief that introducing formal mathematical order makes decision-making more rational is open to question. Clearly, if a particular policy issue is defined in terms of the parameters of a specific model, and if all the actors in the policy formulation agree that the structure so defined is really an adequate and accurate description of the issue, then it may indeed at least perform a very useful communication function. If, on the other hand, the policy has to be redefined or the model has to be force-fit to the issue at hand, or if there is no consensus on the model's utility, the attempt to foist such a structure on the analysis of an issue may exacerbate the policy process by adding still another dimension of disagreement, i.e., the analytic technique itself.

The process of segmenting or breaking down an issue into smaller parts (an integral part of the modeling process) is not necessarily an unqualified blessing, either. Making little ones out of big ones may be good for the prison yard, but most modern day policy issues are quite complex and yield to fragmentation, if at all, only with the greatest of care. In fact, it is quite likely that breaking down an issue into component parts so that it can be more readily handled analytically may give the illusion that an issue which is really horrendously complex can be addressed in a straight-forward fashion. After addressing one portion of the policy, issue, or problem at a time, one could, it is hypothesized, integrate the partial results into a full-blown, complete policy analysis. Would that the world were so linear and additive that one could deal with issues in such a manner!

Before I go on to discuss the various types of models that might be used in the policy process, I must stress again the fact that most formal systems analyses, at least as commonly described by their proponents, require that policymakers be an integral part of the decision analysis. Not only are they to set the goals, but they are to sign off on the preferred option from among the various policy choices presented for the implementation phase. If a policymaker's technical training does not include modeling, there is always a plea to "educate" him or her on the design and use of the techniques. As was pointed out in a recent book on the use of models in the public sector, even if one possesses a technical background and is familiar with the use of models in a specific discipline, there is no reason to assume automatic understanding of the modeling techniques or jargon of another field. The I/O modeling of the economist is not readily understood by the engineer until it is explained as an exercise in matrix algebra.[1] Consequently, there are apt to be many levels of education required at the policy level. The question remains as to whether all this education is really necessary or useful in the first place.

In short, using a specific model, or for that matter, any model, may or may not be good for policy analysis. At the very least, claims made for their universal utility have to be examined carefully. Before examining the question of utility, though, let us turn to the general classes of models that decision analysis has available and look at them in summary fashion here.

THEORY, POLICY, AND MODEL STRUCTURE

Theory refers to our understanding of the basic structure to be modeled. For some structures, basically mechanistic and relegated to, say, the engineering profession, there is a considerably well developed and described theory. For others, say, those found in the physiological fields, our understanding, and consequently our theoretical formulation, is less precise. Looking at the concept of theory in another fashion, normally the simpler or more transparent the system, the more amenable it is to understanding, description, and therefore modeling. The more complex, the poorer the understanding, and consequently the weaker the theory.[2]

Almost any action taken in the public sector, as we shall discuss later, can be said to be subjected to decisions which could be called application of "policy."[3] Most major policies have begun to require analyses which are increasingly complex, use either a greater range of, or larger, more sophisticated models (or both), and include investigations of those impacts caused by the policy beyond the more obvious and direct ones.[4] (It should be noted that an argument could be made that more complex analyses are now required largely because there are models capable of meeting the requirements.) There was a time in the not-so-distant past that secondary impacts were not normally considered in policy formulation.

The inclusion of decisions not directly related to a particular policy, but which occur because of the structural shifts that come from implementing the policy, requires an understanding of how our system operates often far beyond any empirical studies done to date. For example, suppose a substantial gasoline tax were proposed to reduce the amount of gasoline used. The analysis of such policy might include not only the best estimates of consumer behavior in the face of the higher prices for gasoline, but since the policy was expected to reduce the amount traveled, the analysis might also address the secondary impacts on the auto industry, changes in levels of air pollution, of urban forms, of people's lifestyles, and so forth. This simple-sounding policy suggestion could result in an extensive research effort, including a very complex modeling project.

To summarize, the statement that we have to understand a problem well to successfully model it is just another way of saying that we require adequate theory. At this stage in the development of policy modeling, however, our theoretical underpinnings (at least in the rather broadly defined area of the social or policy sciences) are becoming better, because we now realize that in our social system, actions can and do engender secondary impacts and that there is real interest in making these impacts known. Further, quite often we know what the areas so impacted are. Unfortunately, even with this feeling for the probable *direction* of the change resulting from a policy shift, too often we still have little or no idea of the *magnitude* of these impacts. This dilemma leads us to an examination of the actual model structure[5] to see where such deficiencies might actually impact the choice of model type to be used in an analysis. If we do not have the information to supply a very sophisticated model, its elegance will not be useful to us in analyzing a policy issue. Consequently, we may be forced to choose a less complete model, from a technical perspective, simply because the cynicism inherent in the policy process would tend to make one conservative as to the variables chosen. There is then an explicit trade-off of a desire for scientific completeness for the purity of what the policy analyst believes he can demonstrate as "hard" data. Often this trade-off makes for relatively small, transparent models.

Types of Models

There are lots of ways one could organize a taxonomy to discuss models. The following table, taken from a book prepared by the U.S. Environmental Protection Agency,[6] relates model form to the type of decision being made. Although instructive, it should only be considered illustrative of the several ways one might go about constructing a summary table to compare and contrast various model types.

In the main, for models which forecast through time, there are really only two generalized types; one of these tells you what will happen if you decide to do something; the other will tell you the best way to do it. The first of these are called simulation forecasting models and include a very broad class of algorithms, model types, and theoretical constructs. In essence, these models are designed to estimate the impact of a policy or set of policies, given an agreed upon description of the system being modeled. Generally, although such models might be used for normative purposes, the outputs are characteristically descriptive in nature and are meant to represent (or forecast) impacts of decisions in terms of specified indices or parameters.

The other class of model attempts to specify what should be done or what path ought to be followed to achieve a "best" result, given a specified goal and known resources and constraints. The techniques consist of procedures in the areas of optimization, queuing models, or mathematical programming, searching out an analytically determined best solution, and using this result to present the decisionmaker with a specific policy choice to an issue. If the question is properly phrased and the model valid, the response could indeed be the best analytic solution to a given situation.

In the formative days of operations research, systems analysis, and other such formal techniques, several professionals made their careers by developing a new methodology or technique and convincing others that this was the way to address specific classes of problems. Like most situations which are sales-motivated (and make no mistake, these emerging modeling techniques were closely competitive and were being "sold"), there was an attempt to maximize product differentiation so as to capture a discernible share of the potential model user market. Most of the variants within the two general categories of models described above were designed to handle a specific type of question or problem. Fundamentally, they were able to be identified as one of the two general model types, and so users could relate to the variations in terms of the issue that was to be addressed.

In the days of selling these models, the developers of a specific model variant would be looking hard for recognition and funding. It seemed obvious that the best way to get both was to get the attention of someone in power. Further, there was pressure put on these technique salesmen by the bureaucrats and foundation administrators to push their products even harder in the policy user community because the money providers characteristically demanded demonstrable evidence that somebody was actually using the product or technique for its intended purpose. This sales-related drive to involve the policymaker in the decision to use a model was coupled with the very logical belief that getting the policymaker to consider his policies more systematically in the decision process would be a seemingly more rational way to narrow areas of disagreement and would, by the way, force models to the attention of the policy level. At the same time, it meant that the technicians would be given the opportunity to improve their own methodologies, in the sense of making them more realistic and more user-oriented by understanding better the goals of the policymakers and the process by which these goals were obtained.

Regardless of the motivation, however, the attempt at educating the policymaker or at having the technician become an integral part of the policy process met with little widespread success. In the end, as with other operational details, the tool or technique used in an analysis was to be the responsibility of the analyst or the policy staff, and the details of each analysis not something that the policymaker could reasonably be expected to keep up with. The fallacy evident in the assumptions made by the modeling technician was that because a policy was important, the policy level would want to become enmeshed in the details of analyzing choices and impacts. In reality, for any given policymaker, there are usually dozens of such issues in the works at any one time and it would be impossible for any human being to find the time to focus on them all. Consequently, there is a need to rely on the technical staff for a considerable portion of the analysis and only to become involved when options are presented and a choice required. On the other hand, the analysis presented to the policy level does focus them on a specific issue, often more detailed than might otherwise be the case.

Of course, some issues get more policy-level attention than others. If we picture a graph with time on one axis and policy attention on the other, there would be a "U"-shaped function. If the issue is very important and there is very little time to do analysis, then the issue is more apt to get the personal attention of the policymaker. Similarly, personal attention is most likely to appear if there is sufficient time to iterate and reiterate the analyses. Whenever time permits, the policymaker can take the opportunity to inject policy guidance to the emerging analysis. The vast majority of the policies, however, are neither instantaneous nor leisurely. These normal analyses are apt to be staff-driven and often leave the policy level little more to do after specifying the original issue than to accept the results of the analysis or reject it, for there is characteristically not enough time to modify it.

MODEL TYPES: A FURTHER PERSPECTIVE

Let us go into the topic of model type in more detail and from a slightly expanded perspective than the one introduced a few pages ago. Picture a stylized continuum which stretches from one end, consisting of simple extrapolatory models, to another featuring heuristic models. By heuristic, I mean exploratory problem-solving techniques aimed at improving performance by self-education, such as evaluating results and having these results institute feedback to cause a decision change. In general, the methods employed in these model types are quite straightforward and known to many undergraduates.

One difficulty with extrapolatory modeling is that it presupposes that the present is much like the past and that the future is likely to be more of the same. So long as this belief is generally a description of reality, the forecasts will be reasonable. Many physical and chemical reactions are of this class, as there is no reason for the passage of time or experience to alter the physical properties of the situation. When the situation, say a policy being modeled, is a changing one, though, these extrapolatory techniques can produce forecasts which quickly become silly. The lack of clear understanding of how most portions of the total social-institutional systems operate when perturbed—particularly when the perturbation (again, a policy change) is of a type or magnitude never encountered before—means that the majority of the observed changes in the development or growth of a part of the economy could be said to be all but random, given what it is really possible to extrapolate solely on the basis of past events. No scientific statement is possible about the accuracy of the forecasted results because of this limitation alone; others shall be addressed shortly.

Many of the generalities made here and throughout the chapter are equally valid whether one is attempting to model a segment of, or the whole social system. The statements made in the theory section on the relative firmness of information in the physical or engineering areas, in contrast to the softer, social-institutional type, also apply here. Research in these latter areas is sparse and less developed than in the physical sciences. Consequently, we often have to use a pitifully small number of case studies in attempting to estimate the expected response to various policies for modeling purposes. In an uncomfortably large number of cases, such estimates have to be based on conjecture due to the lack of any directly related studies, and consequently the coefficients in the model become mere guesses.[7]

Without a clearly defined theory, one approach an analyst might decide to take in model design would be to make the values of certain variables in his model entirely stochastic. This addition to the field of modeling methodology tries to introduce a feature of reality into the modeling process by highlighting the unexpected nature of the human condition. But because there is a seemingly infinite number of outcomes possible from successive runs of almost any large policy model, with the introduction of a number of stochastic variables, the change of the model reflecting reality can be likened to the anecdotal printing of all of the great books of the world by putting several monkeys in a room and letting them bang away at typewriters. The modern day stochastic models tend to combine some of the features of the extrapolatory method with randomly generated variables in the areas of data or theory uncertainty. In the end, the general result is much the same as in the case of some traditional stochastic models; however, the model user has greater control over the model outcome. The weakness is still the lack of information as to how the system will actually respond to any particular stimuli.[8]

Another variation in the modeling art began as a companion to the planning mania which accompanied systems analysis in the Sixties. The philosophical underpinnings of this school rested on the premise that planning was a rational activity which could be used for all sorts of things—conducting war, building cities, running countries.[9] The planning methodology discussed looked amazingly similar whether the output of the project was to be a bridge or a new administration. The backbone of the concept was disarmingly simple: (1) state where you want to go; (2) name a goal (or some goals) the activity is supposed to accomplish; (3) with this in mind, produce a description of the current system; and (4) come to an understanding of how to get from here to there (or now to then).[10]

The principal modeling activity designed to accomplish this exercise was optimization, dominated by a technique called linear programming. This technique was nothing more than a methodology for solving the problem of getting the most output for a given amount of resources within defined limits to actions existing at a point in time. Later refinements recognized that not all (in fact, almost no) human related activities could readily be described by a simple linear relation. Thus, more sophisticated forms were designed. As a capsule summary of this technique, I noted earlier that if all of the significant variables were included, and if adequate data were available and specified in the model accurately, then the technique could all but replace human decisionmakers by defining a "best" solution to any problem in its domain.[11] A technocrat's dream! One of the biggest problems in applying this technique in the real-world policy arena has been the inability to state the objective function or goal (critical to the model solution) in precise mathematical terms.

A refinement to these forward feeding or oscillating models was formalized with the birth of Systems Dynamics.[12] Variants of this technique have been used on almost every conceivable problem type, from business to urban to global problems.[13] Although purists would be able to point out numerous fine distinctions between this and other model methodologies, the principal clear addition made to the art by Systems Dynamics was the introduction and legitimization of the concept of feedback noted earlier.

In some ways, this model type was a product of its times. Many early model builders, such as economists, knew of the existence of feedbacks in their theories and constructs, but neglected to include them because they did not have any idea of where to get the data which could give them any confidence in the results obtained from their introduction. The inclusion of feedback in Systems Dynamics was based concretely on the logic of the engineer, where cybernetic reasoning is more familiar.

The value of the feedback loop was not so much what it told the engineers who used the early Systems Dynamics in human-related models, but rather the fact that it was used. The use of such feedback meant that the future forecast could (and normally would) be very different from the straightforward past-present-future paradigm of the extrapolatory school. Still, it has been the subject of endless debate as to whether the information generated from these models is really worth much. We have already noted that the reason feedbacks were neglected was not because they were not known, but because there was no real research done on how they operated and what impact they would have under varying situations (such as policy choices). Without such information, the addition of feedback and the specification of its numerical value were pure conjecture. Because of this fact, the argument about the value of information generated by a model which deliberately leaves out feedback because of the lack of information versus the model that includes it and guesses its specification is almost pure metaphysical.

Finally, there is the modeler's delight: the heuristic model. This form of model is a little bit of each of the above forms, but has the added feature of being able to correct itself—to get the best it can get from given resources, yet keeping within prescribed limits. Once the model is begun, it will set and reset its own goals based on a programmed learning algorithm.[14] Military and aerospace applications were the early leaders in this field.

There are several variants of each of these model types and a few others (such as the I/O models of the economist noted earlier)[15] which could be said to have been left out of the continuum. But for our purposes, most of the classical types have been mentioned.[16] The question now shifts from a cursory review of model types to what's new in the area of model design, especially those used for policy purposes. In the first place, without looking very hard, it is possible to find one or more examples of the above modeling types in a single "policy" paper, and at first glance one might conclude that all types of models are used equally in policy analysis. My own reading of the literature and discussion with other policy analysts has led me to the following hypothesis: If the results of a model have to stand up to serious criticism or scrutiny, or if time and money are an important consideration, most analysts feel more secure if the model they use is closer to the extrapolatory end of our continuum of model types. If, on the other hand, these same analysts are giving professional papers, writing journal articles, or otherwise trying to advance their careers by impressing their peers with methodology (as opposed to findings), they often prefer to work with models which are more toward the heuristic end of the scale. In the area of large-scale policy models (where my own expertise lies), those actually used in the policy arena certainly conform to this generalization more times than not.

BUILDING MODELS: SOME FACETS

Over the past decade or more, the changes in computer models (indeed, in computers themselves) have been great. For example, the first computer with which I had some association was the IBM 650, although, like many of my colleagues, I often made use of the then-ubiquitous mechanical card-sorters.

The 650 was an unwieldy beast. It used tubes rather than transistors and was kept in an air-conditioned room (so cold that it felt like an icebox) to prevent overheating and to help prolong tube life. Because of the number of tubes, the statistical probability of having the machine operate for hours at a time was small indeed. A further joy associated with the beast was that it had instruction boards that had to be hand-wired for each program. It was only much later that the hardware and software existed to allow the use of present day computer languages.

Speaking of computer languages, I recall that the first two 650s I ran into were at the U.S. Department of Agriculture in Washington, D.C., and at Cornell University. I worked for USDA as a field man assigned at Cornell at the time. USDA was teaching its interested scientific staff a language called SOAP and required its use when submitting jobs to the Agriculture Computer Center in Washington. I became versed in SOAP before going to Cornell.

As part of my field research at Cornell, I had a set of questionnaires that I had coded and keypunched. I wrote a simple program in SOAP to sort them and to calculate the mean and standard deviation for several sorts, and submitted it to the Cornell Computer Center. No one at Cornell recognized this language! They were using a version of FORTRAN which the USDA did not adopt for another year or so. Things were so confusing even at what is now a trivial level that a major professor on my Ph.D. committee would not permit me to take computer-related courses because he felt that computer simulation was a fad that would pass—or in any case that was likely to remain in too chaotic a state to be useful to anyone but electronic engineers.

This latter point identifies one early difficulty with computer model building; the relationship between the programmer and the computer seemed to be almost spiritual. Few in the social science community were trained enough in their own field to develop the insights that model building requires and at the same time to translate them into usable computer form. The field of policy science did not yet exist as a formal discipline. But the social sciences formed the basis for much of the later work done in policy science and analysis. As for my own experience with this phenomenon, I participated in that domain of the early modeling era that was concerned with spatial analysis and land-use models. I led a team of analysts attempting to do man-machine modeling and computer gaming of the urban area. Our early work was done on an IBM 1130. For those who have never used this machine, it was sold (or rented) to users who wanted a dedicated facility but could not afford a large system. Because time-sharing was not then universally available, if you wanted to use a computer, you bought or rented one.

The IBM 1130 was a nice machine, but it was relatively slow and had small storage capacity. Both these limitations had a great deal to do with how and what was modeled. Often, choices between the algorithm and technical information were made as much on the basis of available space and running time as on the realism of the simulation. With time, larger machines, better software, and several other improvements made the limitations of the computer side of policy simulation a lesser problem.

In retrospect, things were equally chaotic from the social science side. There was a large influx of engineers who transferred into the social science field and brought with them their rigorous methodologies. Unfortunately, these methods and their proponents often tended to bend the available data base to fit their methods, which they were busily transferring to the fields of social and policy sciences. This caused a concomitant loss of some of the meager information available in these two areas. The problem subsided only when almost everyone was able to use a computer and to express his problems in technical terms so that the social scientist could make direct use of and perfect his own data and theories.

Some of the outgrowths of this technocratic approach to analyzing the issues of society are amusing today, given the benefits of hindsight and experience. In an earlier book, I recall trying to describe a city in theoretical terms popular in the pre-Fifties, and then trying to translate this description into algorithms useful for computer programming.[17] I failed, as did everyone else who attempted similar exercises in the social sciences during this period. This was a time of transition. The description of science associated with the social sciences was not applicable to the more precise and rigorous formulation required of the computer age. This is not to say that one formulation was in some way more correct or better than another—merely that it was not possible to transfer the theories directly from one discipline to another. The principal reason that transfer was not possible was that information and data did not exist in the receiving field to specify the theory that was being transferred. Only time will tell whether improved information will bring descriptions and analytic theories more closely into line with each other.

The ultimate theoretical paradigm to describe a city in the above work was one that could not have been formulated using the then-available configurations of the computer and the extensive data sets describing the urban area. It has a better chance today. As an aside, the almost direct transplant of calculus into some social science fields, such as economics, is another attempt to translate the rather primitive theory of social science into a form more amenable to generalization. Whether the mathematically based assumptions of continuity required are useful in a discrete human world—particularly in fields like policy analysis—is still open to question. In the end, though, because our limited mental, descriptive models will ultimately be buttressed by the computer, the theory of the social scientists used in constructing large-scale policy models could possibly become richer and more relevant, as might the models themselves.

DATA

An equally large problem we shall face for some time to come has to do with getting the information in a form to feed the evolving theory and models. But the problem is not simply one of data availability. To paraphrase Coleridge, the data issue can be summarized as: "Data, data everywhere, but not an item to trust." Under the pressure of wanting to know more and more about our society, and because of the seeming ability of our analysts to absorb increasing amounts of information and translate it into usable form, data collection activities have increased steadily for decades. The problem with these mounds of data is that they often cannot be used in conjunction with each other, since they are not calibrated, were not collected using the same assumption, nor even documented so that adjustments could be made post-collection. Until standards are set in the data collection area, this difficulty will continue to plague analysts in most policy fields. Because these data are often not collected to specify a particular theory either, the gap between theory and operating models may well be lessened only accidently.

Models are voracious users of data. For years now, the positive relation of information and improved decisionmaking capability has been posited time and time again. Huge data files have been developed and maintained for almost every discipline and seemingly about every geographic area. Yet it appears that regardless of how a model is conceived, the stages beyond the conceptual design become increasingly frustrating, expensive, and time-consuming as one begins to load the conceptual, theoretically based model with real-world data. Regardless of how extensive the data sets available to build the model, the information these data files contain is always out of date and never quite complete enough to satisfy the modeler's designed algorithms.

A second feature of data is that data collection and use are subject to problems similar to those associated with models themselves. By this I mean that models are eternally excoriated for being either undocumented or not validated. Data sets suffer from the same difficulties.[18] As we noted above, the fact that data sets are undocumented has numerous complications. Without documentation, it is never clear what the data are meant to represent. Not only does this lack of clarity make the use of data for expository purposes risky indeed, it clearly also does not allow one to relate one data set to another. This last requirement is a basic need before data can be used in a modeling environment.

Finally, there is the question of how to use data in the service of models. The heuristic modeler characteristically would specify a model and then search for, modify, or estimate the data needed to fit it. At the other end of the spectrum are the extrapolatory modelers who would tend to build models out of available data only. Neither extreme really makes much scientific sense, although both are in evidence in policy modeling even today. Most models lie somewhere in between these extremes.

MODEL USE

The final item—the one I am most concerned with—is how to use the results of a policy simulation when we have them. Simulation builders continuously cry that no one listens to them. I suspect these cries are rather like those of religious sect leaders who are frustrated that other people refuse to see the "truth"—at least the truth as they define it. Articles and books have been written suggesting how it is necessary to move simulation builders into the position resembling that of "vizier" to the policymaker. The fact is that in present day policy shops, such a perspective is naive. The majority of the people who do policy analysis understand models and the use of computers, and it is these people (not the policymakers) who are the actual clients of the simulationist. These staffers and bureaucrats will be the ones who will take the simulation results (as they do with the results of any contractor) and translate them for use in the policy formulation process. They will also formulate the questions which will be addressed by the contractor modeler and set the specifics to be modeled. The idea that every policymaker would one day have a television screen linked to a computer (known as a CRT) on his desk is a myth of the past. Generally, policymaking is not a technical job.

The situation is such that no decisions are ever made on the basis of computer results alone (nor should they be). Our ability to simulate everything and anything is still under suspicion. The suspicion results not only from the logical unreasonableness of such a situation, but also from a reservoir of illwill generated by a history of computer model analyses that were overpromised and underdelivered. Several books and articles have appeared in the last few years documenting these failings in numerous specific areas and fields. The aphorism of writers—KEEP IT SIMPLE, STUPID (KISS)—has become that of the model builder also.

On the other hand, it is often not possible to make models so elegant that they are reduced to a very few variables. As a policy issue heats up, there is often great pressure to add more and more specifics and to take note of increasingly more variables as they swing into the purview of the analyst or decisionmakers. The simplicity of design that is called for here is then often modified by the needs of the moment. The model grows and adjusts to meet the requirements of the analysis. Often this is preferred to a generalized, comprehensive model that invites force-fitting. This can occur by redefining the issue to fit the model, or by trying to redesign the model to use it on a specific issue, an issue it was not built to handle, or some combination of both situations. A generalized, comprehensive model may be just what is needed if the time for generating the policy analysis is short or the resources constrained in some other fashion. If the model fits the needs of the moment fairly well, then the necessity to readjust the expectations of the analysis to fit the capabilities of the available model may not be as bad as not being able to use much of a model at all.

Search for a Valid Model

There are lots of questions which are outside the capacity of models to answer. We have alluded to several of these earlier. Characteristically for the policymaker, a sample of such queries might run like this: Will my constituency buy the analysis? Will my opponent be able to make hay with the data? Can I live with the results? What good will the results do me politically? These and dozens of other similar perceptions and questions are awfully hard to make explicit in a formal model. Further, the information that could be quantified often is not, or it is done so poorly that the data are little more than a guess. There are lots of reasons for this situation, which have been or will be addressed elsewhere in the book. Even when such weaknesses are realized, however, there is effectively no quantitative technique available to deal with all of them. To handle problems of this sort (model quality), the technical community has developed some methods for validating its models. The question is: How good are these methods? We took a brief look at validity in Chapter 2. Let me build on that discussion and redirect it toward policy models and their validation.

The concept of validation, particularly validation of models which are used to predict the future, is based on very shaky theoretical grounds. Basic questions as to whether it can be done and why it is necessary to do it underlie the issues related to when we should try to validate models and how to do it.

Let us, for a moment, look at the question of when models can be validated from a particular perspective. Imagine an n-dimensional array. Each dimension or axis is so designed that it measures relevant variables describing models on scales from easy to hard, or from small to large. The various axes might be, say, (1) size, (2) type of model, (3) subject matter, (4) time horizon, and (5) number of variables.

(1) Size would refer to the number and type of equations in the model, and would suggest that the more equations a model has, the more complex it would be.

(2) Type of model—from pure simulation through the various optimization techniques. The closer the model tries to come to actually providing a "best" solution to a problem, the more complex it is assumed to be.

(3) Life or physical sciences are better able to state and manipulate their variables than the less quantified social sciences. This is very hard to portray on a single scale ranging from hard to soft science, because many policy models being built today use a mixture of disciplines from both areas. Perhaps a scale could be designed which would array disciplines according to their dependence on human behavior, since changes in human behavior and institutions present some of the greatest difficulties in predicting the future.

(4) Time horizon—the distance into the future the model is expected to forecast. Ignoring for the moment whether any forecasting exercise can be said to have validity, there usually is more information as to what the near future is apt to be like than the distant future, especially in technical areas where developments are kept track of.

(5) The greater the number of variables, the more complex the model, the bigger it is, and the more difficult it is to assure the quality of the data.

There are several other dimensions that could be mentioned, but our discussion can be carried out with these. Validating models is hypothesized to be a function of where these models are located in the space created by these vectors. As a general tendency, the closer the model lies to the origin, the more readily it will lend itself to standardized validation techniques. In other words, the simpler, more transparent the model, the easier it is to validate. Of course, this hypothesis does not in any way speak to the utility of the model or to the efficiency of the validation exercise itself.

It seems clear that the concept of validation applies most closely to simulation models, since they are intended to ape reality. An optimization model could be validated in terms of its causal algorithms, but it is rare in policy studies that the optimality of the predicted solution can be measured. Subject matter and discipline also make large differences. In the natural sciences, observations or experiments are charted and compared to a law or set of known reactions. The comparison of the observed to known relationships forms the basis both for validating the experiment and for integrating the results with a body of knowledge. This latter provides a technique for at least some of the validation work in modeling.

A MODEL AS AN EXPERIMENTAL DEVICE

One of the uses of the concept of validation is to use a model which is a faithful replication of actual events as an experimental device in a series of "what if" exercises. It is the use of such logic, where the underlying natural law is unknown, that is at the root of our concern. Let us assume first that the model we are going to validate is one which concerns an institutional, organizational, or social structure. During the period being covered, there will be times in which the situation described will react to an event or series of events. The greater the number of variables being modeled, the more likely it is to happen. An economic model will have to take into consideration factors normally extraneous to the system being modeled, but which are turning points affecting all subsequent events. World War II and OPEC are examples. A model calibrated to truly mimic these happenings would be one which was a simulation of a series of absolutely unique events. This situation differs dramatically from the natural law hypotheses which allow validation in the "hard" sciences. The use of such a unique event model to test "what if" hypotheses is open to serious question, particularly if there is no opportunity for the model to simulate behavioral reaction to situational changes. Small perturbations in noncritical areas for very near-term forecasts might have some credibility, but any more aggressive tests would be lacking.

A second use of model validation is to provide a basis for forecasting the future. Many of the problems alluded to earlier apply here also. Predictive models can be tested hypothetically to verify whether they perform as designed. They are sometimes compared against historical data and then validated against short-range predictions, if any, depending on the patience and objectives of the modeler. Although validation and historical comparison are not useless exercises, they are a far cry from claiming that a model is proven to have any prophetic capability. Validation would add little to forecasting. Knowing the model operates as advertised means only that in the hands of competent analysts, the impacts of varying certain variables can be explained to other analysts in terms of what might have happened—had such changes occurred in a society much like the one we have, given extrapolated changes in all other variables. Helpful perhaps in decisionmaking, but hardly a substitute for a crystal ball.

VALIDATING POLICY MODELS

If there ever were a modern day search for the golden fleece, it must be the attempt to validate policy models. The search becomes more quixotic (as already noted) as the size of the model increases. The motives behind the search are clear enough. After all, many forecasts of these models help to direct the expenditure of millions of taxpayers' dollars and put the reputations of policymakers on the line. Since the models appear to portray results with such certainty (as opposed to results arrived at by an analyst's judgment, which are assumed to be fallible), it seems reasonable to ask the model builders and users to be able to justify the confidence they have in the model forecasts. Unfortunately, just as wishing does not make it so, neither does reasonableness.

As I have said before,[19] the basic logic which underlies the search for a valid model comes from the natural and physical sciences. Once these scientists have, through a combination of rigorous research methodology, patience, and good fortune, been able to discover a natural law, validation of their forecasting methodology can be so structured as to ensure that it will produce results which conform to the measured data. Because the social and policy sciences have not yet been able to discover such natural laws (or at least not ones recognized by all), the closest they have been able to come to a validation procedure is to replicate the past with a model which purports to forecast the future. This procedure might actually work out pretty well in cases where the phenomenon modeled is fairly consistent from period to period. The difficulties appear when the forecasting algorithms are expected to replicate happenings which deviate from historical trend lines. Forecasting such turning points or "knees" in the trend lines demonstrates the really impossible nature of true "forecasting," and consequently, the frustration of validating such forecasts.

Given current knowledge, we can say two things about forecasting models: (1) anyone who says they are able to accurately predict turning points in a policy forecast is either wrong, naive, or a charlatan. In essence, the promise is equivalent to actually "foretelling the future"; (2) even a model that is so designed that it apes the past completely has nothing in its makeup which gives one any confidence that it will be able to forecast the future. The past is only prologue for *certain* futures, and then only by hindsight.

Large-scale models have special problems which make it difficult for policy-makers and others to use their results with confidence. In the first place, several large-scale models are really large principally in terms of numbers of variables. Recently, we estimated that the Strategic Environmental Assessment System (SEAS), a policy model used in both the Department of Energy and the Environmental Protection Agency, had over 100,000 variables. A model with this many variables can cause statistical problems of uncertainty, suggesting a situation where the results contain so many compounding errors that the information produced on a given run is apt to be in the noise range. An even worse situation can come to pass when one considers the problem of having several such modules, each of which can be identified with a specific error or individual function similarly error laden. The multiplication of each error with the next makes one highly leery of the model results.

In reality, little can or has been done about this presumption of corresponding errors. Even worse, it still remains to be demonstrated that it is possible to specify individual errors accurately in a model before worrying about the potential for making them additive. Regardless of whether one agrees or not with the philosophical proposition that validation is impossible on the basis of logic alone, the sheer size of a model would at least reduce the ease, if not the capability. To even begin to get a very large model down to size where existing statistical tools can come into play is a design problem which has yet to be solved.

Some recent thinking at the Department of Energy has suggested various means of grouping like variables in a fashion which would allow the statistician to operate on fewer parameters. Probably the simplest idea would be to group the variables on the basis of the operation performed on them. All variables which were merely linear (coefficient operations) relations of an earlier forecasted variable could be collapsed to the control variable (as the variation would be a known function of the forcing variable). The smaller the resultant number of variables, the easier the application of statistical techniques. It might actually be possible to prespecify these control variables through fiat or by analyst choice. Or, the variables agreed to be forcing could receive widespread review. In any case, this reductionism may prove to be useful in carrying out rudimentary verification, but has still to undergo considerable thought.

Possiby the greatest hurdle to the validation of large-scale models is that in a purist sense, there are few of them in existence. For example, in the early days of ERDA (later DOE), of the three large models used for policy purposes (MEFS, SEAS, and the Brookhaven model), [20] only SEAS could really be run as a total machine model. The other two required the intervention of analysts between the running of submodels to "massage" the data in order to get a full run of the system. The interjection of human analysts in the forecasts means that any form of mechanical validation is a technical impossibility.

The potential for problems because of human interface with a model comes up in still another guise. In the area of policy modeling, one typical use of these tools is to have a model run as a base or reference case, to change the policy assumptions loaded into the model, and to rerun the model for comparative purposes. This is often referred to as sensitivity analysis. This method of using models places less emphasis on the absolute values of the forecasts, but rather stresses the relative values brought about by the introduction of a given set of policies. The validation issue in this model uses shifts from an emphasis on the forecasted values per se to the reasonableness of the algorithm themselves. [21] As we noted earlier, not all scientists agree with this approach. Probably the best form of validation is still to be found in the judgment of the analysts who have to use the forecasts.

Among the hardest things for those new to policy analysis to understand is the frustrating fact that it may not really be possible to technically "validate" the data or the results from policy models. Because nobody is certain of the future, and because in our dynamic society the past is only a rough indicator of trends, the next best strategy has been to compare the results of a particular model with the results of other models or of surveys which purport to measure the same factors. Although such comparisons clearly do not result in anything but good feelings on the part of the modeler whose projections compare closely to someone or everyone else's, they are at least useful for pointing out where further analysis may be necessary to explain the results obtained. On the other hand, these comparisons do not shed much light on validity in cases where the results from various analysts are more spread out (i.e., the results are not in such tight agreement). Still, this form of comparative analysis does at least give the user some insight into how risky his results may be thought to be in the world of science and policy—close clustering would suggest less risk than would a scatter. Neither case should be mistaken for validity, however, as all that is being tested is consensus, not fact. Except possibly in a pure democracy, truth is not a commodity subject to vote. [22]

WHAT USE WOULD VALIDATION BE TO THE POLICYMAKER?

Possibly the most difficult question for the topic of validation is not how—or even whether—it can be done, but what to do with it after it has been done. Let us assume, in spite of the reservations we have discussed earlier, that somehow or other methods are derived to perform the feat of validating model results. Let us further assume that the current trend toward models which are increasingly complex will continue. By complex, I mean not only are the models large in terms of the numbers of variables, but that they are multidisciplinary: not simply economic, or environmental, or engineering, but containing variables and algorithms from several fields. But without empirical evidence, we can still only hypothesize, on the basis of logic and experience alone, the inescapably questionable results of such model validations.

First, any honest researcher is constantly humiliated with how little he really knows in any area. The scientist remains unwilling to commit himself to a research conclusion because a little more investigation, experimentation, and data are seemingly always needed to more fully understand a phenomena. Second, as sparse as our knowledge is of any single phenomenon or discipline, the ignorance we have of the relationships of a particular area to any other is significantly greater. Third, our knowledge of causality is weak in many of the social and behavioral sciences. Not only is this true at the most rudimentary levels of analysis—say, historical cause and effect for actions and reactions that actually happened—but we have almost no clue as to what might take place if cause and effect relationships were to be hypothesized for assumed actions. We simply do not really know much about many of the fundamental relationships that underlie the system in which we live.

But to make policy, we have to make decisions. Because of our technical training, many believe that decisions are better the more information is available. Ignoring information overload, whether there is even enough information, or whether it is the correct information, probably such a belief is more right than wrong. It is this belief which drives analysis toward becoming even more precise, and to try more and more to relate policy options to impacts.

The intersection of our desire for more information and our lack of basic data and relationships suggests that even without rigorous tests of validity being in practical use today, many models would show (if they existed) that their forecasts have to be taken with large margins of error. In many cases, these margins of error would be so large that there would be some question as to the utility of the forecast at all. Therein lies the dilemma for policy models and validation.

VALIDATION TESTS ARE A PANDORA'S BOX
FOR POLICYMAKERS

The question boils down to how one tells a policymaker about validation tests. All kinds of issues bubble to the surface when this pandora's box is opened. For example, should one tell the policymaker the error expectations associated with each analysis? If yes, how much should one then go into the technical derivation of such information and the attendant error analysis? Wouldn't subjecting analytical methods (particularly complex ones) to a rigorous validating procedure bias the decisionmaker toward accepting nonrigorous, seat-of-the-pants estimates which are not presented to them with error bands?

Actually, questions such as these are handled pragmatically. A good analysis staff always tells the decisionmaker how much confidence they have in their analysis, regardless of how this confidence was arrived at. Even if the confidence is low, if a decision is to be made on some basis other than random choice, the data and the analysis—regardless of how suspect—will normally form the basis for choice. Although decisionmakers do sometimes use analysis to leap to a preconceived conclusion, such bias cannot possibly be universally ascribed to the incredibly large number of decisions these people have to make. Assuming some rationality, the decisionmaker has to trust the inputs from staff, based on whatever information there is available at that time. Although the quality of the data may impact the form of the decision, it will seldom determine whether a decision is made. Because decisionmakers are not omnipotent, their decisions are usually forced by actions taken elsewhere. The option of not making a decision because of a lack of high quality information is a luxury the decisionmaker normally cannot afford.

RIGOROUS VALIDATION NEITHER PRACTICAL NOR USEFUL

In summary, it is clear that from a practical viewpoint I have had little of hope to say for rigorous validation. Although a technical background would lead one to applaud the effort to discover and perfect such procedures, I hold little hope for their being found, especially for large-scale, complex models. Further, the use of validation to give credence to forecasts is a modeler's fantasy and requires careful handling. Even if this Holy Grail is discovered, it will likely have little real impact in the policy user community in situations where there are questions about results of a model but nothing else available on which to make a decision.

Although there is some cause for despair about the analytical postulations we have presented, the practical utility of the results should not appear startling. No practicing policy analyst or experienced decisionmaker ever takes any analyses as gospel, regardless of how derived. Our institutional structures are designed so that major decisions can be revisited and revised as more information becomes available or as experience changes the perceptions and goals. Finding out analytically that we are not very sure of what will really happen if a particular policy choice is made is not news to the experienced. What it may do, though, is to possibly allow those "dastardly" policymakers who have a preconceived notion to ignore the results of analytical investigations on the basis of validation findings and turn to their own subjective notions. This is the very event that early modelers were trying to avoid with such procedures as systems analysis: an interesting, but unvalidated speculation with counterintuitive results.

USE OF EXPERTS

Even if we were able to completely validate formal models, there would still be places where quantitative judgments would not be complete or sufficient. Normative situations aside, there are several times in the run of any model where specification of a decision rule for the computer to operate on is in the neighborhood of "difficult" to "impossible." To handle such cases, the technicians who build models may resort to a formalism called man-machine simulation. What this entails is planned interaction between the computer, as it works its way through a model, and the professional who is supplying it with some of its parameter values. Technically, there is no reason why this human interface could not consist of inputs from several people, fed through an individual to the computer. Although the programming of the model may have to be slightly more complex to accommodate an interactive man-machine linkage, conceptually the idea is pretty straightforward. Instead of having the values for the parameters used in a model specified as part of the computer code or calculated by the model, the model could ask for a decision or value for a parameter. The known input values are then combined with those specified in the model and acted upon according to the rules specified by the algorithm. This technique is tailor-made for those analysts who believe that analysis results are improved if there is explicit input from an involved decisionmaker throughout the analytic process.

One major weakness in the methodology is that even if a single decisionmaker could be identified for a particular issue and was willing to spend the time linked to a model, it would probably not be a satisfactory situation. For one thing, the professionals operating the model are likely also feeding in their judgment as to what the qualitative inputs should be, to the extent that data have to be interpreted to fit the model. To the extent that the input should be reflective of a particular policymaker, it cannot be under such conditions. To the extent that it ought to be representative of some general or average opinion, it will not be. To the extent that it is supposed to be agreed-upon scientific judgment, it is unlikely to be. In the end, the concept of a man-machine simulation is apt to work like what it sounds like it is: a mechanical fix.

The other extreme is to have a group of experts gather together and ruminate over the issue at hand, without any computer at all, pronouncing their judgment as to what ought and ought not to be done. If these groups of people are truly up to snuff on the topic at issue, if they have the time and resources available to look at an issue or facets thereof, if they are *truly* objective, and if they are able to work together—then they may be able to help with the analysis. On the other hand, the joke about camels and committees is told and retold because it is so close to reality. The process of compromise and bargaining is a poor substitute for information. There will likely have to be considerable negotiating as the opinions or judgments of the group of experts become a part of the political process. There is some question about whether adding deliberate compromise at the information phase as well as the decision phase serves the policy process well. Further, the caveats noted above as to the most favorable circumstances for group interaction almost never come to pass. Experts and prima donnas are often synonymous. To get several such people to pull together is a very difficult chore; it is worse if there is any competition or professional disagreement among the members of the group. In general, the reality of the situation is that it would be unlikely indeed for all of the conditions to be met that are necessary to have the most effective use of this combined talent.

With all these potential problems, the researchers have suggested an additional difficulty. In addition to the issue of compromise and the resulting loss of individual or at least minority opinions, there is the feeling that most such meetings tend to get dominated by a single individual who cows the group and forces a result in a specific direction. This fear of domination, added to the belief that there is no such thing as an "unbiased" expert, has led to an attempt to ritualize the process in terms of a technique called Delphi, already discussed in chapter 2.

SUMMARIZING TECHNIQUE

Let me summarize some of these points. It is my contention that the research in modeling and its allied fields is indeed far advanced. Further, the frontiers being explored as a part of this research may be of great utility to those who will eventually have to use models for theory-building analysis and the like. Looking across the full spectrum of model applications, there are a very large number of models in actual use or development. Depending upon the function intended, almost all of these models could be considered proper applications of the art. I contend, however, that once the discussion of the use of models is narrowed by requiring that only those constructs which are able to be used for policy purposes be considered, the rules for determining what is a "proper" model change. This change consists of a need to choose models that are more fully tested and that contain algorithms which have greater degrees of consensus as to their correctness in terms of representing reality among those who are considered the cognoscenti in the subject area being modeled. Given this test, it means that it will normally be years before the models available today for, say, research purposes, become widely acceptable for policy use.

In short, the potential for further advances in the state-of-the-art of the narrowly defined area of policy models resides largely with models which are in existence today. It is only by reviewing these policy models that one can refer to their weaknesses and limitations, rather than dragging the whole field of modeling into the discussion. Further, by assessing the potential for correcting the shortcomings of policy models in the near future, it is possible to realistically forecast the probable advances to policy models in the future. [23]

Policymakers and Policy Models

A recent lecture delivered at the International Institute for Applied Systems Analysis by George Dantzig [24] contains some sample quotes of selected key personnel in Washington, D.C.:

> A good Assistant Secretary knows when to use a number. He knows when a number is good and knows where and to whom to go to get a good number.
>
> Staff people (of a senator) are not influenced by models, except if they conform to a point of view that they wish to promote.
>
> Senators are advocates. Few if any of them know anything about the technical details modeling folk talk about. They don't talk the same language.
>
> PIES (the main planning model of the Department of Energy) is irrelevant to anything we do around here. No one, and I mean no one, takes it or any model seriously.
>
> At best, a senator has a 6-year time frame, but we are asked to look at analysis within a 25-year horizon, or more. That is ridiculous.
>
> We need discrete and simple answers, and no model is going to give you that.
>
> The only influence or impact that modeling has is on the incomes of the modelers.

If these quotes are truly representative, then there is little need to bother trying to convince the policy level that models are something they personally should become involved in. However, usually they have somewhat less of a problem being concerned about the use of models by their staffs.

The most potentially controversial parts of this chapter center around the terms "policy" and "policy model." Policy, reduced to its essence, is an official statement of "how things are going to be done around here." In the strictest interpretation, all federal policy resides with the president and Congress, but because the government could not operate at all if they alone had to make all decisions, the responsibility for specific areas is characteristically delegated to others, say, Departments, and then to Assistant Secretaries in these Departments and then on down the chain of command. In the end, as noted earlier, although the formal responsibility for a specific policy is clear, identification of the actual person who makes the policy decision is often not.

The ambiguity associated with who actually makes policy, a point we have discussed earlier and will return to again, leads us directly back into the question of the form and use of policy models. Because of the hierarchical nature of policymaking, it is possible and likely that most analyses include the use of a model or two as the decision passes from one level to the next, although the specific results of a model may not be in evidence at the time the final policy decision is publicized. The higher up the policy hierarchy one goes, the greater is the tendency for the decision-maker to be concerned with the output and the impacts of the decision and less with the inputs of the analysis. Models are inputs. Even cases where there is less time for sequential analysis by several layers of the bureaucracy, there is nonetheless certain data pulled together to arrive at the ultimate policy decision, and again, it is likely that models will have something to do with the derivation of this data even if they were not run specifically for the particular analyses at hand. There are, in short, few cases where models are highly visible and intimately involved at the cutting edge of policy decision (though there are noteworthy exceptions).

The Federal Energy Administration Project Independence Model created a wave of federal activity in the energy area that was coordinated by the now defunct Federal Energy Administration (FEA). The report used to prepare and support the administration's policy was based largely on the analysis contained in the PIES system.[25] Further, there are highly visible models—say, the econometric models used as a part of several economic reports—but these are less clearly a driver of federal policy.

As a final example, let me turn to a model I helped construct: the Strategic Environmental Assessment System (SEAS) used first at the Environmental Protection Agency and now at the Department of Energy. This model was the backbone of the 1975 Cost of Clean Air and Water Report to Congress.[26] Although it is unclear whether one would consider such a report to be a policy document, it is certain that the data contained therein will be used by others to formulate positions which will more obviously be the basis of policy.

These are all large models, though. More modest models also make contributions to policy. For example, I gathered a sample of books and reports which are anthologies of models and divided a few of them into three categories for purposes of our discussion here: environment, spatial analysis, and energy. The two works in the environmental area[27] make it clear that throughout the air and water pollution fields, there are dozens of models used for planning and policy. Although we might get into an argument over whether planning is policy formulation, the fact is that models are used all the way from setting pollution control standards to promulgating guidelines, and are published by EPA as tools to be used by state and local governments when they publish their State Implementation Plans (that the Clean Air Act requires) or for the part of their section 208 regional planning documents. Combined, these documents must describe upwards of a hundred models in use today.

In the energy area, there is at least an equally large number of actively used models. Recently, the Electric Power Research Institute (EPRI), in an attempt to sort out the claims of the model builders from the reality actually produced by the models themselves, set up a workshop to study the problem. It became a forum to analyze the results of models used to study the same policy question. This innovative experiment in model comparison and evaluation is still in progress.[28]

The Department of Energy, like EPA, uses dozens of models to predict resource availability and to stimulate technology performance. Another publication by the Office of Planning, Analysis, and Evaluation of the former U.S. Energy Research and Development Administration lists over fifty models used merely to assess the impact of energy development.[29] Although there is little attempt to specify what models should be used by localities that wish to measure energy budgets, the types of models catalogued are from a class developed for spatial analysis, our last category.

Three additional publications I chose for this section, *Urban Development Models,*[30] *Models and Techniques for Urban Planning,*[31] and *An Introduction to Urban Development Models and Guidelines for Their Use in Urban Transportation Planning,*[32] are somewhat redundant in terms of content, but they do cover the majority of the models of this type used by the Department of Housing and Urban Development (HUD) and the Department of Transportation (DOT) for urban planning. Reports like these, or some portions of them, are made available by these federal agencies in one form or another to local planning departments who wish to prepare plans for both their internal use and to apply for federal funding. Whether or not the funding use of models is considered policy at the national level, the use of these models in local jurisdictions clearly is.

We can see, then, that lots of models are used in policy formulation. This is because much policymaking is normally a long involved process requiring input from numerous people over extended periods of time.

Most of the models covered in the reports mentioned have characteristics of engineering models and are usually sufficiently transparent so that an average user would both understand the algorithm and know where (or how) to get the data to run the system. As a class, they are not overly large or complex.

FURTHER USES OF POLICY MODELS

In the opening paragraphs of this chapter, I suggested that it has seemed recently that nearly every policy analysis now makes use of models. This statement, upon reflection, is even truer than it first appears. While looking out the window, I chanced upon an analogy which made the phenomenon clearer to me. I pass it on to you. Almost everyone, or so it seems, drives a car. At the turn of the century, when the automobile was a new phenomenon, however, the owner and driver of a car was a fairly unique individual. He not only drove the car, he normally had sufficient skills to be his own mechanic (or he didn't drive the car). Today, this is no longer required. Cars are generally more reliable and repairs are readily available.

We can say the same thing about the computer and the model builder. Early enthusiasts had to understand considerably more about computer hardware and software than do modern day computer users. In fact, today's more advanced hand calculators have programmed circuits often times more complex than the average algorithms tackled by many early model builders. With such relatively strong calculating power so readily available, it is no wonder that everyone seems to use models in policy analysis.

The analogy between the automobile and the computer was developed merely to make the point that the early pioneers in their use had a "hobby" atmosphere surrounding them. Auto touring and building models have had much in common. Today, because of the advances in the technology and because our institutions have changed to accommodate this development, both products are fairly commonplace. The computer model, however, is some stage removed from the automobile, in that the advertisement for its use has not been totally divested of its science fiction-like aspect, although the growing home computer market is moving in this direction.

To say the same thing in just slightly different terms, those who are gifted with foresight almost always steal the thunder from reality. Reading Leonardo Da Vinci would tend to take the wonder out of flight or submarines; Jules Verne, out of trips to the moon, and so forth. Similarly, those who predicted or painted the future of computers and models have left us a challenge that we shall be many years in actually achieving. In short, we often find that our theories and speculations in model development are far ahead of the state-of-the-art we use for policy purposes.

One of the additional reasons for the widespread use of models is that most universities teach their use as a proper way to do problem analysis. This probably has more impact on model use than almost any other single factor. As in the case of management information systems, a great mystique grew up around the question of who actually was the ultimate model user. The popular belief always was that it had to be policymakers; after all, they are the source of permission for the expenditure of funds and also have the responsibility for making the ultimate policy choice. With this hypothesis in mind, it was only logical for technicians to want to brief these decisionmakers regarding their models.

Over the years, I have been present at (and presented) dozens upon dozens of such briefings. It is only in recent years that it has become clear to me what the actual outcome of such briefings has been. On the one hand, the briefings serve as a pacifier to the policymaker in the sense that he receives some feeling of assurance that at least one of the numerous problems he is facing is under control. The more complex the briefing and the better the salesman who gives it, the more this feature is served. Model quality, validity, and so forth characteristically enter into such discussions almost not at all. If the briefing is poorly handled or the administrator does not have confidence in the model team or leader, little is accomplished by such presentations. A second outcome of such briefings is that the policymaker is given enough information to be able to present some version of it to others, often giving the impression that they have the situation in hand.

Although such statements sound somewhat cynical, they actually represent all one might realistically expect as the outcome of many technician-policy level interactions. For example, at one agency where I worked, the decisionmaker was most apt to have been a classically trained lawyer, representing a field where almost no instruction is normally offered in the analytical arts. In other cases decisionmakers, even if they have scientific training, cannot really be expected to be familiar with the subject matter of all the technicians under their supervision. The broader or more technical the issue being modeled, the less familiarity one might expect them to have with the total breadth of the subject. As a result, often the only tools the administrators have at their disposal are their own logic, whatever knowledge they may have of the subject being modeled, and their faith in the ability of the technicians (or their supervisor). The latter faith is buttressed by how well the analytical team (or individual) appears to have the issue being modeled defined and whether the output can be presented in a form that the decisionmaker can use.

The latter point, I believe, is the link to model use in the policy area. Because the administrator cannot normally be expected to have enough expertise to pass scientific judgment on model development and validity, this task is delegated to advisors who are trusted to provide it. They, too, often have similar limitations and delegate such questions to those who work for them, and so on down to the model developers themselves, who find that they are apt to have considerable latitude and say in the model structure.

This rather long discourse now can be tied back to the point that most universities teach—that models are legitimate ways to do analysis. Graduates either recommend them or actually proceed to use them when they are assigned a particular piece of policy analysis. The administrator, at the receiving end, is correctly pictured as someone concerned with the output of such analyses, not with the inputs in the form of models.

Once this stage has been reached, the way becomes open to break the final stumbling block to widespread model use: cost. Model development costs a lot of money. Data acquisition costs a lot of money. Validation costs a lot of money. Two factors are responsible for springing these funds loose: (1) the administrators must be convinced that the analysis will improve understanding (or selling) of the issue or policy and, (2) they must have faith in the staff which advises that the only (or best) way to produce a particular analysis is by using a model. If these conditions are met, somehow the funds normally follow.

Before proceeding to the last portion of this chapter, let me investigate a brief aside in the area of model use—the tendency toward building larger and more complex models. I have discussed above my concern that those who develop and use models justify their huge expense by presenting the model results as "forecasts" in the sense that the results actually describe the future. The dangers of these perfectly human defense mechanisms are obvious; for those who are interested, they can be read in a paper entitled "The Developing Forecasting Hoax."[33] For our purposes here, it is sufficient to say that the legitimization of model use has another effect: it has become easier for those who claim to be able to expand models so that they cover "everything" to get a hearing by a policy type. This feature of human nature can spring up because of all sorts of things. Cost and time arguments are often used.

In any case, once a model is used, it has a tendency to develop a life of its own and to require constant updating. A model is successfully used for one purpose and because of the political, financial, and technical capital it already represents, it gets modified or expanded to handle another problem. Or someone in the chain of model development sees that there is a problem with the model that has to be corrected before it gets used again. Or the model has to be updated to reflect more up-to-date data or policy. For any of these reasons (or excuses), there is the tendency to sell and resell existing models which have been accepted through use for more and more applications—naturally after increasing their size, complexity, and cost to use.

WHY USE MODELS? A REVIEW OF CONVENTIONAL WISDOM

As we have already noted, models are now used extensively in federal and regional policy analysis. Let me recount some of the reasons for their use. In the forefront are environmental quality estimates and long-range energy supply and demand projections. As recently as the early Seventies, there was a widespread and heated debate about the appropriate use of models. In these debates, many people defended models as a proper technique in policymaking. Typical promodel arguments include:

- The use of models allows for more rigorous analyses because the procedures used to build and apply models are both detailed and explicit. Algorithms have to be specified and can be reviewed for structural sense. Also, data must be found and restructured to operate the model.
- The formalism of model construction and validation processes met the scientific-methods paradigm, since others can replicate the model analyses to check the results, and can then perform their own analysis using their own assumptions.
- Often, alternate analysis techniques are not feasible or are too expensive in terms of available resources if a computer model were not used. In particular, "long range" projections can be simulated, allowing impact analyses of specific options by modeling.
- Allied to the above is the possibility of efficiently performing multiple "what if" analysis options which can be used to rank impacts of most likely alternatives; or to provide ranges of plausible estimates.
- The scope and detail of analyses could also be more complete and internally consistent in the sense that more variables can be considered in single analysis format and more secondary impacts can be measured.

- A related point is the belief that having models available can reduce the level of adversarial confrontations that polarize issues but are apparently lacking in facts—or, at least, a sufficiently complete set of facts.

There are other benefits ascribed to model use, but the ones above serve to give a flavor for them. Generally, there is a belief that use of detail and rigor in models means that analyses and decisions will be strengthened.

I will not speak now to the quality of final decisions as such, but rather I want to review enough of the process of arriving at one decision to consider the merits of model use in policy analyses generally and to ask (1) whether these are realized; (2) if not, why not; and (3) what can or is likely to be done to improve the situation. Let me turn to a case study.

A CASE STUDY OF MODEL USE: THE DECISION TO SCRUB COAL [34]

Since the invention of the computer, practitioners of social and policy science have held that decisionmaking in the public and private sectors could be improved substantially by providing more and better information to those who make the decisions. To be sure, common sense seems to be on their side. Those who engage in policymaking on a day-to-day basis, however, seldom seem to make their decisions on strictly quantifiable bases. Those pushing more quantification suggest that this is simply because not enough is yet available or known—when more data bases and models are made available, then decisions will be made which rest more completely on these results.

Recently, a major policy exercise was carried out involving environmental/energy/economic trade-offs. It had to do with the 1977 Amendments to the Clean Air Act, the use of coal, and inflationary impacts. Clearly, these are all significant policy issues. The debate was carried on with high visibility for nearly two years and was one where the policy analysts made extensive use of computer models. My intention here is to explore what difference, if any, the extensive use of such models made in the final decision.

THE POLICY SETTING

In the remaining decades of the twentieth century, coal will be the primary resource to solving America's need for energy—coal for electricity, coal for industry, coal converted to transportation and home heating fuels. But coal is dirty and our gains in environmental clean-up must not be lost.

One of the areas of concern is the emissions of sulfur dioxide (SO_2) from fossil fuel combustion. The majority of sulfur dioxide emissions in this country are produced by coal-fired power plants (they accounted for 62 percent of the total SO_2 in 1975). By 1990, present and future coal plants are projected to produce 60 percent of all sulfur dioxide, 11 percent of particulates, and 32 percent of nitrogen oxides emitted. For this reason, the Clean Air Act Amendments of 1977, in establishing the requirement for review and revisions of New Source Performance Standards (NSPS), set detailed procedures and stringent revision criteria for steam electric fossil fuel plants.

Congress, on August 7, 1977, as part of the Clean Air Act Amendments of 1977, made the first NSPS revision requirement mandatory within one year and redefined the standard criteria to be used for the steam electric industry. The new NSPS for criteria air pollutants were to be set to include two control tests:

- as in the earlier version of NSPS, a maximum weight of emissions per unit of potential heat input; and
- a requirement that, no matter what level of content of a pollutant in the fuel as mined, a percentage of emissions reduction using continuous controls to be achieved even when this reduces the emitted weight below the first criterion.

My discussion will consider only those major issues concerned with (1) coal-fired conventional steam electric boilers, and (2) sulfur dioxide emission standards, even though the debate ranged to other areas. Here is a short list of some of the big issues:

- To what level of percentage emission reduction have scrubbers that may be in operation as early as 1983 been adequately demonstrated?
- What are the economic impacts and fuel type (e.g., oil) usage impacts among the options?
- What are the regional coal mining impacts, environmentally and occupationally?
- What is the level of environmental improvement and how do these improvements balance against other impacts?
- What is the relation of the federally set national standard (NSPS) to state set, federally reviewed permitting processes required under Prevention of Significant Deterioration rulemaking?

If there were to be any satisfactory quantitative analyses of this policy, other than projections of technological feasibility, there seemed to be no choice but to use projective modeling of regulatory alternatives and relative impact analysis of these long-term projections. Certainly, from the modeler's perspective, this is a case study that is almost ideal to permit a fair, adequate test of the utility of models. Even the study time was adequate: well over a year to perform. Therefore, let us consider the models actually used by the several groups in the public debate.

We focus on three models used primarily in the comment period from February 1978 to mid-December 1978 to project utility capital plans and develop, at the national level, the energy/economic/environmental trade-off projections. The models were developed by: Teknekron,[35] ICF,[36] and the National Economic Research Associates (NERA).[37] The ICF model was used by EPA and DOE (jointly), CEA, and Interior; Teknekron by EPA; and NERA by the Utility Air Regulatory Group (UARG), a utility industry group. There were many stated reasons for the choice of the model used by each group. Although the technicians who developed these models and the policy technicians who used them would engage in debates about which of the models was "best," it appears from the documentation provided by the developers that they were all quite similar. More than that, it also appears that it would be possible to convert one model to include all the special capabilities of any other with a relatively modest expenditure of funds and effort. They all cover pretty much the same variables, Teknekron's being more detailed in the environmental impacts area (originally contracted for by EPA); NERA's emphasizing detail in the financial area (used by the utilities); and ICF's detailing coal usage (built for DOE's environmental and coal offices; see Table 3.1). In each case, the emphasis bias noted appears to be a function of the original client more than a basic design criterion of the model.

In general, these models are balancing routines which take a supply sector consisting of types of existing power plants and coal availability by region and type and match them to a demand for utility products by region to project additional future utility plant characteristics. In varying degrees, the models consider more detailed aspects of these general areas such as coal types, number of resource and demand regions, existing and new capacity, other fuels, utility demands, pollution generated, industrial fuel demands, and transportation links. ICF and NERA are linear optimization models solved on a 5-year projection basis, whereas Teknekron balanced a prespecified demand schedule with variable supply capability schedules as a simulation on an annual basis.

TABLE 3.1   Comparison of Model Parameters

Supply	ICF	NERA	Teknekron
Supply			
Number of Regions	30	19	12
Number of Coal Types	40	24	24
Existing Capacity	X	X	X
New Capacity	X	X	X
Coal Washing	X	X	X
Other Fuels	X	X	X
Utility Demand			
Number of Regions	39	21	96
Utility Environmental Impacts			
Air Pollution Emissions	X	X	X
Ambient Air Quality	–	–	X
Water Use	–	–	X
Solid Waste	–	–	X
Non-Utility Demand			
Metallurgical	X	–	–
Export	X	X	–
Industrial	X	X	X
Residential/Commercial	X	–	X
Synthetic Fuels	X	–	–
Transportation Costs	X	X	X

X = Included for consideration.

– = No specific output

REGULATORY OPTIONS CONSIDERED

In the steam electric NSPS analyses, more than two dozen regulatory options were analyzed and many more variations were proposed. Three general option formats, however, were stressed. These are defined next for our analysis results:

- The present NSPS standard is that promulgated in 1971 and currently in effect. This regulation, assumed for all plants starting operation from 1976 to any year of analysis, serves as the baseline of the present trend.

- The full scrubbing option is so named in that its primary differentiation from other new options is that it requires "full," or a constant, rate of scrubbing for all coals, no matter what level of sulfur is in the feedstock coal blend.
- The sliding scale option, or the partial scrubbing option, differs from the full scrubbing option in that after a certain minimum threshold level of sulfur dioxide emissions (by weight) is achieved, then a less-than-full rate of scrubbing is required. Therefore, high sulfur and most mid-sulfur coals are scrubbed to remove at least 85 percent of the sulfur dioxides, but a low sulfur coal could be scrubbed at rates as low as 33 percent.

COMPARING MODEL RESULTS: AMONG THE MODELS

As a first comparison, we compare the results of three models for a single projected year (for results submitted at about the same time: August 1977). Certainly, the models are not exact replications, nor are the input data necessarily exactly the same. However, any differences are usually subtle and in most cases would not leap out at the average policymaker in a comparative review of these results. I chose 1990 as the year for comparison, a year for which all three models provided results (see Table 3.2.)

- For sulfur dioxide annual emissions—by all utilities—all three sets of data are similar in that, as compared to current NSPS standards, either alternative would cause a drop of 2.4 to 3.2 million tons (12 percent to 16 percent), yet the difference between the two alternatives is less than one-twentieth of the drop from current NSPS. That is, although the general new form of the standard makes a considerable emissions savings over the current NSPS, the difference between the alternatives is negligible. One model, however, projects the sliding scale as lowest, while the other two have it higher than the full option; thus, the choice of the sliding scale versus the full option is not clear cut.
- In the financial statistics (rows 2 through 4 of Table 3.2), the results between the alternatives are small and mixed. The only common point is that either of the alternatives (being more stringent) will cost somewhat more now than the present standard. Certainly, the absolute values among the models vary sufficiently that a decision-maker might modify his choice based on which model results he uses.
- Concerning changes in coal production (or for Teknekron results, utility coal usage), the differences in coal use between all three cases is small (1 percent to 2 percent) and the sliding scale case is always

TABLE 3.2 Model Results from August Analysis Period for Selected 1990 Projections

	ICF			NERA			Teknekron		
	Present	Full	Sliding	Present	Full	Sliding	Present	Full	Sliding
National SO$_2$ (10^6 tons)	21.4	18.9	18.8	20.0	16.8	16.9	19.7	17.3	17.4
Difference	—	-2.5	-.1	—	-3.2	+.1	—	-2.4	+.1
Incremental Cumulated Capital Costs	—	0	8		N/A			13.9	13.9
Incremental Annualized Cost	—	1.9	1.7	—	3.3	2.1		N/A	
Average Monthly Bill ($)	43.9	44.2	44.5		N/A		34.4	35.8	35.7
Coal Production (10^6 tons)	1525	1502	1517	1509	1486	1492	919*	932*	937*
Difference	—	-23	+15	—	-23	+ 6	—	+13	+ 5
Utility Western Coal Burned in East (10^6 tons)	149	118	117		N/A		235	140	179
Oil/Natural Gas Consumed by Utilities (10^6 gal/day)	1.2	1.5	1.4	.7	.9	.9	.8	.8	.8

Source: Department of Energy, Office of Environment, "Briefing Paper: Proposed Revisions to New Source Performance Standards (NSPS) for Electric Utility Steam Generating Units," October 1978.

145

somewhat higher than the full scale. An anomaly appears in the Teknekron case—here the present standard compared to either new option is predicted to use less coal. Thus, once again, small but cross-over variations exist among the model results that would be likely to change the policy if it were based on this parameter.

• The differences in oil and natural gas used by the utilities are larger between the present standard and the alternatives (the Teknekron result has an opposite direction), but it must be recognized that the differences in the alternatives are small. Again, a quandary for the policymaker.

Although the set of differences is often small, a policymaker who had to choose, based on the information of a single model, between the full and sliding scale options could well change his decision as a function of which model output he had. Equally important, the model developers and users actually added confusion to the policy debate. Although the results shown here were quite close by the time the debate was a year old, they were not so close early on. Individual modeling groups, because of their expertise, the strengths of their models and data bases, and their client interest, stressed different variables as being *the* most important ones that the policymakers should consider. Further, at professional meetings and in government circles, there was much bad-mouthing of the other guy's techniques and results. The early differences in results, the variation in what the models predicted, and the general professional in-fighting reduced the utility of the model findings, especially to those who were not trained in the analytical arts where such discrepancies are often seen to be more significant than they really are.

COMPARING MODEL RESULTS: OUTPUT OF A SINGLE MODEL AT FOUR-MONTH INTERVALS

During the public debate, the ICF model was used in a collaborative effort by EPA and DOE, in that the general data used in this model were approved by both organizations as being the best available *at each time* of simulation, and both federal units agreed as to how data representing each option should be entered as independent variables in the model algorithms. In 1978, this was done three times (April, August, December) and each time, the data were updated to represent latest accepted information.

While it could be argued that the results should not be compared over time since the last period represents the "best" information, it can also be stated that federal policymakers in any given time period would have to make decisions on model results available at that time. Since this often occurs (and it did for our case study), it is appropriate to see how the simulation results changed in one model over the time period of analysis (see Table 3.3).

Table 3.3 provides the following insights:

- Nearly all values underwent significant adjustment and the patterns are not in one direction.
- Of the seven statistics, two maintained the same direction of change, three reversed direction, and two were mixed among the options.
- For four statistics, the amount of change was much smaller in the second time period than the first; for two statistics, the changes were similar and small, while monthly household expenditures showed a much larger increase over the second period.
- Among the three standards, the amount of change appears reasonably consistent when compared in each of the options. In the April-August phase, this is almost universally true; in the second period, this is less true for sulfur dioxide emissions and the financial measures.

Thus, the general statistics appear to suggest that major changes did occur during the year, although results appear to be converging as information is gained. The policymaker has to use information based on a moving target for incremental decisions on the proposed NSPS. As evidenced in a public meeting in October, there was considerable skepticism on the part of public groups about the changes in the April-to-August results and about model results in general. Of particular note were the projections of cost to the utilities and the consumers. The early results suggest a much larger cost (30 billion dollars) than the final results (6 billion dollars)—if, say, the DOE or EPA decisionmaker had based his concerns on the size of the financial impact of the industry regulations that his department was stimulating, the sizable shrinkage of the financial impact as happened here might well have changed the intensity of departmental concern, as well as modified the selected position. In DOE, there was frustration by the policymakers and the supporting policy analysis groups because of the changes in the data and, in the end, because of the relatively small differences in outcome among the alternative options. From the time of the October public meeting, DOE noted similar frustrations in other interest groups over how to compare outputs from different models.

CASE STUDY RESULTS

It would appear that in this case study, the models did not differentiate well among the alternative regulatory options. In fact, the need to improve the input data over the year made changes in outcome that easily masked

TABLE 3.3 Values of Selected Output Statistics from ICF Model During NSPS Analysis Period

	Present Standard			Full Control			Sliding Scale		
	April	August	December	April	August	December	April	August	December
National SO_2 Emissions (10^6 tons)	23.3	21.4	21.5	21.1	18.9	19.5	21.3	18.8	19.6
Incremental Cumulative Capital Expenditures ($B)	---	---	---	10	0	2.5	15	8	5.5
Incremental Annualized Cost ($B)	---	---	---	2.0	1.9	2.1	1.3	1.7	1.5
Monthly Household Bill ($)	45.3	43.9	50.5	46.4	44.2	51.4	46.2	44.5	51.0
Total Coal Production (10^6 tons)	1767	1525	1441	1711	1502	1437	1755	1517	1444
Utility Coal Moved East (10^6 tons)	455	149	84	299	118	64	346	117	62
Oil/Gas Consumed by Utilities (10^6 bbl/day)	3.0	1.2	1.9	3.3	1.5	2.2	3.1	1.4	2.0

Source: EPA and DOE sponsored analyses as published in *Federal Register*, 19 September 1978 and 8 December 1978.

the differences in the options. Further, based on comparative results among models, the selection of a model and the time the model was chosen could have had a significant impact on the ultimate policy choice— or at least in the positions of one or more of the adversaries.

Perhaps the greatest achievement of the models in this case study was to show a high degree of consistency of *relative* results among the three options. No matter which model was applied or which vintage data were being studied, the results ended as being small differences. If these results had been so close in the beginning of this policy exercise between models, and if the final model results of a single model used had been consistent through time, *there is some reasonable doubt whether the policy issue would have been joined at all, and a serious question of whether it would have engendered so much heat and resulted in so much expenditure of effort for what turned out to be a decision where not enough was really known to analyze. Possibly the models actually added to the confusion and heightened the adversary process—the direct inverse to what the early proponents of models envisioned.*

The result was not a panacea: on the contrary, at the level of detail and resolution of the results, *these models did not clearly distinguish among the options. The final judgments of the policymaker had to be supported from other rationale and sources.* For example, a factor in the formation of the final refined options was judgmental information collected in the public meeting on the relative merits of the options. Those who advocate a more "rational" approach to policy formation have said repeatedly that having better information available would make the opinions clearer and allow more of an objective, dispassionate choice among alternatives. Given this issue and the experience of the public inputs received by DOE, it would be hard to find such improvement in this case. By the time these public meetings were held, the NSPS issue was almost a year old, and models and data had played a considerable part to that point.

In summary, then, it is possible to become cynical and to hold that models, even when used extensively, have little impact on the policy-setting process. Such a statement is as exaggerated in one direction as the early claims about the utility of models were in the other. On the other hand, a policy decision had to be made because of the timing of a Congressional mandate and the data, good or bad, were all that was available for model use in supporting this decision process. And, let us acknowledge that this particular analysis was superior to what was for-mally done for other significant policy decisions.

The real lesson is that models are not and should not be expected to be "the be-all and the end-all" but that they continue to help and play a role in the complicated decision process. Because the policymaking process is an interesting one, using the existing information and opinions of all the interested parties, the final refinements will continue to be subjective. But, as shown in this case, the model results did serve this process and did allow a greater focus by the policymaker on detailed issues.

Thus, we suggest that our case study has reaffirmed the general consensus of models used today:

- models are often needed to help form insights and discussion points that could not be available otherwise;
- their results should not be overly interpreted, especially when the data base is weak or changing; and
- they can support continuing debate on controversial issues and often provide highly plausible relative impact assessments of options as these options are being refined.

This case study shows clearly that there was a real reason to be skeptical of the ultimate utility of model inputs into the policy-formulation process. *On the other hand, if planning is seen to be a form of policy analysis, then models are being used, and used repeatedly.* The next case study looks to some of these models in the energy area.

"DEEP SIX" ALL MODELS?

Because all models have inadequacies does not mean that we should never make use of them. It does suggest that these techniques have often been oversold and that some attempt should be made to reduce their capabilities to life-size. The most suspect of their vaunted capabilities is to be found in the suggestion that somehow they are able to "predict" or "forecast" the future. With a little reflection, it will be clear that such claims are subliminal desires for the legendary crystal ball and not readily available to any but Merlin. There are legitimate uses of models to extrapolate known present day conditions into the future. In this sense, one can say that given what we know about the system today, what we suspect may happen in the future, and what reactions will come to pass because of a specific policy or set of policies, the present will likely proceed to the future in anticipated fashion.

To summarize, let's take a look at a few specific types of modeling efforts that we could use in the policy area:

- Models could be used to perform impact analyses. By this I mean they could do standard "if x, then y" experiments. Many of the examples in this book are of this type—environmental impact analyses of energy policy.

- Models could be used as the front end of an interest group matrix. Such a matrix would be used to make explicit the concept of whose ox is gored. In this analysis form, the success of an issue is explicitly matched against its assumed popularity with representatives of the general populace.

- A modeling form could be developed which is designed to match the decision logic of many policy leaders. As such, it could be thought of as a maze or hurdle algorithm and be used to test whether an idea is "good enough" to survive a series of tests. If so, then regardless of whether it is best or not, it would be eligible as a policy.

- Finally, a formal variant on the above would be the ecologist's carrying capacity model. In this instance, the test is to see whether there is sufficient resiliency in the system to absorb the impacts of a proposed policy. We shall return to this concept in a couple of chapters.

In general, modeling is here to stay. It is also potentially a highly useful technique that can provide insights into the effects of policies not otherwise evident. Much needs to be done to refine the techniques though, and efforts are required to reduce the tendency toward normative sounding pronouncements on the part of the practitioners. As it becomes more of a secular and less a religious position, its utility will grow.

The Future of Policy Modeling

It would be inappropriate for me to assert that the statements I am about to make on the future of policy modeling are the result of any deeply held conviction or of careful analysis. On the contrary, they are more in the nature of observations and opinions based on several years of modeling experience—most of it in the federal policy community. Because of the nature of some of these opinions, I should also make the point that I do support further research in the modeling field. I have always been a strong proponent of such research and have found model development to have been among the more intellectually satisfying activities of my own professional career. This chapter, however, is restricted to the area of policy modeling. Once this use of models is stressed, experimentation with models should cease. Policy analysis is no place for developing and testing theories of basic science.

With these two caveats out of the way, let us proceed to discuss the potential future for policy models. Since we are discussing the future, where certainty is a goal rather than a possibility, I have chosen to present the few ideas I have in this area in terms of individual points.

- There has not been a serious attempt made by anyone to discuss where the balance exists between maintaining data sets or models that are already developed vis-à-vis redeveloping ones that are more narrowly focused each time we need them. This leads to a couple of related points.
- The data sets available (and the models) never appear to be quite right or adequate to deal with a given emerging policy question. This is not surprising, since most policy questions are either new questions or new ways to address old questions. In any case, new data (or algorithms) always seem to have to be developed.
- Our puritan heritage has endowed us with a "waste not, want not" conscience. With this perspective, it becomes difficult to throw away anything, either old newspapers or old models, for fear that we may need them again someday.
- Similar arguments are made for the staffs which build the models or gather the data base. Getting together multidisciplinary teams and undergoing the interpersonal dynamics that transforms them from a group to a team is painful. There is a reluctance to disband such teams (particularly on the part of the members of the team) after an analysis or model development is complete. This often leads to attempts to extend the life of a model (or data base) in order to get work for and keep together the "team."
- A disturbing characteristic of groups or agencies often appears when they must depend upon analyses generated with captive, in-house models. These agencies begin to define their policy problems in terms of what it is possible for the models to produce or analyze. Such habits mean that all policies tend to gravitate toward a homogenized amalgam.

In the end, as experience is gained, I believe that we will find that interdisciplinary teams are generally no longer all that difficult to put together, and indeed often a fresh perspective is gained by starting over. Also, keeping up large data bases which are only partly used may turn out to be much more expensive than bringing them up to date when they are needed. And finally, building small, special purpose models may actually turn out to be cheaper and preferable to modifying existing systems in a vast majority of cases. These three hypotheses all have proponents and detractors on both sides of the issues. It will not be too many more years, however, before there is enough accumulated experience to give better guidance on these questions.

- Most model algorithms are still pretty crude. If we divide the types of issues addressed by models into two categories—things we *could know* if we had more research and things we *would like to know* but it is not clear how we are ever going to—then it is possible to engage in some guesses here also.
- In the first category, if the research should improve, we are almost certain to be eternally faced with the catch-up problems alluded to above, i.e., never quite having the exact data or algorithm required to answer a specific policy issue. Further, there appears to be a multiplicative law which says that the more one knows, the more one wants to know. In short, policy models will continue to approach "perfection" as a constantly moving target. The experience slope, however, is positive and for several years has been improving rapidly.
- The second category—the search for models which foretell the future—is like the search for the philosopher's stone. The more models are designed to amplify the sometimes disorganized storage and retrieval capability of the mind, and less to predict actions and reactions in a way no analyst would, the better off the models will be for policy use. Larger, complex models which are difficult to understand are possibly useful for research purposes but are normally of limited use in the policy arena. If it is not clear why a particular analytical solution was arrived at, and the solution is still used anyway for policy support, then a model has inappropriately taken the place of careful policy analysis and leaves the resulting policy decision open to question.

Even the design of models as extensions of known logic can lead to some funny results. As one example, just as it is impossible to predict changes in all the various parts of our system through time, it is equally problematical to merely extrapolate current trends. Almost no variable associated with human actions could be found to be represented by a simple function, though. Why then should we expect that the anticipated results of any actions taken today would be so in the future? It is the *changes* which are both decisive and impossible to accurately predict. The model which attempts to forecast such change is consequently also impossible to validate. It becomes then largely a matter of opinion. With time, models will likely be used to pinpoint plans and institutions that the policymaker might want to consider altering if a particular policy is put into place as opposed to "predicting outcomes of the policy." For example, the prediction obtained by a model analysis which implies "running out" of a specific resource might mean that better data were needed, or a new technology, or a form of conservation, or some other solution. The primary result, therefore, becomes the starting point for more analyses rather than the ultimate basis for an immediate decision. Startling results or ones that suggest drastic change would send us back to the drawing board both to check the analyses further and to design mitigation strategies. It would force policy pronouncements to handle both the immediate and secondary problems associated with a particular issue.

With this in mind, let me offer a few generalizations which are by way of being personal predictions:

- Models and data tend to cost more and more to build, use, and maintain these days. This clearly suggests that the more interest groups focus on their ever rising popularity, the quicker the bureaucratic "bean-counter" will get into the act to help determine when models "cost too much." In the end, they may have as much to say about which analysis techniques are used as the technician. Given current trends, though, it seems probable that the final outcome will be more and more money allocated to the analyst's coffers.

- The emphasis on classical validation per se will all but die out in the policy model community (although such exercises will remain visible in other modeling activities). Interest will continue to shift toward better documentation. This shift, along with the growing facility of the policy analysis community in dealing with models, will mean preliminary validation in the nature of comparative results and taking a look at the data and documentation to see if variations can be explained reasonably. Because I have already asserted that policy modeling is no place for model research, the documentation and data information should be enough to let most analysts judge the utility of the output of a specific model run.

- Increasingly, models which receive a great deal of publicity find their way into the policy arena. Many such models have assumptions built into them which are those of their designers, and often these assumptions tend to proselytize a particular perspective. This tendency to use models as harbingers of the future will eventually require careful policing on the part of the modeling community itself- possibly by widespread discrimination of the builder's model assumptions in professional journals or by setting up a professional committee to review models.

• The notion of a "simple" model I have preached here should not lead the reader to replace the term with "trivial." Because of these models and general advances throughout our knowledge industries, what is fairly generally known (and therefore simple) is seemingly increasing daily. The policy questions that several of the federal agencies struggle with are not ones they were created to solve (energy, agriculture, commerce, and so forth), but are ones which occur when the policies of their own agency impact, in a way that has come to public attention, with those of another agency. The current energy and environment debate is but one example of such a crossover. Our theories across discipline and subject matter lines are still in the formative stages. Unlike the use of models per se, the universities have not made great strides in legitimizing research and institutions in areas which are not clearly in the domain of one department or another. This is slowly changing, though, and as it does, "simple" models will become even more complex.

I guess the bottom line on this whole chapter is that the changes we can actually expect to see in the area of policy models are already on the horizon or pretty much in place. Nothing really new or startling is expected, and the next several years will see us trying to live up to the promises made by those who built and sold policy models in our recent heritage. More to the point, in terms of model form and validation at least, we shall not even see the day when present state-of-the-art research models will advance to the stage of reliable policy tools, let alone the advances which are being and will be made in the future. Lots of work remains, but if the question is, "What's new with policy modeling?" the answer is "Not much."

NOTES

1. Op cit., U.S. EPA.

2. G. D. Brewer, *The Politician, The Bureaucrat, and The Consultant: A Critique of Urban Problem Solving* (New York: Basic Books, 1973); or D.B.J. Lee, "Requiem for Large-Scale Models," *American Institute of Planners Journal* (May 1973).

3. E. S. Quade, *Analysis for Public Decisions* (New York: American Elsevier, 1975).

4. Jay Forrester, "Counterintuitive Behavior of Social Systems," *Simulation* (February 1971).

5. See Harold Chestnut and T. B. Sheridan, "Modelling Large-Scale Systems at National and Regional Levels." Report at the Brookings Institute, Washington, D.C., February 1975.

6. Op cit., U.S. EPA.

7. See H.S.D. Cole et al., *Models of Doom: A Critique of the Limits to Growth* (New York: Basic Books, 1973).

8. Although the statements of the section on stochastic modeling and those to come on other more sophisticated modeling forms are harsh, the castigation is aimed primarily at their performance in the public policy arena, especially where human decisions have a large part in the predicted outcome. On the positive side, these techniques have often proven highly useful in military and business applications where it was possible to specify the total situation to be modeled with greater clarity and certainty.

9. Not everyone has been enthusiastic about systems analysis. The most famous critique was done by Ida Hoos in *Systems Analysis in Public Policy: A Critique* (Berkeley, CA: University of California Press, 1972).

10. International Research and Technology Corporation, *Forecasting, Planning, Resource Allocation, Source Book* (Washington, DC: n.d.).

11. Roger Sisson, in the *Guide to Models in Governmental Planning and Operations,* extols optimization models and suggests that models are both simulations and optimizations.

12. Although the father of this methodology as applied to social and business policy analysis was Jay Forrester of MIT, the best exposition on the use of the technique can be found in John McLeod's "How to Simulate," *Simulation in the Service to Society* (September 1974).

13. The most recent use of the technique to gain widespread attention was the development of the so-called COAL-II model. Its principal developer is now at the Department of Energy. See Roger Naill, *Managing the Energy Transition: A Systems Dynamics Search for Alternatives to Oil and Gas* (Cambridge, MA: Ballinger, 1977).

14. See Peter W. House and E. R. Williams, *The Carrying Capacity of a Nation* (Lexington, MA: Lexington Books, 1976) for an example of this model type.

15. Clopper Almon, Jr., Margaret B. Buckley, L. M. Horowitz, and T. C. Reunhold, *1985: Interindustry Forecasts of the American Economy* (Lexington Books, 1975).

16. The reviewers of early drafts of this chapter reacted very differently to the above section. Some took exception to my description of particular modeling methodologies as being too caustic—although the objections were not consistent enough to reflect any sort of consensus. To set the record straight, I react in this section to the well-known claims of the model builders who touted specific model methodologies, promising great benefits from acceptance of their technique. It should be clear to almost any impartial observer that considerable overselling took place (although the term "overselling" is not meaningful in retrospection), and that the reality finally arrived at today is less than promised. Nonetheless, the capabilities of some of these techniques, for specific applications, are often great indeed.

17. Peter W. House, *The Urban Environmental System* (Beverly Hills, CA: Sage, 1973).

18. See "DATA" (Report of the Working Committee on Data) in D. U. McAlister, *Environment: A New Focus for Land Use Planning.* Report on an

NSF/RANN-Sponsored Workshop-Conference, Boulder, Colorado, 1972, p. 456; or the various reports of the "National Commission on Supplies and Shortages," *Government and the Nation's Resources* (Washington, DC: U.S. Government Printing Office, 1976), which dealt in detail with the data question.

19. See Peter W. House and John McLeod, *Large-Scale Models for Policy Evaluation* (New York: John Wiley, 1977).

20. See the Chestnut study for a brief description of the models or the more recent Martin Greenberger, Mathew A. Crenson, and Brian L. Crissey, "Public Decision Making in the Computer Era," in *Models in the Policy Process* (New York: Russell Sage Foundation, 1976).

21. See the Annual Environmental Assessment Report (Washington, DC: U.S. Department of Energy, 1977) for an example of the use of this technique.

22. A recent RANN study by L. Granessi and H. Peskin, *The Cost to Industries of Meeting the 1977 Provisions of the Water Pollution Control Amendments of 1972* (Washington, DC: NBER, 1975). This is an example of such a validation attempt. In the end, it merely resulted in pointing out that different models yielded different results, but did not demonstrate the absolute or relative "correctness" of any one.

23. A number of the reviewers of an earlier paper on which this section was based argued that the changing emphasis from model "technique" to how models are used for policy analysis is a major reemphasis in policy modeling interest. Probably so, but my hypothesis remains that the classical facets of the modeling field are not apt to change radically in the near future, provided the focus is just on policy models.

24. G. Dantzig, "The Role of Models in Determining Policy for Transition to a More Resilient Technological Society," IIASA, Vienna, Austria, June 12, 1979.

25. Federal Energy Administration, *Project Independence Report* (Washington, DC: U.S. Government Printing Office, November 1974).

26. U.S. Environmental Protection Agency, *Resource and Pollution Control*, EPA 600/6-79-010, September 1979.

27. U.S. Simulation Modeling Advisory Committee, SCOPE, Simulation Modeling Assessment Project, *Environmental Simulation Modeling and its Use in Decision-making: The United States Experience* (Indianapolis: Praeger Press, 1976); and Office of Research and Development Decisionmaking and Office of Planning and Management, U.S. Environmental Protection Agency, *Environmental Modeling and Simulation* (Washington, DC: USEPA, 1976).

28. EPRI Workshop for Considering a Form for the Analysis of Energy Options Through the Use of Models. Special Report, Stanford, California, 1977.

29. Office of Planning, Analysis, and Evaluation, *Models and Methodologies for Assessing the Impact of Energy Development* (Washington, DC: USERDA, 1977).

30. Highway Research Board, *Urban Development Models* (Washington, DC: National Academy of Sciences, 1968).

31. Douglas Lee, *Models and Techniques for Urban Planning* (Buffalo, NY: Cornell Aeronautical Laboratory, 1968).

32. Federal Highway Administration, *An Introduction to Urban Development Models and Guidelines for Their Use in Urban Transportation Planning* (Washington, DC: U.S. Department of Transportation, 1975).

33. Peter W. House, "The Developing Forecasting Hoax," Simulation Councils, Inc., 1977.

34. Peter W. House and Ted Williams, "On the Efficacy of Mousetraps: A Case Study of Use of Models to Refine Environmental Emission Standards." (unpublished)

35. A. Van Horn, "Utility Simulation Model Documentation," Teknekron, Inc., 1979.

36. "Coal and Electric Utilities Model Documentation," ICF, Inc., 1977.

37. "A Description of the National Economic Research Associates Electricity Supply Optimization Model," NERA, Inc., 1979.

CHAPTER 4

THE ART OF POLICYMAKING

Policymaking in Action

Which of the following statements do you believe a Congressman or the president would make at a press conference?

- I understand that my decision to select this alternative is expected to result in 50,000 excess deaths.
- Of the three alternatives I had offered to me, the one I chose should afflict or kill the fewest number of people.
- I have decided that it costs too much to make this policy any less risky than it is at present.
- There were not enough funds available to solve the energy crisis in a risk-free way, so I have decided to do nothing.

All of these statements seem bizarre, overdrawn, or examples of re-ductio ad absurdum when put in the framework of taking statistically derived risk conclusions and presenting them as a political statement. Yet there is some reason to believe that the political process often forces a decisionmaker to make a choice between several seemingly poor alter-natives, and the big question is how to handle the public announcement in the least damaging way. Most times, those issues which are simplest to solve are handled simply and routinely. The decisions in the public sector which require the special attention of those in the political scene are abnormal—often, as Mel Webber of the University of California calls them, "wicked." They are complex and interrelated with other issues, and the policies proposed have notable numbers of proponents and opponents, meaning that each decision usually results in the formation of political factions.

In an atmosphere such as this, it is entirely understandable that the average politician is reluctant to present decisions to the public in terms which highlight probable damage levels that can be used by his opponents to discredit him. It would seem that such information, in fact, is tailor-made for political embarrassment at least or is a potent weapon to encourage the veto of a candidate policy. Unless one does nothing, there are bound to be decisions which will have as part of their impact the potential for killing or injuring people. If one is adamant that risk be added to the decision process, here are some of the kinds of questions we have to face:

(1) Is it ever possible to reduce risk in our society to zero?

(2) Is it possible to convince people that, on the average, they are only worth some finite amount of money to society and that society should not invest more than that amount to protect and maintain that person?

(3) Is it possible to transfer to the nonmilitary sector the wartime philosophy that some attrition or human injury is necessary to achieve an objective?[1]

Questions like these come about, in one guise or another, every day in some portion of the public sector. The ones I chose to introduce this chapter were supposed to direct the reader to the oft apparent contradiction between the pragmatists on the one hand and the seeming naiveté of some technicians on the other. Earlier chapters alluded to this problem but spent most of the time with questions of "what if?" Chapter 1 was designed to question the logic behind the whole field of formal, highly analytic policy analysis. It did this by taking an introspective look at the field to see if the assumptions and expectations that have grown up around it for the past couple of decades have really been borne out by actual experience. Chapter 2 went behind this theme and zeroed in on the limitations of analysis as a formal process for decisionmaking, using case studies to demonstrate that formalism has not been, and indeed cannot be, all that successful. Chapter 3 narrowed the perspective even more by reviewing and analyzing the use of and successes with computer models. This chapter will begin the task of resetting the policy formulation process in a more realistic fashion to prepare the way for some suggested modifications discussed in the last two chapters. I want to try to bring to bear some case studies and examples in this chapter which show the dynamics of the policy process and elaborate the discussions begun in these earlier chapters. Let us get on to looking at the more pragmatic side of policymaking.

THE SITUATION IN WHICH A DECISION HAS TO BE MADE

Some writers seem to describe the task of decisionmaking as akin to choices of whether or not one would have an extra piece of toast for breakfast. In the public sector, at the federal level, nothing is quite so simple-minded. Decision choices are confounded by several features, for example:[2]

- The power to make decisions in Washington is deliberately divided among at least three major branches of government. Under the constitutional doctrine of separation of powers, none of these branches of government has complete decisionmaking authority. The proliferation of commissions, authorities, and the like have complicated this division of power even further.
- Further, although there is considerable power at the federal level, the ultimate ability to make and carry out a decision is further shared with two other levels of government, the state and the local. Again, each of these levels has some ability to make its influence known in the policy process.
- Modern day decisions are very complex. The advent of high technology, especially rapid communications and transportation, means that decisions are more widely discussed, their implementation expected more quickly, and evidence of their success or failure widely sought, often unreasonably soon. Further, the fabric of modern industrial society is so tightly interwoven that it is really inconceivable that a candidate policy could be discussed which did not impact one or more areas of interest: economics, education, environment, energy, and so forth.
- Many of the public policy issues that arise daily are presented with heavy overtones of "emotional" or "crisis" or "political" postures rather than on the basis of information produced by analyses or using other formal information processes. To the extent that this is so, it is hard to address such issues in what an empiricist would consider a rational manner, as quantification of these postures is not presently possible.
- The idea that decisionmakers represent some group referred to as "the public" is largely rhetoric. It is clear to anyone who does policy analysis or who is in the political arena that as policies are segmented by issue, so their supporters and detractors are similarly segmented into varieties of interest groups. The response at the political level to an issue in the name of "the public" is usually a response to one or

more of these special interest groups. Congress, for example, is deliberately designed to represent, at least, different regional areas. The Executive branch has departments which focus on various specific areas such as transportation, energy, agriculture, and the like. In addition to other functions, such departments become advocates of these interest areas, at least to the extent that they compete for shares of the total federal budget.

- The question of whether an issue "makes sense" or not is a non-question. Issues are whatever rise to the policy level as items that they have to address. The driving force for a particular issue seldom comes from the scientific or technical spheres and is not usually resolved by highly rigorous analysis alone. It is usually an "issue" because somewhere there is a threatened shift in the relative distribution of the existing power structure or other potential changes in the present distribution of resources.

- Finally, the policy process, as it is presently structured, is largely defined from the perspective of a legal model and, as such, is adversarial. The rules that govern this process are set to ensure that a contestant wins a particular point, whether or not he is right according to some technical or moral criteria. As such, the focus of issues is deliberately restricted to as narrow a perspective as possible or necessary to make a case, and then a particular position is argued based on the most favorable interpretation of one of these narrow positions. Winning is seldom enhanced by attempting to exhaustively check a position (or policy) against all the possible impacts a decision might have. In fact, the relevant impact is normally felt only by the contestants. Secondary impacts on others (such as other interest groups) are seen as somebody else's responsibility, and as elements which unnecessarily muddy the issue debate. Further, the legal profession places great reliance on precedent. In an arena where much of the decision structure is based on logic, and which puts great value on being able to trace a proposed decision through a linked chain of decisions stretching far into the past, there is little room for wide variation in the positions (or policy choices) actually adopted.

Let me begin with some definitions. There will be no attempt exhaustively to define these terms, but rather an effort to give the reader some indication of a class of variables that, although not expressly dealt with in specific analyses, are nonetheless often critical to the actual impact of the resulting policy, and therefore should be considered when the policy is being analyzed. Most experienced decisionmakers intuitively incorporate these factors into the total decision process. Thus, we might say that such factors pertain more to the "demand side" of policy analysis than the "supply side" noted above. I categorize them as circumstantial, conditional, and methodological:

- *Circumstantial*—the environment extant at the time a policy is being reviewed, internal or external to the policy unit. Such factors as an agency or department's present policy position, the current public attitude toward such items as, say, the unemployment rate or inflation all could be considered to be policy-related, but beyond the scope of an individual policymaker's ability to influence them fully or directly. These types of factors are not expected to change greatly during the course of an analysis.
- *Conditional*—the provisional situation under which the analysis is performed. Examples are the amount and kind of resources available for the analysis, the time before the analysis is needed, and the personality or approach of the person receiving the information. These factors are often set at the beginning of an analysis and could be changed during its course.
- *Methodological*—the method(s) adopted to perform an analysis. There is rarely any clear-cut methodology ideal for performing policy analysis of public issues, although entire professional careers are often spent trying to develop particular approaches. As we noted earlier, methodologies range from so-called optimal solutions, produced through one or more computerized algorithms, to those produced through a less rigorous political process—a sort of "muddling-through" approach to be discussed in Chapter 6.

Public policy operates in a highly complex, but not always fully empirical, rational world, and must give equal weight to a number of factors not easily obtained objectively or by quantitative analysis. A review of the incommensurables noted in Chapter 2 will give some indication of the kind of specific variables one might want to consider. Of course, the need to include so many subjective variables in the first place leads some to dismiss the quantitative side entirely and others to throw up their hands and exclaim that the nature of our system precludes good decisionmaking. Neither is true.

The fact that a decision cannot be fully quantified does not mean that we cannot make any decision or even that a good decision is impossible. As far as energy and environmental trade-offs are concerned, political and administrative problems make the development and use of comprehensive, large-scale, or combined models very difficult. This does not, however, mean that quantitative analysis has no place in the decision process. Such an environment merely indicates a need to redefine the trade-off techniques. The quantitative framework, and the drivers within that framework, which frequently describe a closed system to policy analysts, must instead be viewed as a subset of the larger political process. If one takes into consideration the political assumptions and public perceptions which are the front-end drivers of our policy system and which have a great deal to do with determining the eventual decision, then one can put quantitative analysis into a proper framework. This framework would require that models be used for backup data and information to show the potential feasibility, popularity, or success of a particular decision. Used in this manner, any one or a combination of several quantitative techniques may well be appropriate. To be appropriate, however, they may have to operate at a microlevel, providing the policymakers' advisors with the detailed information that will allow them to appraise the accuracy of the results and to make those results available to the policymakers for them to interpret with the nonquantitative aspects of a decision.

Unfortunately, problems like these are seldom discussed openly and seldom remembered when the debate is over. The neatly reasoned and structured process portrayed in textbooks does not exist at times of stress, while forces often not articulated do come into play. The mismatch between theory and practice, however, is not unique to policy analysis.

A REVIEW OF THE ANALYSIS PROCESS

Almost everyone else who has been seriously interested in how to do policy analysis at some time or another is likely to examine the literature for applicable techniques and guidelines. Methods abound, as we have seen, nearly all borrowed from a variety of more traditional disciplines—economics, systems analyses, operations research. One of the clear perceptions obtained in such a search is that almost all guidance derived from these fields recommends highly analytical and technical methods for supporting policy decisions. On the other hand, the literature of public administration provides largely descriptive solutions, usually relegated to personnel or administrative matters. Guidance from the policy science field is often so highly structured that public policies *appear* rational—the products of models and computers that presumably have very effectively removed the biases and politics of human judgment and interplay.

The search for guidance becomes increasingly disappointing as one gains experience in actually producing public policy analyses in the real world, and relies on this experience to pinpoint methods that might be useful or workable. On the other hand, to be fair, analysis of major public policies is, as we have already noted, an incredibly complex process. In some cases it resembles more an art than a science. In many decisions that must be made daily, it is. This feature of policy analysis suggests that almost every situation is unique, and attempts to structure the process tend to add a dimension not useful to the actual practitioners. This is an overstatement, of course, but it does suggest that some attention should be paid to those practicalities that often make application of conventional paradigms messy. The process of analysis begins when a decisionmaker calls for an analytic structure on which to base a policy decision. What follows depends on consideration of a variety of factors that can influence the way the analysis is performed and used.

A final policy decision may have little to do with the options suggested by rigorous analytical techniques. A mystique has arisen in the public (and often, private) bureaucracies that seems to attribute supernatural capabilities to the various quantitative techniques which had their roots in systems analysis and operations research. In spite of the fact that few policies have ever been formulated solely by following these techniques, texts and college curriculae perpetuate the myths surrounding their use. One technique, mathematical programming, discussed in Chapter 3, is representative. This method requires specification of (1) the present situation; (2) the final situation desired; and (3) a listing of the so-called boundary conditions preventing immediate solutions. Computer programs are devised to demonstrate to the policymaker "the" solution which would yield the greatest payoff, or the least loss. How handy it would be to have a computation show, unequivocally, what should be done!

Again, let me mention that no posture is implied as to the value of analysis per se. Some of the lessons of the previous chapter, however, can usefully be summarized here:

- Data or information should only be a part of an analysis if the user is fairly certain of such factors as causality, magnitude, sign, and so forth. Highly speculative relationships, values, and the like, or concepts and theories which are known to be in the formation stages have no place in a policy analysis, although they may be useful in a longer-range, properly designed research or assessment piece.
- At times, a taxonomy of effects and impacts may be all that can be presented in a trade-off analysis. In areas where emotional impact is inherently present in the nature of the subject matter (e.g., jobs, religion, health), great care ought to be exercised not to present incomplete or even unreliable findings regardless of how well-meaning or virtuous they might seem to those who wish to make "all" information available to a policymaker.

- When the analyst is stretching hard to come up with enough information to say something meaningful about a particular trade-off, it
  is fruitless to suggest he use very sophisticated techniques which rely
  on there being available even more richness in the data or information bases; for example, by adding stochastic and distributive measures such as confidence limits to the findings. J. Menkes[3] has held
  that:

  > human beings are not particularly well suited for or compatible with
  > making decisions on the basis of merely probabilistic information, suggest-
  > ing that these more sophisticated techniques, even if technically possible,
  > are not really useful to impart information to the policy level.

Menkes thus adds a further dimension to my view on adding sophisticated
error or probability measures. My statement is that it is not really possible
to specify such probabilities in a large majority of the policy analyses. It
may be that they would not be well used even if it were.

In addition to these three general rules or limits placed by the professional on anyone who is trained in a technical fashion and wishes to
responsibly carry out policy analysis, there are other realities introduced
by the political/bureaucratic system. Although none of these is absolutely
constraining in the sense that policy must always be made with every one
of them in mind, it is nonetheless instructive to note that the following
situations are representative.

PRACTICAL CONSIDERATIONS AND FORMAL METHODS

If the situation surrounding the decision to be made is accurately and
adequately described, the goal correctly articulated, the future forecasted
correctly, and the boundary conditions completely specified, then the
computer model's results might indeed suggest the decision(s) that ought
to be forthcoming. Unfortunately, such a situation hardly ever exists in
the area of public policy analysis. Consequently, policy analysis must
depend upon the skills of humans who use less than perfect tools to
articulate the possibilities for resolution of an issue that requires a decision. The ways that this can be done are myriad, and yet depend on a
traditional set of factors that must be considered for a credible job to be
done. Many of these are obvious and are stressed by those who promote
policy analysis as a highly structured science, e.g., the use of data and/or
models information. These might be defined as pertaining to the "supply
side" of policy analyses, as discussed earlier.

There is, however, a set of other real-world factors that are nearly always taken into consideration, such as specific advantages and limitations to most quantitative techniques used to compare the impacts of different energy technologies. As we have noted, quantitative models in general usually have inherent problems when their results are used to formulate policies in the public sector. In the next several pages, we will discuss the deficiencies associated with the practical application of a selection of the types of analytic techniques discussed in the previous chapters. Our concerns are generic, not with data availability or the applications of a specific model or technique to analyze any given issue. We shall assume that in individual situations, the model used and its results reflect the best that can be done with available information. Nor am I concerned here with inappropriate conclusions that result from an oversimplification of the analytical process. Problems of this nature do indeed relate generally to the utility of the various quantitative analytical techniques, but have been more appropriately discussed elsewhere in other chapters. Rather, we are concerned with broader problems related to the mismatch between the analytical design and the way the results may really be used in an actual policy situation.

There is probably no way to design, say, an energy/environmental/ economic paradigm that adequately allows trade-offs to be made between real energy, environmental, and economic considerations. Certainly, a paradigm (or even several paradigms) can be conceptualized and designed. When such a design is finally displayed to portray the essential elements of a major policy issue, however, a number of cells will always be vacant. The vacant cells may have little to do with the traditional technical deficiencies such as the complexity of the process, the availability of the data, or the appropriateness of the data. In this instance, the vacant cells show us the points where other less analytically definitive processes become dominant; for example, cultural habits, societal choice, institutional relationships, and politics.

The well-bound decision world in which most of the analytical methods originate is, unfortunately, characteristically different from the public policy world. The economic and efficiency paradigms used by the private sector are not necessarily useful for the general welfare issues of the public sector. The "bottom line," seemingly so clear in the private sector, is less obvious. Although one can legitimately argue about the relative importance of the simple profit motive in private decisions, still, profit is a necessary, but often not sufficient condition in most private sector decisions. No such clear-cut objective function or "bottom line" exists for the public sector. Consequently, techniques which incorporate concepts tied to the profit motive (e.g., rate of return, value of labor, economic efficiency) do not usually transfer well into the public policy arena. This brings us back to the inclusion of the incommensurables in comparative analysis discussed in Chapter II.

In addition to the vagaries introduced by the world of people and politics, there are a series of factors that are related to the background and agenda of the policymakers themselves. Let us continue to look at these in greater detail, first reminding ourselves that policymakers are people.

SOME HIDDEN POLICY QUESTIONS

Implicitly or explicitly, the policy- or decisionmaker might address questions as they come upon them by asking themselves a series of questions that help focus the issue. Among them might be:

- Can I get away with the policy? If not, what can I get away with? "Whose ox is being gored?"
- Will this idea really work? If I can't get assurances in this regard, will it at least appear to work so that I can at least get credit for addressing the issue?
- Will this policy make me look good?
- Will this policy give me maximum flexibility in case I have to reverse or modify it?
- Will adoption of this policy put my job in jeopardy? If yes, will it nonetheless improve my chances for a better job elsewhere?
- Is this policy supportive of my own personal basic goals and ideals? Does it do damage to any of them?

None of these questions are posited as being noble or ignoble, bad or good per se. They are, however, among the types of questions that human beings who are also decisionmakers have been known to ponder as they make choices among policies.

The Process of Public Policy Analysis

Public policies are often elusive beasts. They can range from decisions to go to war to the way civil servants should interact with the public. What is policy for today may not be in vogue tomorrow. Although it is often confusing, this seemingly endless flux is the way we tend to operate our public sector, at least at the margin. In fact, the purpose of public policy is to make "steering corrections in the ship of state" and to change them as the "weather" requires. Although hundreds of policies, big and small, are formulated and modified every day, the perception of "how things get done" typically appears stable. The reason for this is that the numerically large number of policy shifts is relatively small compared to the existing institutions and operations they attempt to adjust.

Most individual public policies seeming to have little direct effect on how most of us live; this is fortuitous or sad, depending on one's viewpoint. On the other hand, the direct and secondary impact of many individual policies and the combined impact of the multitudinous decisions made by all the public sector decisionmakers have profound impacts on the way we approach our daily lives. Some realize how great an effect their actions usually have on individuals and strive for informed and thoughtful decisions.

Formulation of a public policy that deals with a complex and far-reaching issue is normally supported by analysis of the source of the issue, criteria for setting the policy, alternative decisions that might be made, the impact of these decisions, and the institutions and groups affected. The way such an analysis is carried out can often significantly affect the final policy decision.

POLICY ANALYSIS IN PRACTICE:
INSTITUTIONAL PERSPECTIVES

Decisionmaking in the public sector is really dependent on several factors and should not be expected to be done in a like fashion in every sector of the economy. For example, if one were to compare the expected decision processes in such areas as the public nonmilitary, the military, and the private sectors, there would be apt to be several areas of dissimilarity.

- The military and other public areas are similar in that they receive their mandates from several sources, e.g., Congress, public interest groups, and the courts, so that to the extent that the demands of these spheres of authority are not the same, neither will the responses be. This leads to a tendency to make more foggy the programmatic plans and a putting forth of a face to the citizens which often appears that an agency has promised to rush forth in all directions at once, while remaining steadfastly rooted to one spot. Because the constituent groups that the private sector responds to (the stockholders, the workers, the customers, and the government), although possibly as numerous, all have a more uniform idea of what profit-making firms should do, the private sector is able to plan a strategy for survival with more certainty as to who to please, how, and when. In contrast, the public sector managers may very well find themselves in situations where satisfying one mandate often gets them in trouble with another.

- The commitment of the senior management level could be postulated to be different between the private and public sectors. The decision level of the public sector, after all, consists of political appointees who have taken the job for various reasons and may evidence varying degrees of commitment to the long-range goals of organizations. The private sector managers will likely be around to face the consequences of any activity they start. The public ones probably won't be. For example, former Secretary of Transportation Coleman did a long-range transportation plan that was declared obsolete within months after the new incoming Secretary replaced him. Examples such as these abound around the time of an administration change.

- The interpretation of the goals of the public sector changes by administration, often by a department in the administration, or even by an organizational entity within the individual department. The Carter Administration's commitment to protect the environment, for example, was seen as meaning something different by the Council on Environmental Quality, the Environmental Protection Agency, and the Departments of Energy or Commerce. Within the latter two departments, there are environmental officers who often find themselves in an adversarial position during a single decision process concerning an environmental and industry hassle.

- Finally, the clearest manifestation of differences is possibly the fact that the "make a profit" or "win a war" goals of the other sectors are more specific in the nonmilitary private sector. The bottom line for the managers in the public sector is vague, and consequently it is difficult for these managers to gauge the potential for their own successes or failures before an action, or even to measure it afterward. Often, the vagaries of public opinion or political factors can change a perfectly rational action to a disastrous mistake, even while the implementation of the policy is in process. The reader can surely think of several examples of one promised policy goal running smack into another. Normally, even after the embarrassment of these seeming contradictions is made manifest, there is an explanation or strategy devised to reconcile them. But for a period of time, it is obvious that there has not been the coordination necessary for the smooth functioning of the public sector. During recent testimony in the Piceance Basin in Colorado supporting the last administration's position on oil shale production, a local politician reminded this federal witness that the larger growth expected in oil shale would require a lot of water, and getting this water would require impoundments—and that the federal government had just reinforced its policy not to support any more impoundments in the West!

POLICY ANALYSIS MANAGEMENT: SOME PRACTICALITIES

I have already talked a great deal about the various institutional realities surrounding the development of policy results. One that could stand a little extra emphasis, though, is the situation surrounding those who manage the resources used to produce the requisite analyses: personnel and money.

Personnel: There are two ways to obtain the people to carry out any particular piece of analysis: use in-house talent or hire it. Since hiring it is tantamount to managing money resources, we will get to that next. The use of in-house resources poses a number of interesting problems for the manager.

- *Never Enough:* Policy issues gobble resources at a prodigious rate when they are hot. At that stage, every available body is mobilized and put to work on some facet of the issue. Long hours and a frantic pace characterize this period. After the analysis, there is likely to be a lull where, in a relative sense at least, there is nothing to do. If the organization has staffed up to the level of support required during the peak of a crisis, then there are a lot of idle resources around. To some extent, the situation is akin to that of the armed forces which has to develop the optimum size of a standing army versus the size of one in a wartime situation. Staying with this analogy, one of the biggest problems of military management is keeping the troops busy when there is no war to fight. Policy shops are similar. Consequently, prudent management strategy suggests that a less than full-strength work force be assembled—particularly in the civil service, where shrinking it again is so difficult. Consequently, there is never enough help when the heat is on.
- *Typical Days:* The people who do policy analysis are not really different from anyone else, in that they like recognition for the work they do. Generally, the only difference is that many of these people sometimes get hold of a very hot issue and go right to the center of a maelstrom of activity. Recognition, excitement, challenge, and other wonderful things abound. An experience of this sort often turns a person into a policy junkie.

  This fact means that there is a constant push on the part of those analysts who are not center stage to get there. Since anything could potentially be an issue, if the policy level takes notice and chooses to make it one, there is a constant push to find a hot candidate analysis and hype it to the policy-level attention.

Although not fatal, the understandable desire to be center stage ofttimes means that pulling together a team to work on whatever issue has surfaced defines winners and losers in the attention-getting sweepstakes. In some cases, reluctance to leave a project which might blossom into an issue can create artificial scarcities for the policy group. Along the same lines, this understandable desire to get attention for an issue (and thereby, the analyst) may push an issue into the limelight that did not surface in the fashion anticipated by the traditional policy formulation model; i.e., the issue specification is the prerogative of the decision level, and the analyst is expected to be solution- or option-oriented. We have built an argument here, however, that there is real pressure to at least influence this initiation process from the analyst level.

- *Hiring and Firing:* It is not impossible to fire a civil servant, but it might as well be. Although the detailed procedures differ by agency, grade, and the interpretation of the personnel management system, the procedure for dismissal requires such things as specific (usually in writing) criteria for performance, including expected output, quality, and timing; and a respectable period for monitoring the performance, which includes frequent interactions between manager and employee. The counseling sessions should include explicit statements about the areas of dissatisfaction, required improvement, and finally, written unsatisfactory ratings to the employee. To ensure objectivity, this process is often monitored by people from the agency's personnel shop. At best, the process takes months and is subject to layers of review, including court action. Attrition usually occurs, not through this process, however, but by means of the employee, unable to withstand the harassment, finding another job. It is equally difficult to hire a new civil servant. One would think that it would be possible to interview a series of applicants and offer one of them a job. Not so. First, assuming a slot (position) is available in the policy shop, a description of the job has to be prepared. This position description serves to specify the duties of the job and is the basis for classifying the pay level to be offered. Once established, the description becomes the basis for selecting a candidate.

From the potential employee's side, there is a standard information form (SF-171) to be filled out. It is used to rate the salary level eligibility and specify the technical capability of the person.

The job is advertised (for up to a month) and interested applicants (plus some others added by the Office of Personnel Management) send in their SF-171s. After the advertising period, all the applications are rated according to a set of criteria specified at the time of the advertisement. Each of the criteria are given a certain number of possible points (all adding to 100). Veterans and disabled applicants are given an extra five points each. The top score is to be offered the job first, and then on a rank-ordered basis, each of the others is called. It is easily possible that a person chosen by a route outside this one would never score high enough to even be considered.

This process could take from three months to a year or more.

Resources: The people difficulties of the analyst manager are obviously real and potentially serious. But they're only half the problem. Suppose one tries to solve the problem of controlling variable workloads by contracting out the work at peak times.

- *Buckets of Gold:* Ordinarily, contracts are awarded in the public sector by having proposals selected on a bid basis. Since the contract and procurement law is written in such a way that the logic is as good for buying chairs as paper studies, any technically qualified contractor (regardless of how much better they are than another qualified group) is still ultimately judged on the basis of the lowest cost. Because this institutional model did not make sense for several of the services the government required, other forms of getting technical information were instituted. Universities, for example, and selected other groups can get grants. These are based on some mixture of quality and resource availability. Or, if one can demonstrate uniqueness, then a sole source contract can be issued. These are relatively difficult to pull off. One variant is used heavily by shops which aid in policymaking. Instead of being very specific as to what is needed from a contractor, what is called "task order contracts" are let. These contracts specify a level-of-effort and allow the policy shop to specify the individual task when an issue surfaces. A good first step; now all one has to do is guess the initial, overall level-of-effort for, say, a year. Unfortunately, if one is wrong in his guess and not enough funds are put in a particular bucket, then all of the problems of procurement just noted come to the fore at the time that the effort is going on to produce a policy analysis. The average policy analysis lasts for days, possibly weeks. The average procurement in most agencies is from six to nine months, start to finish; an obvious impedence mismatch.

- *Potential Control:* There is no guarantee, regardless of the amount of time spent checking the qualifications of a contractor, that the product produced will be of acceptable quality. Even if one checks credentials and makes a practice of meeting with the contractor frequently, there is no assurance that the resulting product will be good enough to be usable by the policy shop. For one reason, after all the coordination is over, someone has to write it down. Unfortunately, there are people who communicate well verbally and seem to be organized, but who are congenitally incapable of writing an English composition. Although it is contractually possible to return the product as unacceptable, the time pressure of the policy world does not normally allow such luxury.

  Recently, there has been an emphasis on making sure that there is no conflict of interest entailed in carrying out a specific piece of policy analysis. Further, there is a drive to ensure that as much policy analysis as possible is done in-house. Often the more extreme interpretation of this interest makes responsible management difficult. When a specific task is suggested to a contractor, in theory a written order is prepared and the contractor goes away and produces a product. To ensure that the task is of high quality, relevant, and responsive to shifts in the policy focus under investigation, the contract is monitored closely and written products required. If such checking is done very frequently, the contractor begins to act like a member of the public service rather than the public. The uncertainty lies in striking a "reasonable" management strategy on the part of the government.

- *Congress, Office of Management and Budget, and Budgets:* Each year, the many parts of the executive branch participate in an exercise which results in a budget for an individual policy shop to operate on. After this budget is estimated by the policy shop, it is argued through higher and higher levels as the amount needed to perform the work. In the end, if it is approved, it is hard to argue that one did not know what he was talking about when the money was requested, and to return a surplus. Imagine the difficulty of handing back a surplus at the same time one is requesting funds for the next budget period. In short, there is great pressure to spend the money—all the money—in any given fiscal year.

In summary, it is a complex management problem for the policy shop manager to bring to bear his personnel and financial resources on the continually changing set of policy issues that must be addressed during a given fiscal year. The requirements of the job are such that in-house staff is necessary to do the analysis, but the optimum size of this staff fluctuates depending upon the frequency and intensity of policy issues. The resources required are equally difficult to predict. Both resources and personnel, due to the vagaries of the regulations and customs of the federal establishment, have to be utilized somehow, even when there is no burning policy issue to employ them.

Some Specific Examples of Policy Formulation

Up to this point, this chapter has been concerned with some general perceptions of how policy analysis is actually carried out in the federal sector and what hidden rules and constraints do to the carrying out of these analyses. Now let us turn to examples of how some specific policies were made (or evolved) and what impact analysis had on these decisions. The first will be a discussion of environmental standards setting, specifically the Prevention of Significant Deterioration (PSD). The second, the setting of the New Source Performance Standards (NSPS) for electric utility boilers from a different aspect than model use (covered in Chapter 3), the third, other rulemaking issues and issue areas, and fourth, the setting of a commercialization strategy for the Department of Energy.

ENVIRONMENTAL STANDARD SETTING: PSD

It has become increasingly clear to those who work in the public sector that whether analysis is complete or not, without regard to the quality of the analysis, or how applicable the information used to perform the analysis, sooner or later a decision will be made using whatever information is available. Most supporters of analysis suggest that careful, scientific analysis should improve decisionmaking. I, for one, heartily agree with this pious hope, but I am less sanguine about our ability to implement our desire for scientifically supported decisions.[4]

It is the theme of this section that many of the more problematic issues in policy analysis are evident in the trade-off space of energy and environment—and that here none is more intractable than policies promoting the use of coal and maintaining the goals of the Clean Air Act. I will cite some examples of problems that have surfaced when the public policy communities have attempted to be faithful to the goal of promoting coal as our nation's transition fuel and to using it in an environmentally acceptable fashion. Although several papers have been written on one or more aspect of the problem, the perspective I have adopted in this section is to look across several instances of past and emerging energy/environment trade-offs and suggest that in meeting environmental regulations, the primary issues facing the energy industry today are uncertainty of rulemaking and of supporting data, and complexity of legislation and court actions.

Complexity: A major difficulty of analysis and rulemaking is that of complexity. The Clean Air Act was amended twice in the Seventies alone—and its last amendment set a mechanism for further amendment in the early Eighties. The Act has taken on increasing complexity with each amendment, and the courts have found more convoluted legislative intentions than appeared obvious from the stated language. That is not to say that the elements of the Act are not complex in and of themselves, but that in addition, actions taken under one section of the Act often cause major revisions in rulemaking or permitting of other sections. Let me first pursue the history of a single concept of the Act, the Prevention of Significant Deterioration (PSD) in areas of the country presently meeting the National Ambient Air Quality Standards (NAAQS), as an example of this complexity.

The concept of prevention of significant deterioration of air quality has had a long and litigative history. Its roots are traced to a 1971 legal determination by the Environmental Protection Agency (EPA) that it did not have the authority to regulate deterioration of air quality in clean air areas under the Clean Air Act as amended in 1970, despite earlier rule-makings by EPA incorporating such a policy. The Sierra Club challenged this EPA determination on the grounds that the Clean Air Act could not be interpreted as to allow pristine air areas to be polluted, even to the levels of the secondary standards. In a landmark court decision (Sierra Club vs. Ruckelshaus), the District Court upheld the Sierra Club's position and enjoined EPA from approving portions of State Implementation Plans (SIPs) that did not provide for the prevention of significant deterioration of air quality in those regions that have air cleaner than the secondary national ambient air quality standards.

Subsequent court decisions provided little guidance to EPA. On appeal, the Supreme Court had a deadlocked vote of 4-4; no written opinion was issued and no Supreme Court precedent was set. Since the Supreme Court was deadlocked, the lower court's decision stood. The Appeals Court did not issue a written opinion. As a result, the "rule of law" meant the original District Court opinion—a procedural order which was in fact a ruling on an application for a preliminary injunction instead of a ruling based on the actual merits of the case—would stand as the final guidance on this issue.

While the PSD regulations have produced an incredibly complex maze for implementation, the underlying concept is relatively simple. The country was divided into three types of areas. For each type, a limit of additional allowable pollution was set. Class I areas, essentially pristine areas including major National Parks and Wilderness Areas, allow the least amount of incremental pollution. Class II areas (into which the whole country except for the parks was initially placed) allow moderate levels of pollution growth. The original definition for Class III PSD areas would have permitted the most growth of pollutant levels from present conditions, allowing air quality to deteriorate up to the secondary ambient air quality standards under the 1974 regulations, but this has since been modified. States, Indian tribes, and federal land managers have the option of petitioning EPA to reclassify areas from Class II to Class I to prevent air quality deterioration, or from Class II to Class III to encourage industrial development. For example, the Northern Cheyenne Indians have petitioned successfully to have their Montana reservation classified PSD I. No states have asked for a PSD III classification for any of their areas.

Each major new pollution source was required to obtain a PSD permit by going through a very complex review process to determine, through modeling and monitoring of emissions, whether the allowable increments would be exceeded if the facility were operated. The 1974 regulations, in their entirety, withstood the court battle which ensued. However, they were based upon the 1970 Clean Air Act. In 1977, Congress amended the Act and affirmed and strengthened the court's position on PSD. Because of these modifications, EPA went back to the drawing board and new regulations emerged on June 19, 1978.

The predictable occurred. Both sides—industry and the environmentalists —went hurrying back into court to seek changes in the new regulations. The 37 separate challenges were consolidated into a single court case, Alabama Power Company et al. v. Costle. No less than 15 major issues were studied, argued, analyzed, and decided upon by the District Court of Appeals. A preliminary opinion of 43 pages was issued on June 18, 1979, more litigative comment was sought, and the final opinion, a tome of 160 pages, was released on December 14, 1979. The issues covered a wide spectrum, including technical issues of the definition of a polluting source, what constituted "potential to emit," interstate transportation of air pollutants, when monitoring or modeling of emissions is an acceptable information base, if fugitive dust should be included in determining whether a source is major, what the baseline date is for initiating use of allowable increments, how a stack's emissions will be monitored or modeled, and whether a concept of net off-setting adjustments within a source should be allowed.

On September 5, 1979, between the final court statements, EPA proposed new regulations based on the preliminary court ruling. They are technically and administratively complex. The preamble (explaining the regulations) is twice as long as the regulations themselves. Parts of the regulations will undergo modification due to public comments and some changes in the court's final opinion; further, the economic and energy impacts of the proposed regulations have not yet been calculated as required by the Clean Air Act.

Rather than try and go into the above issue or surface several others in any meaningful way, our purpose in providing an example of an emerging regulation can be served by noting the potential difficulties surrounding the requirement for including fugitive dust as an element in PSD permitting. The issue is complex, possibly involving several industrial sectors, and there is concern that resolution will be attempted for this ruling without adequate environmental, energy, and economic analyses. Quoting from the DOE comments to EPA:

> Furthermore, we are deeply concerned about the implications of the proposed fugitive dust policy for surface mines. The proposal appears to subject surface mines to PSD review where a power plant or synthetic fuel plant is proposed to be collocated with the surface mines. (See Proposal 40 CFR 52.21(b)(5) and (20).) Additionally, adoption of future NSPS for surface mines would have the effect of subjecting all new surface mines to air quality impact review for fugitive dust. If this did happen, the cumulative regulatory impact could occur without a proper assessment of the economic and the energy impacts of the PSD provisions. We believe that the full assessment of the potential impact of the modified rule on fugitive rulemaking activity at a later date. *The potential impact of the present PSD proposal could be the prohibition of large new mine-mouth facilities and strip mines.* Surface mine facilities are essential to national energy objectives. They should not be jeopardized lightly, especially when there appears to be evidence that adverse health effects from the generally large non-toxic particles generated as fugitive dust by such operations are limited or non-existent.

> A study[5] recently completed for DOE showed that surface mines are major emitters of fugitive particulate matter, but most of the particulates are in a size range with little or no bearing on the

infringement of human health. Application of current EPA modeling techniques on a Western mining area showed ambient concentrations of particulates of over 100 ug/m^3 in areas near the mines. Modifying the model to allow for the natural deposition of particles, the predicted ambient impacts were reduced by a factor of two. Annual increments for TSP could still be exceeded in the locality of a mine producing 10 million tons of coal per year.

The impact of the proposal on the Nation's synthetic fuels program could be major. Mines associated with synfuel plants are large (10-20 million tons of coal per year). The energy program outlined by the President on July 15, 1979, included 1.0-1.5 million barrels per day (MMB/D) of synthetic oil and gas capacity from coal and 0.4 MMB/D capacity from oil shale. Most of this capacity would be jeopardized by the proposal, as well as future surface mine-mouth power plants.

With the future adoption of a New Source Performance Standard for surface mines, *all* new surface mines (not just those directly associated with an energy-related plant would be subjected to PSD review. The potential impact of such an eventuality is that no major new surface mines could be permitted. This impact would be catastrophic since our Nation derives over half its coal from surface mines.[6]

We can expect that no matter what the final regulations look like, environmental and industry opponents will be back in court arguing one or more of the many issues. And so uncertainty continues to hang over this air quality issue as we look forward to the possibility of new amendments to the Clean Air Act in 1981 or 1982, requiring new regulations and producing new court fights. Not only does PSD and its developmental history exemplify the uncertainty issue, but the detail noted in both the court rulings and the preliminary regulations is noteworthy. Again, this requirement is only one of the many potential environmental, health, and safety regulations that those who would use coal may have to contend with.

Thus we have a short history of a decade of increasing complexity in fuelmaking for a single, rather straightforward environmental concept—if air in an area is now relatively unpolluted, its quality should not be allowed to undergo significant deterioration. If the complexity of the implementation of this single concept is appalling, consider now some other concepts, also simple by themselves, that do or will impact on PSD.

- If any part of the Act sets a rule concerning any new air pollutant, then PSD must consider it—the turmoil noted above deals with rule-making for only two pollutants (TSP and SO_2).
- Permitting new or modified pollutant sources in areas exceeding NAAQS requires control technologies from any source to be considered, regardless of economics. PSD permits must consider such state-of-the-art technology (but now economics are considered).
- PSD permits must consider within the control technologies a set of minimum national performance standards for new source emissions that are to be reviewed and revised every four years, and are to force improvement of control technologies. This forcing process, the New Source Performance Standards (NSPS), is itself embroiled in controversy and litigation, especially as it concerns coal-fired electric utilities. I will pursue this further in the next section.

The complexity of rulemaking imposed by the legislation cannot be ordinarily offset by simply applying extensive, high quality analysis. To continue with our argument, I shall use the recent (June 1979) promulgation of New Source Performance Standards for electric utilities as an example of a thoroughly analyzed energy/environment issue to illustrate the hypothesis that even with extensive analysis, it is not always possible to predict where a policy decision—in this case, changes in promulgation of environmental regulations—will come down. Next, I shall sketch some present uncertainties with regard to evolving environmental regulations. I shall then proceed to highlight two areas where, by looking at the protection of the environment from an energy perspective, we can develop some interesting insights into what new issues might come to the fore. Finally, there is a summary where I suggest some steps in reducing these uncertainties. Now let us turn again to the NSPS for electric utilities.

THE ELECTRIC UTILITY NSPS: UNCERTAINTIES OF DATA

New Source Performance Standards have been set by EPA for over two dozen specific industrial categories, including steam electric utilities. Additionally, a general NSPS applies to large industrial boilers without regard to the product of the facility. For each industry category having an NSPS, the standards must be reviewed at least on a 4-year cycle to determine if adequately demonstrated control technologies exist to cause performance standards for control of any (or all) air pollutants to be made more stringent. If the review findings are positive, a formal rulemaking process is carried out to increase the NSPS stringency. The rationale for the general NSPS rulemaking, and specifically, the NSPS periodic reviews, is to ensure that the best adequately demonstrated control technology is used in new facilities and in major existing plant modifications. A secondary impact of the process occurs, however, because the review cycle is short compared to the time to design and construct a several-module utility facility. This impact increases investor uncertainty because a new NSPS may increase facility costs, thus causing a major modification of rate of return to surface after the investment decision is made for the first module (even assuming that subsequent module control costs will not escalate).

The NSPS process has a further general impact in that control technology choices for plants in PSD or nonattainment areas, as required by the construction permit granted by the state or EPA, cannot be less stringent than the analogous NSPS performance standards then in effect. Therefore, the technology-forcing provision intended by Congress carries over from the NSPS process, in that minimum performance standards for the nonattainment and PSD-permitting process are automatically set by the NSPS.

An industrial boiler NSPS is presently under study with the expectation that there will be a final rulemaking in 1981. For large industrial boilers, the performance standards are likely to be similar to the June 1979 electric utility standards; smaller boilers that use coal as a fuel may have somewhat less stringent controls. The complexity and uncertainty issues within the rulemaking process are not really put to rest when everyone goes to work on analyzing these impacts, either. In fact, there is some evidence that all the high-powered analysis surrounding the most recent setting of the electric utility NSPS (EUNSPS) actually heightened the uncertainty.

There are those of us who were involved in the analysis of this issue for almost two years of our professional lives. EUNSPS may be one of the more heavily analyzed decisions made in the public sector. It represented the expenditure of considerable analytic resources from both public and private sectors, had high-level policy attention throughout the executive, judicial, and legislative branches, and had lengthy statements of an analytically sophisticated nature from numerous parties. In the more detailed evaluation of the resulting analytic discrimination presented in Chapter 3, the conclusions reached are somewhat startling. On the basis of the evidence, it is possible to conclude that, due to the state of the information available, the presentation of modeling results that include preliminary input data to the decision level at the Department of Energy may have resulted in policy involvement to a level that was greater than justified. Further, even after a considerable amount of analysis and public involvement, the final EPA regulations were based on purported scrubbing capabilities of a technology (dry scrubbing) that was specifically excluded from the earlier analysis produced for review during the public comment period. Demonstration of the continuing operational feasibility of the central technology of the comment period—wet scrubbing—was probably the fundamental issue surrounding the whole debate from a technical perspective. It and all the other analyses were essentially ignored during the final promulgation. Let's look again at some of the findings of the earlier chapter on NSPS.

The review of this issue in Chapter 3 suggested that using models, even in a very technically credible fashion, does not necessarily mean that better decisions will inevitably come to pass. The very detailed policy analyses performed shifted the focus of the policy issue from the type of coal to be mined and the area of the country it would come from to the cost of compliance and the reliability of the pollution control equipment. The use of sophisticated analysis, however, as we noted earlier:

- is often needed to help form insights and discussion points that could not be available otherwise;
- results that should not be overly interpreted, especially when the data base is weak or changing;
- can support continuing debate on controversial issues and often provide highly plausible relative impact assessments of options as these options are being refined.

Several other basic conclusions can be drawn from the NSPS exercise.

(1) The data (information) available for most of the analyses done in the energy/environment area are of variable quality. In many instances, the desired data are completely missing or of questionable utility. Health effects data often fall into this latter category. Or, where data appear to be available, their applicability must be carefully reviewed. For example, EPA made much of the fact that prior applicants for PSD permits to build utility boilers often promised to scrub SO_2 emissions in excess of 90%. DOE, on the other hand, argued that promised performance based on engineering estimates did not substitute for hard data based on operating experience. In fact, a disappointingly large amount of the data that *all* policy decisions use in the energy/environment areas (and particularly for emerging technologies) are of the engineering estimation, rather than monitored performance, type.

(2) Most of the policy discussion which surrounds energy/environment issues is based on forecasts of energy demand and supply, and associated environmental impacts for years, often decades, into the future. Although no one purports to believe these forecasts absolutely, the reported analyses seem to put considerable faith in their veracity, even to make calculations to 3- to 4-digit detail. Consider that even a single coal-fired plant takes nearly a decade to design and construct. Also consider that the real focus of the trade-off mechanics we have been discussing lies at the state and local levels of government, or at the industry which has to come up with the capital to build it, or both. I find it hard to believe that many people would take the institutional or organizational arrangements and perceptions of these political units as being constant (or even predictable) over a decade of decisions.

(3) The regulatory climate, particularly the fears introduced by yet-to-be-defined regulations, is important. In most instances, Congress signals intent and scope of action to the public and private sectors that something is to be done to achieve a particular national goal. Generally speaking, after regulations are promulgated (and even more so when they are litigated), industry settles down and meets these often stringent but achievable requirements.

The experience with the promulgation of the NSPS regulations could lead some observers to question whether, even with extensive analysis and attention on the part of interested parties, anything in the environmental area is ever really settled. With all this attention to one single regulation, what is to be expected from those which are still to be promulgated? The "horror stories" based on potential worst cases before the actual regulation is set are often what make the private sector and politicians most nervous.

The review of the analysis of this very specific section of the Clean Air Act has suggested that there is reason to be suspicious of the help formal analyses gives us in making such decisions. The situation in terms of the various sectors of the economy attempting to adjust to the Clean Air Act is likely to be much worse than the problems suggested by this single issue, though. As flawed as these analyses may have been, at least they were attempting to address an issue. There are other areas, so complex and potentially immeasurable that no analysis has even been done. And yet it is in such areas that really significant impacts lie for our nation. We shall look at samples of these areas; uncertainty, long-range transport, and intermedia impacts.

YET-TO-BE- DEFINED REGULATIONS:
UNCERTAINTIES IN RULEMAKING

This next section will not be an attempt to treat, in any rigorous fashion, the whole panoply of emerging regulations. In fact, I continue to focus mainly on the Clean Air Act, although I must mention solid waste regulations necessitated by air pollution control. Unless there is a significant change in the mood of the nation, environmental, health, and safety standards, regulations, and permits will continue to be a basic part of the reality of doing business. Likely also will be increased laws and regulations with time (CFR Title 40, Protection of the Environment, has increased from one volume to four volumes since 1971). To make the point that uncertainty is clearly an important and justified concern of energy technologies, we shall note three evolving regulations and comment briefly on one or two portions of these. The two chosen are Visibility Impacts on Mandatory PSD I Areas, and the Resource Conservation and Recovery Act (RCRA).[7]

VISIBILITY

All major particulate, sulfur oxide, and nitrogen oxide emission sources, which would include all steam electric fossil fuel plants, large industrial boilers, and shale and coal conversion processes, may be subject to yet undeveloped regulations to prevent visibility degradation, especially in the West, near all federal PSD Class I lands. These regulations may lead to air emission controls more stringent than would otherwise be considered for PSD-permitting, including BACT determinations. The visibility regulations could lead to new pollutant control criteria (e.g., particulate emission controls by size, sulfate controls, and more stringent nitrogen oxide controls). Significant new control costs plus constraints on facility size and location could also result.[8]

These regulations are expected to be promulgated in late 1980. In essence, they could provide more stringent control of emitters in or near PSD Class I areas than the PSD regulations in force. Although the following issues will likely be made less stringent when these regulations are finally promulgated, there was considerable concern as to what impacts could occur if the regulations were issued in their most stringent guise, and this concern has resulted in substantial uncertainty. Three of these very environmentally conservative postures are:

(1) The definition of "baseline" from which all effects would be measured could be defined to mean the visibility imagined to have been in an area *before the imposition of man.*

(2) The law requires that "significant" impairment of visibility be regulated. One potential definition of "significant" proposed by EPA for comment is *any perceptable change* from baseline.

(3) Finally, the question of "vistas" has arisen in conjunction with observation points in the PSD I area. It is unclear whether Congress intended the visibility to be only within the Class I areas or whether it was expected to be extended to include the views to any outside horizon. If the latter (or any close approximation) is adopted, there are portions of the West where such "vistas" would require regulations to protect unimpeded visibility for areas up to 150 miles around Class I areas, especially if definitions 1 and 2 above are also applied.

Even though I could be criticized for pointing out a caricatured horror story which simply is not expected to come to pass (in the sense that EPA would not be likely to put forth such stringent definitions and standards), the fact remains that such regulatory options were presented for public comment in December 1979, and these do heighten the worries and uncertainties of energy developers. The spector of overly stringent controls may be doing more harm to the environmental movement than the reality of the regulations themselves.

No amount of formal analyses could reduce the uncertainty associated with this issue. It is strictly a political matter, based on factors aligned with the real or perceived desires of the American populace (or its representatives in some organized lobby). There is no training that could be designed to address such issues. The analysis may show the effects of policy on items such as land area or vistas, but these data would likely have little real effect on the policy outcome. The next area of uncertainty is an example of how information might truly help in making a better decision, but where the needed information would not be available in time for the legislative requirement for the promulgation of the regulation.

RESOURCE CONSERVATION AND RECOVERY ACT

Although the Resource Conservation and Recovery Act is not directly impacted by the Clean Air Act, one of its regulations will potentially have a considerable economic effect on the disposal of scrubber sludge and fly ash from air pollution control requirements. Fuel conversion processes and faulty air emission control equipment will lead to the generation of high volumes of solid wastes. Further, the treatment of water effluent streams may result in collection of concentrated wastes in lagoons or treatment streams. Included in the waste streams from all processes—biomass, coal, and oil shale conversion—are organics that require characterization and testing to determine if there is a carcinogenic or other health-related risk, and if overall waste management regulation is satisfactory.

A primary concern to investors is that the applicable regulations for the handling of energy process wastes are not in place and may not be promulgated for two or more years. Tests to determine if the wastes are hazardous are undergoing revision. For some technologies, even if a waste stream is declared hazardous, it may be subject to less restrictive management practices that would be proposed later this summer. Finally, the hazardous waste disposal costs are not well-defined at this time. If a high volume waste stream is declared hazardous, the cost associated with meeting the regulations could have a substantial impact on the economics of the technology.[9]

The most important provisions to DOE under the Resource Conservation and Recovery Act of 1976 are those that apply to the identification of hazardous wastes and performance standards for the treatment, transportation, storage, and disposal of hazardous wastes. Based on current test protocol proposals, some coal-burning wastes have the potential to be classified as hazardous wastes. The EPA-proposed hazardous waste regulations would increase disposal costs and impose siting constraints on coal-burning facilities, as compared to the revised sanitary land-fill state regulations.

When the hazardous waste regulations were proposed in December 1978, EPA considered a "special waste" designation for high-volume energy wastes identified as hazardous. This designation would reduce the cost impacts; however, special wastes may be subject to the environmentally sensitive area provisions of EPA's proposed hazardous waste regulations. DOE's March 1979 comments to EPA on the proposed hazardous waste provisions urged EPA to broaden the "special waste" designation to include many other energy process wastes. There are indications from EPA that the "special waste" may include all coal liquid wastes. EPA's proposed "special waste" regulations require monitoring and record-keeping of the waste. Further guidance from EPA regarding specialized waste designations is expected late this summer.

This again provides an example of a case where the potential impacts of the regulations are uncertain and can be quite alarming if a worst case is assumed. Due to the volume of power plant fly ash and scrubber wastes or the spent shale wastes of retorting, stringent forms of special waste provisions are seen to be expensive per se. Without them, there is some reason to question industrial economic viability for certain processes or means of delivering energy.

As problematical as these and other emerging regulations are (such as the short-term NOx standard and the Toxic Substances Control Act (TSCA)), there is another class of uncertainty coming to pass which can be viewed from the perspective of a single industry—energy—rather than looking at all industries from the perspective of a single environmental issue at a time. Several such examples could probably be constructed. I shall only note two here in the most preliminary fashion: long-range transport and intermedia impacts.

These examples are again important to us to understand with regard to the actuality of how policy is formulated. The few environmental regulations we discussed thus far, and particularly the last two, might or might not be addressed in an improved manner if formal analysis were looked at. What the next section will suggest is that there is a high probability that the fundamental and underlying issues will not be looked at at all, and that failing to address such seminal issues leaves the analyst in the field of environmental regulation open to the criticism of only addressing symptoms of the problem of environmental pollution control.

LONG-RANGE TRANSPORT

The phenomenon of long-range transport is not adequately addressed by the Clean Air Act. In fact, tall stacks, one of the early control strategies approved by EPA (and since prohibited by court decisions and the 1977 Amendments to the Act), may have actually exacerbated the problem of long-range transport. In a nutshell, certain of the pollutants from combustion (TSP, NOx, and SOx) are released into the atmosphere as fine particles or gases which convert to particles in the atmosphere. This pollution is then carried long distances and becomes either the primary culprit or a major contributor to several environmental issues being debated and researched today.

- *Acid Rain:* The entry of NOx and SOx derivatives into the ground level environment has increased the acidity of lakes and other water bodies and has had measurable impacts on crops. The phenomenon has international implications. At present, there is still not enough data available to clearly identify cause and effect relationships for regulatory purposes, but enough information has been gathered to spark active speculation that additional legislation and regulations will come to pass in this area.

- *Health Effects of Particulates:* There are studies[10] which suggest that the really bad actors in the particulate waste stream are the fine or inhalable ones. It is these that are breathed deeply into the lungs and increase the risk of (or cause) cancer and other respiratory disease. So far, definitive health studies are yet to be done and there is some question as to whether these "fines" can be controlled adequately, as many of them escape as gases (not caught by scrubbers, electrostatic precipitators, or baghouses), forming particulates through atmospheric physical and chemical changes.[11]

- *Visibility:* We have discussed visibility earlier. It is enough to note here that it is postulated that a significant amount of the visibility impairment is due to fine particulates. As we have already noted, these particulates are susceptible to movement considerable distances from the source.

- *Nonattainment and PSD:* There has been discussion in several places in the East that the growth levels allowed because of existent pollution levels are inequitable because the source of the emissions causing the ambient violations is not in the locale. For example, in a November 1, 1979 position paper, Secretary Jones of the Department of Environmental Resources, Commonwealth of Pennsylvania, stated:

Pennsylvania is experiencing serious adverse economic and environmental impacts as a result of advected air pollution across state boundaries. These impacts result from the long distance transport of air pollution from the midwestern states and short-range transport from upwind states. . . . Thus, the construction of new industry in many areas of Pennsylvania may be prohibited unless the amount of advected pollutant is significantly reduced.

Pennsylvania is currently in litigation of EPA's approval of SO_2 emission relaxations for two power plants in West Virginia. Other states are believed to be considering litigation as a recourse to receiving pollution from beyond their jurisdiction.

In summary, these issues taken one at a time are potentially problematic and will require considerable deliberation. If long-range transport is assumed as the driving issue, however, then treating each issue as part of a composite means new difficulties coming to the fore. For example:

- Who and how to regulate transported pollutants?
- How to establish cause/effect relationships?
- Who sets the standards and how are they enforced? By whom?
- Is there enough scientific evidence to back these pollutant conditions in court?

- How does one provide relief to those who are impacted from afar?
- After present and proposed BACT standards, how much fine particulate emission is there?
- With the switching to coal, how much worse is the problem?
- Will the anticipated development of portions of the West make the problems worse? Where?

These and other such questions are apt to surface in the near future as more of these questions are asked and as analysts begin to realize the commonality between the various issues.

INTERMEDIA IMPACTS

As with the above case, this can hardly be said to be a new issue. Anybody who understands the chemist's concept of mass balance recognizes that all of the elements that are present when a fuel is used to produce energy will have to be accounted for after the energy is produced. After acknowledging that this fundamental truth was valid, the regulating agencies went about their business of looking at the environmental problem media by media, issue by issue. The results of such a strategy are all around us. The Congressional laws are segmented by media as is the organization of EPA. Other environmental legislation is carried out in other departments altogether (surface mining in the Interior, for example).

Early environmental interest in the public sector (say, around 1970) centered around pollution regulation in air and water media and so discussion of intermedia impacts were not seriously addressed. As EPA rulemaking progressed through the media and pollutant areas, highlighting first one, then another area, and attempting to implement the sometimes "foggy" but always demanding will of Congress, a pattern emerged which may or may not have been intended, but which might appear threatening to someone in a specific industrial sector. It seemed to some that you "can't put it anywhere."

Let me highlight the gist of this notion by skimming across the impacts. They come about, in a nutshell, by demonstrating that as time goes on, the materials balance notion will become more important in an economic sense because of the fact that each of the media or sources are being or have been addressed by disparate regulations, not in any cohesive or comprehensive fashion. For example, the Clean Air Act requires scrubbing of all coals. This practice results in considerable fly ash and scrubber sludge. The Clean Water Act of 1977 not only prevents putting this into the nation's waterways, but requires that many industries achieve "zero discharge" by 1985. The sludge in the settlement ponds is a new waste product. Neither of these wastes can be put into the ocean (except under permitted conditions) because of the Ocean Dumping Act. And the Safe Drinking Water Act prevents indiscriminate injection of these wastes below the ground surface. Finally, the yet-to-be-promulgated Resource Conservation and Recovery Act provisions will limit how these wastes may be handled on the land.

Clearly, in and of themselves, each of these provisions is beneficial and indeed laudable. The difficulty arises in that they are promulgated, administered, and enforced separately, often without any conscious interest in their combined impacts. Such practices may result in very costly strategies for energy production, the choice of relatively inefficient processes, great uncertainty, and some risk to the environmental movement at large because of backlash. As with the example above, the time may have come to consider industry- or regional-specific pollutant criteria. But because these ideas have not been tried either, they too will have problems. The only certain fact is that the present practices will, in time, likely generate more and more complexity and uncertainty in both environmental protection and energy production.

Examples of the kinds of regulations and issues actually found in the public arena are good indications of the potentially limited role very formal analysis might have on their outcome. There are some institutional arrangements attempting to make way for good analysis and to position decisions for its use. Following is one example.

WHAT NEXT?

After performing broad-reaching surveys like the one above, the reader has a right to ask, "OK, what do we do about the issues you raise?" In general, when the problems are as knotty as those I have surfaced, I am tempted to respond, "How do I know?"

Through the years, I have heard many ideas that, if implemented, might have created some improvement. For example, if we were to start the whole environmental movement over again, we might want to think of the secondary and tertiary impacts of decisions. Or, if Congress were not so specific in the laws it wrote and allowed the executive branch some modicum of discretion in implementing them, or if the decision process could be more straightforward and less adversarial or regulatory in nature so that posturing could be reduced, then maybe things would be less complex and uncertain.

The case studies presented to this point are pretty negative. This is not to say that no efforts are being made to do anything about the difficulties of the energy/environment trade-off. One problem is in the area of trying to provide the best information possible. Recently, both DOE and EPA entered into a Memorandum of Understanding (MOU). Specifically, the MOU is stated:

> It is understood by EPA and DOE that the purpose of this MOU is to aid both EPA and DOE in their mandated missions so that EPA is able to set environmental protection standards for emerging energy technologies in the most effective and timely manner and DOE is able to bring environmentally acceptable emerging energy technologies to commercialization as expeditiously as possible. Both EPA and DOE recognize that it remains EPA's statutory responsibility to set environmental protection standards and that it remains DOE's statutory responsibility to promote development and commercialization of emerging energy technologies in an environmentally acceptable manner. This document applies to all emerging non-nuclear energy technologies and sets forth those activities along the environmental standards setting process at which EPA and DOE will consult and exchange information on a timely basis, thereby enabling:
>
> (1) DOE and EPA to assure collectively that necessary research and development (R&D) is done to provide that information in a timely manner needed for setting environmental protection standards and for internalizing environmental requirements early in the development of an emerging energy technology;
> (2) DOE and EPA to avoid duplication of R&D and technical activities through well-defined procedures and coordinated R&D programs;
> (3) EPA to develop appropriate EGD's prior to the demonstration stage, and standards prior to the commercial state of emerging energy technologies;
> (4) DOE to take cognizance of relevant EGD's and existing and projected standards at the earliest possible stage in the development of an emerging energy technology; and
> (5) DOE to reflect environmental protection measures and costs and associated health and environmental impacts on technology development decisions and programs.

Although attempts such as these are not totally adequate to handle the problems of complexity and uncertainty, they are steps in the right direction. Such attempts, along with improvements in our information base, should make strides toward making it more feasible to actually deliver the energy the nation needs in an environmentally acceptable manner.

The MOU went through several drafts and after almost two years was finally signed by both agencies. After all this fuss, one might expect that the resulting document would be around for a while. But situations change. The EPA attempted to expand the use of the document, beyond that of helping the DOE plan its energy technology research, to offering the Pollution Control Guidance Documents (PCGD) as references for locales doing permitting of energy facility sites. At the same time, the legislation bringing into being the Synthetic Fuels Corporation (SFC) came to pass. One of the interesting anomalies of this occurrence was that technologies that were "emerging" suddenly became "commercial" and therefore eligible for financing under the SFC. With these two events, an MOU that was wholly acceptable earlier suddenly became a problem. DOE, or at least parts of it, seemed to be concerned that "too much" information was going to be available on EPA's part (as opposed to the paucity complained about before the MOU) and wanted the PCGDs slowed down—seemingly, until several first-round synfuel facilities could be sited. Same needs for information on the part of both parties—only the political/institutional situation had changed. No formal assessment method could have predicted this outcome.

Clearly, the world is not going to be restructured overnight just because of overlap, inconsistencies, or mandates which are seemingly impossible to implement. There are dozens of ways one might go to rerationalize the goals of energy and environment, and for all of these one might devise strategies to carry out such goals. My crystal ball is not much better than anyone else's. Having criticized the present, however, I take some responsibility for suggesting directions for solutions. For example:

- Regulations should be studied so that their combined impact on any single industry would be noted in a systematic fashion.
- Alternate material balance flows should be analyzed from several aspects; environmental, energy, future economic potential, and so forth.
- Clear signals should be sent by Congress as to which areas are meant to be discretionary in implementation.
- Data uncertainties should be recognized and their impacts included in regulatory and planning scenarios.

- The legislative branch should provide more precision in their purposes and areas of assigned discretionary actions to elements of the executive branch, and continue to set broad policy with some room for creative implementation.

Such lists could go on forever.

The purpose of this chapter, though, is not to provide policy suggestions to improve environmental decisionmaking, but to use the examples of these decision processes to place the use of formal analyses in proper perspective. Indeed, not only might decisions in the energy/environment area be better if such improvements were made, but the changes might facilitate the use of better analytic input. Clearly though, such changes may only be necessary but not sufficient conditions to make better use of formal information.

The last example is a more complete case study of the formulation of a major Department of Energy policy: the selection of "commercial" energy technologies. The exercise was carried out at the Assistant Secretary level but had considerable input from the involved staffs. Even with a very "logical" and formal decision mechanism, situation and politics ruled the day.

A FEDERAL AGENCY AS A BUSINESS ENTERPRISE

It is a self-righteous myth that federal departments are supposed to produce something. The Department of Defense builds weapons and conducts war. The Department of Transportation builds roads. Others, like State, Commerce, and Agriculture, are less apt to come up with specific products, but are expected to provide services to their constituencies, and of course, to the nation. Specified portions of these departments are not required to produce products or services as part of their day-to-day existence, but are expected to come up with the material from which tomorrow's products will emerge. These are the research and development (R&D) arms of the departments, whose missions and budgets devoted to R&D or RD&D (the last D standing for demonstration) differ substantially.

DEPARTMENT OF ENERGY STRUCTURED TO MARKET ENERGY TECHNOLOGIES

Recently, the Department of Energy (DOE), responding to the widespread belief that the Nation was truly in an "energy crisis," was structured as an institution to maximize the potential for moving ideas and research on technologies in the energy area to the marketplace. At the time of its birth, there were four organizational components in DOE at the Assistant Secretary level, accounting for 71% of the total budget. They were designed to move energy technologies from the concept stage to commercialization.

- *Office of Energy Research:* This office conducts the fundamental research programs of the Department and provides the overview for the remainder of the research program.
- *Office of Energy Technology:* This office is responsible for resource/supply/conservation research, development, and technology demonstration in all fields of energy.
- *Office of Resource Applications:* This office manages the major departmental operational programs of energy production and supply. It also manages the incentive activities of the Department designed to spur the commercial deployment of developed supply technologies and the demonstration of energy technologies deemed to be at the stage of commercialization.
- *Office of Conservation and Solar Applications:* This office carries out conservation programs and certain commercialization programs related to solar energy.

To push all technologies toward commercialization, each one is classified as to its present stage of development. This classification scheme has been made the backbone of the whole program planning process for the funded programs of the Department of Energy.

MAKING THE DOE SYSTEM WORK: STAGE I

Just as wishing does not make it so, neither does an institutional structure. Starting in April 1978, soon after the appointment of a Deputy Under Secretary for Commercialization, a formal task force in the area of commercialization was instituted by the Under Secretary. This is not to imply that no one in the various groups which made up the Department of Energy was interested in commercialization, or that the early days of DOE did not see effort in this area. In fact, one project, done under the Comptroller's Office, carried out an exhaustive study of two technologies as test cases to a full-blown market analysis. In spite of considerable effort on the part of those who performed these experiments, little tangible results occurred in the way of real impact on Department policy.

The lack of definitive results stems from several sources. In addition to the fact that there was not a clear indication of which technologies would pass from the RD&D stages at DOE into the private marketplace, there was a real internal organizational difficulty which centered around the question of how to set up a process which would transition technologies smoothly from one Assistant Secretary to another as they progressed along the development chain. The early exercise, although formally being carried out by the Comptroller, was the brainchild of the new Assistant Secretary for Resource Applications (ASRA). There were several bureaucrats who interpreted the ASRA's inputs as being less than totally objective, since he would be the prime beneficiary of the decisions to transfer program elements to the commercialization stage. Therefore, the question reduced to one of dividing up the research budget and setting the research priorities of an evolving department. Of particular interest was the allocation of projects between the Office of Energy Technology and the Office of Resource Applications. Without formal adjudication of almost every stage, there was no easy formula for moving technologies from one program to another. Certainly, it could not be expected that the Assistant Secretaries would voluntarily relinquish manpower and dollars without some quid pro quo. It appeared that the Department design would come to naught as it actually tried to function as it was designed. With this as background, let us discuss the commercialization task force itself.

On April 4, 1978, the Under Secretary issued a memorandum to the six major Office Directors carrying out RD&D under his responsibility (the so-called outlay programs). In essence, it (1) formally put into being the task force, (2) required the active participation of each of the principals from these six Offices, and (3) outlined the functions of the group. They were as follows:

The committee will screen those processes and products at present in the pipeline for their categorization with respect to the new system acquisition definitions. In addition, it will examine each process for its:

Technology feasibility,
Economic potential,
Environmental acceptability,
Market and institutional acceptability, and
Proper lead assistant secretary, and categorize and prioritize them as
    follows: push now, pick up later, defer.

Push process recommendations will not exceed twenty (20) in number.

Following this action, a concept statement will be submitted outlining the assumed commercial or national benefits to support each push recommendation. The concept statement is a tightly written factual document of not over five pages which contains a full description of the product, including its physical characteristics, features, costs, and end benefits.

The Deputy Under Secretary who was to chair this group issued his own memo on the same date. In addition to reinforcing the tone of the Under Secretary's memo, and establishing an agenda for the first meeting, the memo set a very rapid pace for the Assistant Secretaries to follow. He desired that each Assistant Secretary bring to the first meeting a series of candidates for consideration by the whole group. Each technology was to be described succinctly but cover similar facets including:

- Descriptions of process or technology including a summary of work completed to date.
- Description of principal technical or commercial features which provide potential for market penetration.
- Technical risks remaining, with short assessment of effort required to remove them.
- Market potential (including regional differentiations when appropriate).
- Environmental or institutional concerns, if any.
- Cost history and projection of further capital required based upon a specific market share target.
- End benefits anticipated.
- Legislative, direct investment, or incentive programs which bear upon market penetration.
- Status of market development plan or planning.
- Suggested market or commercialization approach.

NATIONAL ENERGY SUPPLY STRATEGY (NESS)

Department efforts were also underway to prioritize the research for DOE. One of these, called the National Energy Supply Strategy (NESS), was begun by Secretary Schlesinger in response to Congressional criticism that his 1980 budget plans contained "nothing new," i.e., nothing that was not already in his much troubled 1978 National Energy Plan. The NESS was an agency-wide effort to identify those technologies which would become the backbone of the 1980 budget thrust. The technologies, 17 in number, were: Liquids; SRC-1; SRC-2; H-Coal, Donor Solvent, Shale Oil, and Methanol from Coal; Gases, Geopressurized Methane, Devonian Shale; Tight Sands; High Btu Gasification and Low Btu Gasification; Renewables; Low Head Hydropower, Wind, Passive Solar, Wood Combustion, Biomass, and Urban Waste.

As a result of the NESS effort, the technologies that were being chosen by this budget exercise received favored treatment regardless of whether Assistant Secretaries believed they would actually be available by the year 1985. Similar external pressure was put on the group to add several solar technologies due to the widespread popularity that these were receiving. At the end of a full day of discussion, a list of 20 candidate technologies had evolved. They were: Low Head Hydro, High Btu Gas, Medium Btu Gas, Geothermal-Hydro, SRC-1, SRC-2, High Efficiency Motors, Cogeneration, Small Wind, Oil Shale, Enhanced Oil Recovery, Unconventional Gas, Solar Hot Water, Electric/Hybrid Vehicle, Passive Solar, Advanced Electric Generation, Retrofits, Air Fuel Ratio Regenerator, Large-Scale Wind, and Energy from Urban Wastes.[12]

Each of these 20 technologies was to be summarized in a paper not to exceed five pages, including these elements:

- *Product, process or technology description.* Succinct identification of energy source or feedstock, process operation features and conditions, product characteristics, and other key process parameters or unique features such as throughput, temperatures, pressures, cleanup systems, as appropriate.
- *Brief history and description of product/process development,* including key operating features demonstrated to date. Key technical, economic, institutional, environmental, or other questions should be flagged. Constraints on commercialization should be assessed.
- *Identification and summary description of organization presently in product/process development* with a brief description of commercialization strategy options that have been identified and analyzed, including a brief statement of the federal role in commercialization.
- *Summary schedule and cost projects,* including downstream "mortgage," and taking into consideration potential commercial options. Estimates of uncertainties in both areas.
- *Commercial market appropriate for the product/process,* including a description of regional or national markets, probable time frame, and other distinguishing market characteristics.
- *Identification of any policy implications or potential policy conflicts* inherent in the production process.

The culmination of the several meetings among the members of the task force was to be a presentation to the Under Secretary, at which time he was expected to reduce the number of candidates to ten. Technologies so chosen would go on to be studied by other agency task forces (made up of employees of the various Assistant Secretaries' Offices) which would present their findings to the original task force members (the Assistant Secretary level) for review and further screening. The report to the Under Secretary took place in early May 1979.

MAKING THE SYSTEM WORK: STAGE II

The first real meeting of the Assistant Secretary-level task force took place with each Assistant Secretary presenting his candidates for commercialization. By earlier agreement, each presented ten. Before very long it became obvious to all involved that some basic agreement was going to have to be reached in some fairly fundamental areas before the group could do its job in a rational manner. Several people present had been in similar exercises in the Energy Research and Development Administration (ERDA) during the MOPPS study.[13] The feelings voiced at the meeting were that this earlier study degenerated into a "quad" (Quadrillion Btu's) battle, with those technologies professing to have the greatest potential for producing quads as being the ones the Department would focus on. It was the sense of the group that such criteria were entirely too limited, and that other factors had to be considered also.

Although the idea of the term "commercialization" struck similar cords in all participants, the unspoken understanding of the task force proved to be too unwieldy as an operational concept. Hence the good intentions expressed by the task force and its leader began to crumble almost immediately.

The ultimate meeting with the Under Secretary six weeks later made clear that the influence of the NESS exercise had wrenched the commercialization exercise off track. Because of political pressures generated from elsewhere within the Department, many technologies were being considered under commercialization which might otherwise not have been. For example, the Assistant Secretaries had pretty much agreed that a technology was to be considered commercialized (and a part of the effort of this task force) if it was generally available by the year 1985. Widespread use and availability precluded from analysis those technologies which were in the pilot or demonstration stage, regardless of the size of these test facilities. It was expected that no more than three to six technologies would be available. However, during this meeting no one seemed to remember these original goals. Eventually, every technology passed muster and was sent on to Stage II, the stage at which it was to be determined whether there were serious barriers to its commercialization.

As a part of Stage II, a new set of task forces (one for each technology) was established to design and report on what came to be called "market plans." These task forces were made up of professionals and contractors from across the Department. The reports themselves were carefully scoped again by the Comptroller's Office. Great care was taken to ensure that each technology used the same data base and the same formula and assumptions for calculating cost, resource use rates, and the like.

The reports were to have three sections: a technology description, a commercialization readiness assessment, and a market plan. The first step, the technology's description, included its technical readiness (operational status, capital and operating cost experience, and tests and demonstrations underway); its market/economic readiness (including competing technologies and barriers); its environmental readiness; and its institutional readiness (including infrastructure needs). As one important component, the barriers to the development of these technologies were identified and discussions were to be presented as to their seriousness and potential mitigation. The costs and benefits to be gained from the introduction of a given technology were to be presented in such a fashion so that the stakeholders were clearly identified and so that at least a qualitative comparison of the relative costs and benefits could be assessed. Finally, a concluding section was to be produced which covered the commercialization readiness of candidate technologies and the recommendations of the task force members.

MAKING THE SYSTEM WORK: STAGE III

The outline and instructions for the third phase of the commercialization effort were about as well coordinated and thought out as any effort of this type can be. A standard format guide was prepared which was to be used by the various task forces to prepare their reports. The reports were to agree with a complete description of the technology, to be followed by its development history. As we shall see later, this component of the report was to contain sections on the potential "show stoppers" felt to constrain the commercialization of the technology. Finally, this introductory section was to deal with the assessment of where the technology stood in relation to its ultimate goal of commercialization.

It is important to make explicit here a part of the exercise that makes it relatively unique from other Departmental efforts. Specifically, the task forces were not only given a "straw man" report to emulate, but were supplied with pages of data and formulae to be used in making it possible for the Under and Assistant Secretaries who reviewed the ultimate task force reports to compare among alternatives—as the technologies were all presented on a more or less consistent basis.

The staff from the Comptroller's Office that actually run the exercise were careful to see that all their suggestions were reviewed by everyone who would be involved in the actual preparation of the task force documents, and to give some room for everyone to make a contribution to the final plans. By the time the exercise actually entered its third phase, everyone clearly understood what was expected of them and how their outputs would be used. In this case, the exercise was paced by the 1980 budget cycle and was expected to be an important input.

The interests of the policy level of DOE centered on some very obvious areas. They were interested in knowing first, if the technology was "ready" in an engineering sense to be put on the market. Second, if no, what had to be done to get it to that position. If yes, was there any reason(s) that the market wouldn't embrace the technology after it was proven ready in an engineering sense? Third, if these so-called barriers could be identified, what could DOE do to deal with them? Were there any of such a nature that they should be considered "show stoppers?" Fourth, what actions could or should be taken by other public or private parties outside of DOE to overcome the identified barriers? Fifth, what did DOE currently have and how much did it presently hope to have dedicated to this effort? When did the task forces expect to see their candidate technologies commercialized?

The resulting documents produced by the individual task forces were impressive indeed. They gave a reasonable assessment of the technological facets of the subject technology, although none could be expected to be done from a conservation perspective since almost everyone on the task forces would be fairly classed as an advocate of the technology. Even so, there were some fairly consistent limitations to the reports, only one of which was partly overcome.

Specifically, the technological proponents saw barriers either as something to be overcome or set aside, so that the principal business of energy development could be gotten on with. Further, the reports reflected the professional expertise and biases of their preparers. Quite complete in the area of engineering, somewhat less so on economic barriers, even less on environmental, and all but silent on any other—except for regulatory constraints. The economic barriers identified noted a disparity of the present price competitor, or that some feature of the market made the venture too risky for the private sector. The solutions revolved around methods to peg and ensure the price: subsidies, taxes, and the like, and ways to put a floor under the market so as to obviate the perceived risk; market guarantee, underwriting, and so forth. These economic problems and, to the extent that they existed, technological difficulties, were seen as all that had to be overcome for a technology to be successfully marketed in the time frame projected by the task force.

In all fairness, because of the DOE's interest in the environmental movement as the principal deterrent to its policy plans, all task forces were instructed to report on the seriousness of environmental constraints. Most made an honest attempt to do so, but because of several factors, not the least of which was the relatively primitive state of knowledge about the health and environmental impacts of the insertion of these technologies into the ecosystem, these sections were often pretty skimpy. Further, they were generally optimistic, stating that no show stopper could be positively identified at present. A later exercise carried out by the DOE's Office of Environment[14] made this portion of the report more complete by adding more detailed information on environmental, health, and safety impacts of each technology. Further, research time lines to study these potential impacts were developed and compared to those projected by the technologies for their commercialization. Finally, the cost of abating environmental, health, and safety impacts of future technology development or deployment was estimated and added to the projected cost of the technology. These three aspects were presented to the Under and Assistant Secretaries and, as a result of this briefing, the task forces were told to update their earlier Phase III reports.

WINDDOWN

The task forces, after updating their reports, were dissolved. Although this did not mean that the impact of their reports was zero, it did suggest that regardless of what their initial impact might be, it would diminish with time. With the efforts of the Deputy Under Secretary and a small staff from the Comptroller's Office, document updating and several briefings were arranged. Private companies were called in and the reports used as background to exude an optimistic tenor around specific technologies. This was deemed necessary because the prime source of financing for an individual technology was seen ultimately to be the private sector. In the end, however, the reports seemed to have little impact on the 1980 budget, the DOE, OMB, or Congress. Why?

ANATOMY OF A PIPEDREAM

Although lots of people might differ as to whether the commercialization exercise failed or was a success, it is clear that it did not live up to the very high expectations that many seemed to hold for it at the outset. Before I try and catalogue a few of the reasons for such an occurrence, let me say that in some quarters it clearly did have an impact. It did provide a mechanism for moving people and projects from the Office of Energy Technology to the Office of Resource Applications. Whether other mechanisms could have been found is unknown, and really unimportant. The fact is that it did accomplish this highly delicate and bureaucratically difficult task. Further, the whole exercise legitimized the federal bureaucracies' desire to look beyond a simple cataloging of technical difficulties with a program and to enumerate and speculate on barriers of a non-engineering nature. Seldom before has such a search for the realization of a research end been forced into these areas. If nothing else came out of the effort, this alone may have made it all worthwhile.

Now to the realities, and the problems:

- The Deputy Under Secretary was said to have been a protégé of a senator powerful in the energy area, and his emergence on the DOE scene was reported to have depended largely on this fact. If so, this foisting of a second deputy on the Under Secretary could only have been met with less than wholehearted enthusiasm. Such interpersonal relations cannot bode well for any project that an unwanted deputy might undertake.
- On the other hand, the exercise could act as a lightning rod to be brought out and dusted off whenever questions of the relevancy of the R&D effort were brought forth. Further, there was no harm done provided the output had minimal impact on any real decisions. Witness the almost imperceptible impact on the 1980 budget.
- The Deputy Under Secretary himself was a dedicated man who had little expertise in bureaucratic Washington. He believed in private enterprise and sales ability almost as a religion. In some ways, he seemed to be singularly unprepared for the job he undertook. On the other hand, he worked hard to learn the necessary technical facts and to push the task force findings. In reality, though, neither he nor the project ever seemed to be taken seriously by the senior management of OMB or DOE.
- The involved Assistant Secretaries seemed to take on the historical role of "men-in-the-middle." They sometimes found themselves having to sell technologies and processes that they themselves might not

have wholeheartedly believed in. On the other hand, the techno-
logists on their own staff who proposed and presented the research
were thought to be overly optimistic as to the cost and future of
their products. In general, their superiors were skeptical as to their
own office's products.

- The idea of "barriers" to the development of a specific technology
was taken offensively by some. The Assistant Secretary for Environment in DOE found the term particularly offensive. Also, in an
attempt to specify strategies to overcome these barriers, the bureaucrats in DOE found themselves running head-on into policies not
espoused by the current administration, or else following within the
jealously guarded domain of another department or agency.

- In fact, the drive for the commercialization project also came from
the staff of the Comptroller's Office. In the end, the top two
members of the staff resigned to go on to other jobs, leaving the
project effectively unstaffed.

Summing up, the idea was new (and consequently unpopular), suffered
from no or little internal support, and had no institutional base to have a
legitimized input into the Department's policy. It failed.

This example of a rational, analytic approach to planning was meant to
demonstrate that policy formulation does not necessarily have to be
totally reactive to external stimuli. The Department of Energy, like many
federal agencies, embraced technical rationality in the area of policy
formulation which has to do with its program and budget planning. Such
schemes typically consist of methods reminiscent of systems analysis and
have information gathering, goal statement, ranking, and choice stages
which would be familiar to the policy analyst. Such planning exercises are
very prone to influence by those who are in the policy positions, though.
In fact, the very reason for having policy positions might be said to be to
adjust these plans and budgets. Consequently, their impacts might be
expected to overrule any "rational" schemes. It might be considered an
open question as to whether such overrulings are proper, but clearly it is in
those areas that the influence of the individual decisionmaker's goals
would be expected to have most sway.

Our example above demonstrates not only the influence of those at the
Assistant Secretary level, but the effect of a higher level policy change on
the plans and programs of those below. The shift in this case was immediate and clean-cut. Its influence was, in fact, so profound as to prevent
the total exercise, and to make the analyses and decision schemes employed useless.

Summary

This chapter has attempted to bring into sharper focus the many factors which go into making up a policy in addition to formal analysis. These factors are organizational, institutional, cultural, or even the result of a mixture of various personal idiosyncrasies. It should be clear how unlikely it is that analyses alone will carry the day, regardless of how seemingly complete, technically correct, or sophisticated they are. Toward the end of the chapter, I offered several case studies of efforts undertaken at the Department of Energy which were highly rational in purpose and form at their inception, yet ended with results that could not have been anticipated using rationality as a guide. Having severely criticized the analytic technique and suggested that other features of the policy formulation process may really be the determinants in any particular decision, let us now proceed to see if any possibility exists for performing the art of policy analysis. The next chapter will look at a few short-run solutions. The last chapter turns to more fundamental changes in our analysis process.

NOTES

1. A recent article by Gio Batta Gori (*Science* 208 [April 1980]: 259) makes this point also: "It would seem desirable to think of an alternative scenario, one calling for official recognition that risk is an unavoidable element of life and the common welfare, that all human lives cannot be conserved at all costs, and that carcinogenicity tests in animals cannot be reliable quantitative models of human risk. Essential elements of such an approach have been identified and debated in a recent report of the National Academy of Sciences."

See also David Okrent (*Science* 208 [April 1980]: 375): "In conclusion, if our priorities in managing risk are wrong, if we are spending the available resources in a way that is not cost-effective, we are, in effect, killing people whose premature deaths would [otherwise] be prevented. There is some optimal level of resources that should be spent on reducing societal risk, a level beyond which adverse economic and political effects may be overriding. Finally, there is need for the development of a national approach to risk management, one that Congress, the President, and the public can support."

2. Joseph Coates, "What is a Public Policy Issue? An Advisory Essay," *Interdisciplinary Science Review* 4 (1979).

3. J. Menkes, *Epistemological Issues of Technology Assessment* (National Science Foundation, October 1976), p. 7.

4. The posture I will take here is not one of an advocate of either the environmental or energy positions, but that of an analyst in the role of trying to predict the interplay of impacts of energy and environment policies on each other. Although I personally believe in strong environmental laws for the protection of our

health and safety, I can also see how the present way they are implemented could cause considerable concern to those whose manner of operating is being changed by them. In no way does any statement in this section suggest that any standard or regulation should be done away with; however, it is clear that their intent and success could be furthered by our taking steps to reduce the uncertainty and confusion that appears to be generated by the way we presently try to implement them.

5. "A Comparison of Alternative Approaches for Estimation of Particulate Concentrations Resulting from Coal Strip Mining Activities in Northeastern Wyoming," prepared by ERT, Inc., October 1979.

6. Letter dated November 16, 1979 to the Honorable Douglas M. Costle, Administrator, EPA, from John M. Deutch, Under Secretary, Department of Energy, regarding proposed Prevention of Significant Deterioration regulations.

7. By the time this is published, the details related here will probably have been settled and will no longer be uncertain. However, some other set of regulations will be at the same stage and these will be the ones industry is concerned about. The points we will make about uncertainty will therefore remain valid even though the examples will age.

8. Ibid. No. 2, pp. 4-8.

9. Ibid. No. 2, pp. 5-58.

10. F. P. Perera and A. K. Ahmed, "Respirable Particles: Impact of Airborne Fine Particulates on Health and the Environment," NRDC Report, October 17, 1978. See also "Health Effects Considerations for Establishing a Standard for Inhalable Particulates," USEPA, Health Effects Laboratory Report, July 1978.

11. To a certain extent, the long-range transport issue is tied to these fine particulates and then to the acid rain and other issues. It is the fact of the particle size which allows their wandering ways.

12. The reader will note that all of the NESS technologies appear in this list.

13. MOPPS stands for Market Oriented Policy Project.

14. Separate reports were issued called Environmental Readiness Documents (ERDs) that attested to the present state of the technology from a health, safety, and environmental perspective.

CHAPTER 5

SOLUTIONS FOR THE SHORT TERM

Where Are We Now?

Policymaking is relatively easy when there is plenty of everything to go around. There is a lessened need for stringent budgets, and more comfortable decisions are possible on priorities and trade-offs. However, when the national picture is not one of unbounded affluence, then a whole host of pressures are created and decisions become tougher and more complex. Probably the worst situation is when policies are set to aspirations predicated on plenty, and the administration of these policies must be carried out in a period of scarcity. The latter appears to be the situation in which the nation finds itself today.

Let us look at some of the statistics available to describe the situation facing us in just the areas of energy, economics, and the environment.

- *Environment:*

    (1) Using 1975 air quality data for the 80 most populated Air Quality Control Regions (AQCRs) in the nation, our preliminary analysis showed that:

        - Compliance status of 16 AQCRs was unknown.
        - Seventeen AQCRs violated the NAAQSs for TSP.
        - Sixty-three AQCRs violated the NAAQSs for oxidants (ozone).
        - Only one AQCR complied with the NAAQSs for the three pollutants of sulfur oxides, TSP, and oxidants.

    (2) In the area of water pollution, the country is undertaking its ninth year of effort toward meeting the goals of the 1972 Amendments to the Federal Water Pollution Control Act (FWPCA). This period has been one of great expectation and accomplishments on the one hand, and significant frustration on the other. Water quality in the nation has not reached the levels Congress had hoped, and there are still substantial delays in implementing several provisions of the Act. In fact, the 1985 goal of "zero discharge" will, in all probability, have to be deferred.

- *Economics:* Although the economic picture is extremely hazy and the interrelationships among the parts have never appeared more complex, a few general statistics will serve to highlight its problematic state. Last month, the average unemployment in the United States was 7.5 percent with an inflation rate over the past year of 12.4 percent. The price increases for imported energy continue to grow along with the additional costs of regulation, pollution, consumer safety, and the like.

- *Energy:* Everyone is probably aware of our energy situation, but a few pertinent statistics will help to put matters into perspective. In 1973, the nation imported 36 percent of its oil with payments of approximately $8 billion. By the beginning of 1977, the situation had changed to more than 42 percent of our oil coming from imports, with payments in excess of $34 billion. It may be as high as $100 billion by the end of 1981. By the early decades of the 21st century, worldwide supplies of oil and gas are expected to be so scarce as to severely hamper all transportation sectors.

Although it would be easy to expand the list of areas which are important aspects of our national policy picture, those of energy, economics, and the environment are all that we shall try to address here. In brief, the arguments developed in this section are that in instances where we are experiencing serious problems or conflicts, such as those noted above, attempts to carry out individual policies (1) vigorously, (2) in isolation, and (3) with an eye towards maximizing the goals ascribed to one particular area (say, environment) will tend to lead to unanticipated responses in other areas (like energy or economics)—responses that often are detrimental to the articulated national goals of these areas. Further, the more serious the conflicts or problems, the more rapidly the unanticipated and unwelcome responses are apt to appear. Let us turn to the investigation of these hypotheses.

MORE BACKGROUND

Although there are very ambitious and commendable goals set for this nation in the areas of environment, economics, and energy, it is clear that each of these areas is presently, and has been for some time, unable to actually meet these goals.

During the late 1960s and extending into the early 1970s, a unique turning point took place in the way Americans viewed their resources and lifestyles. During those years, the National Environmental Policy Act was enacted, the Environmental Protection Agency was created, and Congress passed sweeping new laws mandating the cleanup and enhancement of our air and water resources. Subsequently, other legislation was passed to deal with pesticides, solid waste, resource conservation and recovery, drinking water, and finally, toxic substances.

In August of 1977, Congress continued its reaffirmation of our nation's commitment to environmental protection and enacted changes to the Clean Air Act of 1970—the Clean Air Act Amendments of 1977. These enactments have been interpreted as some of the strongest environmental laws ever passed. Yet others feel that because of the seriousness of the nation's problems in nonenvironmental areas, the emphasis must be on refinement and implementation of its environmental laws in a balanced manner. Consequently, the nation faces tough, complex decisions involving the consideration of both risks and benefits in achieving its national goals. Policies will have to be implemented that not only affect lifestyles and pocketbooks, but also health and national security and the relative impacts of these policies on each other is far from clear. For example, during the formation and implementation of the nation's environmental laws, an energy crisis appeared, a problem which was brought to a dramatic head by the OPEC oil embargo of 1973. Subsequently, Congress enacted several major pieces of energy legislation and a comprehensive set of National Energy Acts. Congressional deliberations lead to national policies in the energy area which have major impacts in the economic and environmental areas, all three directly affecting the lifestyles of our citizens.

THE SETTING

Characteristically, each of these three areas (energy, environment, and economics) is more or less assigned to a specific governmental department or agency to administer on a national basis. Each organization has its own policymakers and overseers in the Congress, and an articulate constituency among our citizens. The expected strategy is that each organization will pursue, defend, and enhance its positions and policies vis-à-vis those of the other groups in the public arena. Each group is expected to present its position in the best light possible and to require and fight for positions that maximize its own mandated goals. Other organizations, whose goals present major constraints on a proposed policy, are all too often treated as the enemy. Those whose goals are not directly competitive are often ignored. Such is the structure of the political adversary process. In times of affluence, this decisionmaking process has appeared to work adequately. It is becoming painfully clear, however, that it is not a desirable scheme for resolving the current situation the nation faces regarding energy, economic, and environmental goals.

One of the best examples is once again to be found in the field of environmental legislation: the Clean Air Act which, although apparently very straightforward and specific in its mandate from Congress, has turned out to be very complex in its implementation. This law, referred to frequently in earlier chapters, has been most difficult, particularly the 1977 Amendments to the Act. We have already looked at several aspects of this Act and will try not to duplicate any of our earlier efforts here. However, it is our intent to look again at two aspects of the law: Prevention of Significant Deterioration and New Source Performance Standards. Both of these sections require the use of pollution control technology to reduce emissions from major sources. The use of the best available control technology is required in the case of Prevention of Significant Deterioration and a percentage reduction in emissions for New Source Performance Standards. These two sections of the 1977 Amendments have proved to be particularly difficult to manage and have provided a wealth of examples of all kinds of difficulty one can experience when attempting to implement essentially political goals through a bureaucracy while depending on formal analytic techniques to sharpen the intent and to formulate the regulations.

One general thrust of the Clean Air Act of 1970 (and its ensuing Amendments in 1977) has been for the forcing of technology to develop pollution control equipment needed to meet proposed standards. This philosophy may in fact have worked well with the automobile. By the 1981 model year, automobiles will be emitting less than 10 percent of the hydrocarbon and carbon monoxide emissions per mile as their pre-1970 predecessors. In the implementation of these standards, however, the Environmental Protection Agency and Congress have seen fit to allow year-by-year slippage of compliance with the final standards as well as modification of the original levels. In the original 1970 Act, the ultimate standards would have been in place for the 1975 model year. Some of these standards have now been delayed until model year 1982, with interim standards having increasing stringency being put in place since 1975.

In controlling automobile emissions, the industry developed the catalytic converter which appeared to be a direct result of the technology-forcing mechanism within the original Act. In actuality, catalyst technology was already proven, and the final resolution of pollution control, economy, and performance was a result of rethinking the whole combustion process as it related to the automobile. Under the 1977 Amendments, the Environmental Protection Agency and Congress are now attempting to use the same technology-forcing aspect on other industries within the nation. We need to ask ourselves if this philosophy is sound, i.e., sound for all situations and all technologies.

For example, it seems logical to postulate that the results of tough regulation on the utility industry in terms of Prevention of Significant Deterioration and New Source Performance Standards could well result in the unanticipated effects of a severe reduction in the amount of voluntary coal switching—clearly an unfavorable outcome in terms of the nation's goal to reduce dependency on foreign oil. Specifically, the utility industry is unique in comparison with most other American industries in that it is a regulated monopoly at both the federal and state levels with in essence a guaranteed return on investment. Further, it supplies a product that is necessary for the proper functioning of modern society. Consequently, any major reform in the practices of the industry must be carefully implemented to ensure that the actual effect is the desired one.

A case in point is the goal by Congress and the Environmental Protection Agency to require the electric utility industry to use emission reduction technology to control powerplant emissions (i.e., scrubbers). It has been noted that technology-forcing was a success in the automobile industry, causing the use of catalytic converters to control automobile exhaust emissions. There are very important differences, however, between the electric utility industry and automotive manufacturers. The market structure is different. There is a large amount of competition within the automotive industry, especially between domestic and foreign suppliers, but not between one utility and another. In the area of electricity supply, utilities are monopolies with no market competition. Therefore, the success of forcing technology in the automotive industry may not be directly or as easily applicable to the electric utility industry.

What I have tried to show here is that stringent or extraordinary adherence to individual agency mandates can often lead to results which are quite contrary to the stated desires of other national goals. At the same time, however, all of these policies can be held to be clearly in the national interest.

To illustrate that all of the unanticipated results of industry are not to be found in the environment's effect on energy, let us look at the environmental area which also has some problems caused by attempts to bolster its own position.

For example, in the 1977 Amendments to the Clean Air Act, Congress and the Environmental Protection Agency have attempted to deal with the dilemma of growth and pollution control. Among the more specific schemes is the offset provisions of the 1977 Clean Air Act Amendments in nonattainment areas.

Congress placed a complete prohibition on industrial growth and expansion after July 1, 1979 in those areas of the country where states failed to submit a State Implementation Plan (SIP) allowing for attainment and maintenance of national ambient air quality standards by the end of 1982 (or 1987 in the case of photochemical oxidants). Preliminary analysis noted above (using 1975 air quality data) of the country's most populated 80 Air Quality Control Regions (AQCR) indicated that only one AQCR would be an attainment area for all three of the major pollutants (SOx, TSP, and NOx), and 13 AQCRs had an uncertain status. This means that at best, 56 of these 80 urban areas, representing 75 percent of the United States population, would be precluded from industrial expansion after July 1, 1979, unless a SIP is approved to ensure attainment.[1] These areas are also the places where a significant proportion of the new growth and development of our nation are apt to occur. Any energy or economic growth in these areas increases the possibility for making the environmental situation more critical. In short, given the seriousness of the national situation in each of these three areas (energy, economics, and environment), significant actions in any one of them is apt to result in a response (often counterproductive) in another.

As it turned out, only one State, Wyoming, had an approved attainment SIP by the July 1979 deadline. In fact, a year later, only two states had been approved. EPA has thus far, however, avoided imposition of sanctions by a number of policy devices, such as partial or conditional approval of SIP submittals, where states have made good faith efforts at developing an adequate plan. Nevertheless, some states have not yet even submitted a plan (e.g., Ohio for particulates); growth in these areas may ultimately be impacted.

In general, the nonattainment philosophy is meant to be marginal in impact. That is, it is designed to deal with the situation of allowing a plant or so into areas where violations of the ambient standards would ordinarily be precluded. The reduction of emissions within the nonattainment areas, which are all air quality limited, to "offset" those expected to be generated by the prospective plant, results in an emissions rights market similar to the water rights market in the West which is water-limited. To date, this market has not come into significant play, since 95 percent of all offset needs have been found within the expanding organization; future offsets will demand more and more external intercompany deals.

What happens when the desired growth in a particular area is marginal? Suppose there is a strong effort by the federal government to stimulate economic growth in a nonattainment area, or to effect a policy in the energy field such as coal switching? In these cases, the demand for pollution rights increases dramatically and a market is created for such rights. Normally, many industries would not have paid attention to the value of these rights. But at some level, their value is apt to become sufficiently large to attract attention. In short, rapid and significant demand for these rights in a specific nonattainment locale could have unanticipated results. Let's explore some of these possibilities.

First, there may be an increase in the level of pollutants emitted by the industries already situated in a nonattainment area. This anomaly might occur in situations where there are a number of plants controlling at levels greater than required by the standards. Such industries might find it to their advantage to increase their level of pollution and offer their ability to reduce such emissions on the local open market. This action would have the counterintuitive result of making the ambient situation in a locale worse because of a policy to push energy or economic objectives.

Another economic/environmental aberration that might occur under the situation of nonattainment is one involving the marginally profitable firm. There is extensive literature on the potential problem of environmental regulations forcing local plants out of business. A market in pollution rights might make it attractive for marginal plants to sell their emission rights and go out of business voluntarily. Clearly, such situations could further exacerbate the economic and employment picture of specific areas. The significance of this impact is obviously a function of the relative labor intensity of the marginal industry and the industry replacing it which buys up the pollution rights.

MYRIAD OF ENERGY/ENVIRONMENTAL AGENCIES AND REQUIREMENTS

To make matters worse, several federal agencies are involved with the implementation of environmental statutes. For example, the Environmental Protection Agency implements no less than seven major environmental statutes, including the Clean Air Act, the Federal Water Pollution Control Act, the Safe Drinking Water Act and the Resource Conservation and Recovery Act. The Department of the Interior implements more than five environmental statutes stemming from the several water resources acts to the Outer Continental Shelf Lands Act and the Wilderness Act of 1964. In addition, there are other federal agencies involved in implementing environmental statutes: the Department of Labor (in conjunction with HEW), the Occupational Safety and Health Act; the Nuclear Regulatory Commission, the Atomic Energy Act and the Energy Reorganization Act; and the Department of Commerce (NOAA), the Coastal Zone Management Act.

One can readily see that implementation of environmental statutes is extremely complex from a federal regulatory standpoint. In addition to federal agencies, state and local governments are also responsible for the approval of permit applications for energy facility location, construction, and modifications. In regard to energy development, all existing and emerging energy technologies are subject to a myriad of environmental requirements and standards at the federal, state, and local level. Unless coordination and cooperation occur, the commercialization of new and emerging energy technologies will be delayed or precluded. In any event, environmental requirements and standards will affect the timing, siting, and types of alternate sources of energy utilized and will impact the relative economic costs to the consumer.

Since several agencies at the federal, state, and local levels are involved with implementing environmental standards, the question arises, "How does any one agency handle the wide variety of trade-off decisions involved in determining whether a proposed energy facility is acceptable and necessary?" It is important that the trade-offs between energy, environment, and economics be balanced; but how can one federal agency, with a parochial mandate, do this balancing?

AN ALTERNATIVE TO CONFLICT

The discussion to this point has focused on the anomalies that are apt to appear when factions of our society, as one example, and those at the federal government level as another, respond to a defined constituency which perceives that its area of interest is in grave difficulty, even to the point of crisis. The attempt to overcome the negative effects of this crisis is postulated as often meaning that one segment ignores the impacts of an all-out drive to overcome its difficulties on other segments of the society; e.g., environment on energy or vice versa. This forum of "nationalism" makes policy analyses difficult as analysts become still more the captives of a tendency toward partial analyses, even when they realize that such analyses are incomplete. The ultimate outcome of these segmented analyses is that their conclusions are even more likely not to come to pass and their reputation for being false prophets is made worse.

The discussion which follows has analogies elsewhere in our system. Simply, it is to withdraw from positions of ruinous competition between, say, energy and environmental goals, to one of cooperation. Both the professional disciplines of economics and ecology have carried out extensive studies of the potential for cooperative or symbiotic relationships within a system, although they often ignore political difficulties. The more simplistic presentations of theories of international trade (stressing comparative advantage) or the writings of economists such as Adam Smith who preached specialization and trade at the local-industrial level are two examples. In these and other such theories, the point stressed is that by working in a cooperative mode, each can get more of all of the goods and services they desire rather than going it alone.

The situation as described in the opening portion of this chapter is not directly analogous to these earlier theories, of course. The realization that many energy, economic, or environmental goals actually directly constrain each other (by policy rather than physical means) adds a dimension to the cooperation/competitive model as it is traditionally presented to show how and why scarce resources cannot be used to produce more than one product at a time. In short, the question of efficiency (as a market phenomenon) is greatly complicated by policy constraints being added to the natural workings of the free market. This is not to say that things were better or worse without public intervention in the system, or that the quality of life was superior or inferior before such intervention. Regardless of the outcome such a debate might produce, the fact remains that the institutional mechanism which evolved to handle our economic affairs under free market assumptions does not appear to take into consideration other factors, such as environment or the internal security aspects of energy supply, and apparently they have to be modified to handle these and other additional factors adequately.

The previous chapters have made much of the fact that the formal techniques we have today do not adequately handle the range of human, organizational, and institutional factors that are a part (often a large part) of the policy formulation process. In this section, I have added still another dimension by suggesting that one possible reason the use of existing formal techniques has not fallen into complete disrepute is that there has been sufficient slack in our system to absorb and mask bad policy changes. If there are times, however, when there is less of this slack and the adversarial process becomes more in earnest, then the burden placed on quality policy analyses becomes greater. Possibly somewhat more imagination and flexibility is necessary; clearly, more humility in terms of what formalism cannot do. The following discussion is but one example of some of the ways one might begin to expand the analytic goals of "effectiveness" and "efficiency." There are certainly other areas that could be explored with equal profit.

In the areas of energy and environment, the alternatives to unconstrained competition are evolving as attempts are made to search out strategies which, although they do not yield the greatest potential for achieving the goals of any one of the above areas, satisfy some minimum goals of two or more of these sectors. For a discussion of this, let us take the perspective of the energy policymaker and talk in terms of a few exemplary energy technologies:[2]

- There are several combustion technologies being pursued today which are in the picture both because of their potential for satisfying environmental regulations and their potential as energy producers. Although some people think these technologies have advantages in an environmental sense over more traditional combustion techniques, they are far from being environmentally benign. Much research needs to be done to assess the environmental, health, and safety aspects of the technologies, particularly in light of developing regulatory standards. Three of these might be illustrative: coal gasification, coal liquefaction, and atmospheric fluidized bed combustion. Coal gasification may be regarded as an alternative to the direct combustion of coal with the use of scrubbers and electrostatic precipitators to control the coal-based pollutants. In the coal gasification process, the coal is treated with heat and pressure to produce a clean, low- to medium-Btu gas which can be fed into the powerplant, for example, to drive a gas turbine: a relatively clean-burning combustion with the air pollution control achieved in the head-end process.

  Similarly, in coal liquefaction, coal can be processed with comprehensive environmental controls to produce, for example, methanol and other fuel liquids. Here again, the relatively clean-burning product can be used in a powerplant or other industrial facility. It must be noted that in both cases, a fraction of the initial coal energy is lost in the conversion process, and therefore both of these processes are more energy-consumptive procedures than direct coal combustion; however, there seem to be offsetting benefits achieved in the form of environmental protection.

  Atmospheric fluidized bed combustion represents a third technique to control the pollutants originating from coal combustion. In this instance, the coal is burned in a furnace in a bed of limestone with control of the air flow to ensure excellent dynamic contact between the coal and the limestone. The consequence is that, during combustion, sulfur and some other pollutants combine with the limestone to form a solid waste material which is more readily handled and disposed of than the sludge which is created by stack gas scrubbers. Cogeneration is an arrangement whereby waste heat at an industrial facility is used to generate electricity. The capture of the waste heat is a relatively economical process and results in a "fuel" cost of about $2 per million Btu's. The potential for cogeneration in this country is estimated at about 1.5 quads by 1990 and 3.5 quads by the year 2000.

Solar hot water offers about the same potential in terms of quads for the nation, giving 1.0 quads by 1990 and 3.0 quads by the year 2000. On the other hand, the "fuel" cost of this arrangement is presently estimated at about $12 per million Btu's; but of course there is substantial potential for bringing this figure down with large-scale production of the equipment.

In the case of windmill technology, again the "fuel" cost is relatively high, at about $11 per million Btu's. The contribution to the national energy picture is relatively small at about 0.25 quads in 1990 and about 1.7 quads by the year 2000. Windpower, however, need not be dismissed. In some locations, such as offshore islands and other remote areas where the wind has a relatively high average velocity and alternative sources of fuel are difficult to come by, the windmill has a promising future.

- Matching energy production to energy needs, particularly the use of so-called distributive and appropriate technologies. There are several technologies which might be discussed here, such as cogeneration and solar (say solar hot water as a specific example). Each of these has different reasons for being seriously discussed as potentially useful means of energy production.

The technologies which are collected into the area of "appropriate" appear to be able to satisfy the energy desires of certain users, are said to be less environmentally disruptive (particularly when compared to fossil fuels), and because they are relatively new technologies, have no established large-scale production sector bringing them into being or servicing them. Because of this, there are possible short-run gains in terms of the relative labor intensiveness of producing those technologies without an existing infrastructure and of installing them, when compared to centralized energy production.

- For several years, and under several stimuli, there has been a search for a way to meld the goals of getting rid of municipally generated solid waste in both an economical and an environmentally acceptable fashion. Using the waste as a resource base through various forms of recycling is one way that has been investigated in the past.

Several studies are available which show the potential for "mining" metals from this waste, for example. Although numerous methods have been designed and demonstrated, the generation of energy from waste has not been widely adopted.

Municipal waste can be converted into energy through several procedures. One of these is the direct burning of the combustible fraction. To do this generally requires some separation of the paper, wood, and so forth from the metals and glass to improve the combustibility. Another alternative which has been used is to finely grind the entire mass of trash. It has been found that the Btu content is sufficiently high so that the mass will burn with little or no added fuel.

A second technique to extract the energy value present in municipal trash is by pyrolysis, wherein the materials are effectively cooked at high temperature and pressure in a "pressure cooker." A combustible gas is thereby generated, and in addition, both a combustible liquid and a combustible solid char material are generated which can be used for energizing the plant itself or other municipal needs. A third technique for extracting energy from municipal waste (especially sewage sludge) is through fermentation of the material, thereby creating methane gas which is the major constituent in natural gas. In this way, an exceedingly useful fuel is generated from the waste material.

The economics of these processes depend very much on the kind of bookkeeping system which is applied. If the energy program is charged with the cost of trash collection and trash separation, trash grinding, and so forth, the cost of the fuel is quite high. On the other hand, if it is recognized that trash disposal is a municipal function which must be carried out in some manner, regardless, and has a cost associated with it, then the energy processing might be credited with a figure of perhaps $5, $10, or $12 a ton, representing the normal cost of disposal by landfill, incineration, or whatever. In this case, the economics of the energy extraction processes tend to look quite good.

Clearly, the solution of the problems associated with the conversion of municipal solid waste would be a perfect example of energy production in a relatively inefficient fashion, which may be somewhat more expensive (depending upon the availability of disposal sites) than alternatives, and which may shift the environmental problem from one of solid waste to, say, air pollution. Yet the combined benefits from using this waste to produce energy may well outweigh the costs of doing so. The technology to do this is available in a widespread and acceptable fashion. The analyses to measure the relative costs and benefits are still to be produced, however.

There are numerous other examples which might be alluded to (say, in the areas of pricing practices or shifts in production techniques), but the few chosen above (in spite of the fact that they are weighted heavily in favor of energy/environmental examples) suffice to give some credence to the suggestion that there are already attempts underway to circumvent the need for all decisions of a federal policy nature to be settled by the White House or for a new agency to be formed to adjudicate such disputes.

Although these examples may be useful and satisfy a desire to address more than a single national goal in what appears, on the surface at least, to be a defensible and positive fashion, it is not really possible to "prove" that pursuing such combined goals is any better than pursuing any other set, or that the sum of these combinations is the "best" or even better than any other strategy. The challenge to the policy analysis is therefore increased dramatically.

A Search for a Methodology

The suggestion that cooperative behavior might be more useful than competitive, and the evidence that policies are being carried out in an attempt to mitigate the potentially ruinous conflicts that competitive behavior without compromise could lead to, does not mean that any real solution has been found to satisfy the goals set for each of the areas in contention. The shift from forcing all decisions concerning national policies whose goals or proposed strategies lead to inherent conflict and aberrational reactions on the part of the system to searching for strategies which accomplish several goals in a less than complete fashion leaves us with at least two serious problems.

The first problem is the political one spawned when the various interest groups (say, the environment, energy, or economic ones addressed in this section) are confronted with strategies which suggest that they accept less than full commitment or achievement on the part of the bureaucrats or politicians they support. In general, they will probably be willing to accept, or at least not be violently opposed to, such strategies in direct proportion to the assessment they make of their chances of accomplishing their goals by purely adversarial and uncooperative means. Cooperative strategies are usually entered into: (1) if by doing so, at least one of the parties believes that such an action will divert attention away from its "real" strategies. In such cases, the cooperation is illusionary and a tactic for use toward the achievement of a goal not explicitly stated or not obviously part of the bargaining process. Often, cooperative actions are seen as buying time. (2) when both parties see the move as hedging and as being able to accomplish at least a portion of their desired ends. In the latter case, neither party can see itself as having a present bargaining advantage or else it would see less of a reason to enter into any form of cooperation.

The embracing of solar technologies by members of both environmental and energy communities might be seen as a case in point. The amount of energy realistically expected from this source in the foreseeable future is generally held to be relatively small by some members of the energy community, and yet energy policy is in support of this alternative. At the same time, environmental spokesmen often also support it in spite of fairly substantial land-use and air pollution impacts. These impacts, given some of the scenarios suggested by solar advocates, are so land-consumptive and burn so much wood that there is some doubt whether the scenarios offered would conform to the spirit of the National Environmental Policy Act.[3] Yet, under widely varying degrees of agreement among themselves, members of these two communities jointly support aspects of a technology which might be less than totally satisfactory to either one under other circumstances.

Similar problems have appeared in the area of conservation. Conservation and the reduction of pollution have always been seen as synonomous by the more activist members of the environmental community. Recently, however, we have seen considerable evidence that insulating homes for the purposes of conservation (particularly when considered with the use of wood stoves or formaldehyde insulation) is resulting in alarming levels of indoor air pollution which is hazardous to human health.[4]

The second problem is analytical rather than political. To the extent that analysis is used to help arrive at programs which balance multiple objectives, a methodology has to be adopted for structuring and analyzing various alternatives in order to present options to the various decision-makers.

The reader will recall that the original discussion earlier in this section portrayed a situation where decisions were made in a decentralized fashion by members of more than one federal agency. Further, that there was no apparent reason for these agency leaders to bargain with each other, even though the decisions one of them makes often have disastrous impacts on the policies of the other. This situation suggests a milieu in which analysts from each of the agencies perform analyses for use by their own agency. The alternatives presented by these analysts can be expected to result normally in choices which are most favorable to the analyst's agency, other things being equal.

Because of this fact, traditional solutions to the problem of resource allocation, such as those found in traditional systems analysis, are unsatisfactory. These methods, alluded to above, are often both conceptually and analytically straightforward (at least in their simplest forms). In general, to review their form: a goal is chosen and the resources are identified to achieve the goal. Given the situation extant in the referenced system at the beginning of the analyses, and the boundaries expected with unconstrained use of the resources to accomplish the desired goal, a preferred strategy is derived. Under this scheme, the policies of other federal agencies can easily be conceived of as barriers.

A difficulty occurs when each agency, having done its own analyses, arrives at a solution strategy which not only is unlikely to be the same as any other agency, but if such a strategy were implemented, would redescribe the boundary conditions for the analyses performed by all other agencies. To overcome this difficulty analytically would require either the simultaneous solution of all of the agency models or an iterative procedure which readjusted the strategies of each agency until a solution is arrived at which allows no agency to gain at another's expense—a truly complex analytic solution. Yet as difficult as the specification of this problem might be, or as complex as the solution procedures might be, the real difficulty again is institutional.

A COURT OF APPEALS

Another possibility is the formation of a formal White House-level "Court of Appeals" to settle interagency, cross-policy disputes. The reason one might be concerned with a continuation of the present policy of every agency attempting to carry out its own mission to the best of its ability is that it appeared certain that situations would arise which resulted in system outcomes generally felt to be societally undesirable. It has been suggested that some form of cooperative behavior be entered into, and it actually appeared that such was happening in some parts of the energy and environmental areas. Upon investigation, though, empirical analysis of the types of strategies which might be entered into and the degree of cooperation which might be most beneficial to all brought us right back to a situation where, even if the performance of such analysis was possible, there is some question as to whom one would do it for. On a priori grounds, there does not appear to be any reason for an agency to choose a strategy that is biased toward a compromise position if it can accomplish its major mission of pushing its own goals at another's expense.

If it were even possible for a formalized methodology to be developed to arrive at strategies for federal policy, then the application of this methodology would likely have to be carried out at a high level and in a centralized place—say the Office of Management and Budget (OMB). One possible scenario would be for OMB to use such analytical techniques as a part of the budget process.

In reality, the political process carried on by such institutions as the Domestic Council is set up to do the very kind of "last resort" analysis we have just been discussing. At present, the staff is very small and acts both as the long-range planning arm and the arbitrator of agency disputes. It also handles day-to-day policy issues. Regardless of one's personal opinion of how well or poorly the arbitrator's daily policy guidance role is pursued, it is clear that much work has yet to be done to set in place the necessary mechanism for any real long-range planning. There are some who feel that such a move would reduce the need for some of the arbitration in making day-to-day policy issues.

REALITY TEMPERED BY CONFUSION

Either strategy, as they would result in an appeal of all or most major policy decisions of individual agencies to a higher court, would make for a cessation of the federal government as we presently know it. Both suggest a turning toward a more centralized form of government, a suggestion which has continually met with less than total enthusiasm when it appeared as a solution to other problems in times past.

Something different seems to be called for. It is clear that our society is readjusting its conception of what makes for "the good life" and seems to be adding or emphasizing several factors which are both difficult to quantify and alien to the present institutions for producing the goods and services traditionally desired by our system. Because of this, many of the institutional, organizational, and analytical means of running or guiding our culture and seeing to it that it operates in a fashion which efficiently produces the desired outputs are inadequate and under change. It is truly a period of great uncertainty and potential upheaval.

As an alternative to centralization, the cooperation we discussed earlier is presently being carried out in a kind of ad hoc fashion. Vague limits are drawn by the opposing groups and a stratagem is agreed upon; the various actors are more or less satisfied to live without a complete victory if they can at least accomplish some of their individual goals. Consequently, we have a situation where the stratagem agreed to by the opposing parties is not only not maximal in terms of other possible strategies they might adopt if left to their own devices, but where the compromise stratagem chosen may not necessarily be optimal either. In all cases, this solution to the question of agency conflict under crisis is wasteful of resources, but seems to be the price we are willing to pay to accomplish multiple objectives under a system such as ours.

I could go on at some length citing examples of attempts on the part of one agency to accomplish its mandated goals that have exacerbated a situation already considered intolerable by another mission-oriented agency, but the ones discussed above seem to make the point. Although it is admitted that, in most cases, the nation (as is true with any living system) would essentially somehow adjust to any situation, some adjustments would clearly be less desirable than others. For example, widespread poverty or disease could result from a series of policies. Although the nation might "adjust" to this outcome, politically and morally it would not be acceptable to our citizenry.

Given all the difficulties and realities of adversary policymaking, what can be done to accommodate this structure when it is under apparent strain because of structural problems in one or more of its sectors? A cynical response of doing nothing is not allowed. The next most obvious response is to call for some restructuring of the way the public sector makes decisions. The process used with partial success in the past appears to work less well under conditions of scarcity and trauma. If energy, environment, and economics are all important, who decides where the trade-offs will be made? One possibility is that all resolutions of trade-offs would be passed on to the courts. Although this is the proclivity in many regulatory situations, we shall assume that the decisionmakers will not continue to abrogate their responsibilities in this matter. This means that these decisions will be made in the political arena, since the trend to refer all such conflicts to other or higher authority is further taxing our already overloaded court system and exposes the political community to constant risk. Generating requirements to balance goals which are sometimes mutually exclusive is bound to bring forth the ire of various constituencies, and yet each of the goals are extremely important to our quality of life.

My first inclination in summarizing this chapter, at the risk of being castigated for suggesting further paper exercises for the bureaucracy, was to proffer the concept of an impact statement for each decision area. But this is already required in analyzing environment or energy regulations for government actions and, as noted earlier, directly or indirectly for most other decision areas. The reader can decide how successful this strategy is at present. On reflection, I would suggest that we (1) continue to do the best we can analyzing the issues, examining trade-offs, and communicating our derived information to others concerned at all levels of the public and private sectors, but that we recognize the skimpiness of these analyses; and (2) develop a new mechanism for assuring that policy decisions that have the types of impacts discussed here are based on careful consideration of comprehensive, not parochial, analysis.

Several recent studies suggest that the nationwide energy cost of pollution control is about 3 percent of the total energy budget. This represents about four quads of energy by the year 2000, about a third of the total amount of oil expected to be imported to the United States in that year, or more than all of the energy expected to be required by the nation's steel industry.[5] However, few of the impacts discussed in this chapter are of the type that appear at the national level. Instead, they are localized impacts resulting from trying to force-fit uniform national policies into nonuniform situations. For example, analyses of the regional energy costs of pollution control show that certain areas, like the Northeast and Middle Atlantic states, would have considerably higher percentages of energy expended for pollution control, especially in their industrial areas.

These issues beg to be addressed and institutions set up for their solution. If this is not done, given the severeness of the situations in the energy, environment, and economic areas prevalent today, all the goal-setting, law-passing, and regulation promulgation will not result in a healthy society. It is often tempting to portray complex issues such as energy, economic, and environmental goals in a simplistic fashion. For example, it is unfair, misleading, and inaccurate to say that to favor balancing and meeting our environmental and energy goals is to favor dirty air and to have a scant regard for the health and safety of our people. Instead, the issue is one of cleaning and improving our natural resources, thereby protecting public health, while at the same time allowing for needed economic and energy growth. In other words, we should eschew rhetoric and seek reasoned balancing.

Immediate Fixes

The large number of problems I have noted in this and the previous chapters could make a reader discouraged or cynical. Many of the problems noted cannot be addressed simply. Most will require considerable research and testing before they can become an active part of the policy toolkit. If the thesis of this book is correct and if the current methods are inadequate for policy use, then what can be substituted or added to the methods used at present to aid in policy formulation?

Obviously, it is not responsible to seriously suggest Draconian measures such as not having any thoughtful or analytical inputs as those in the public decision process. First of all, on the most cynical level, there are lots and lots of people whose careers are tied up in supporting the policy level. These people are going to resist mightily any attempt to do them out of a job. We should remember that decisions have been made in the public and private sector for a long time without the benefit of high technology. Wars have been fought and the fate of nations and individuals decided based on the reading of chicken entrails or the phases of the moon. To some people, the use of ultrasophisticated analytical techniques without proper data, theoretical, or reality underpinnings might be seen on a par with this kind of primitive divination. In fact, many reasonable alternatives exist without resorting to the occult.

There are several books, courses, and articles in the academic and popular media that purport to help one make a decision. A recent article in the Washington *Post*,[6] for example, lists some of the factors one might want to take into consideration in making a decision in private life: Set a decision deadline; Get data; Know when to quit gathering data; List "pros" and "cons"; Avoid letting others make your decisions; Catastrophize; Consult trusted friends; Relinquish the decision to your subconcious; Cooperate when making decisions as a couple or a group; and Don't fear indecision. These factors are somewhat obvious to those who find making a decision easy. They are pretty stylized and would have one overly regimented for actually carrying out the myriad of choices everybody makes every day. But such rigor might be useful, at least for major personal decisions.

If one were to systematically list the ways to make a public policy choice, as we have in earlier chapters, there would clearly be some similarity in the lists for personal and public "rules" or "guidelines." The suggestions for gathering data and for producing a choice algorithm, including goals and options, should sound familiar to the reader by now. The newer factors are what we will turn to now—options which are less analytical. Out of this collection of things one might lean on to develop a short-run method for policy formation, a pragmatic, though admittedly incomplete, model should begin to emerge.

- *Experience:* When making a decision in any area, there is no substitute for knowledge gained from experience. Putting aside all of the foibles of human nature, including bias, arrogance, and obtuseness, informed decisionmakers can be expected to be better decisionmakers just as experienced carpenters are apt to be better carpenters than home handimen or apprentices.

The intuitive reaching for someone who has the information at his or her fingertips or who has experienced the situation (or similar ones) before is common practice. The most serious drawback is that experience is obviously human-based, colored with individual bias, and consequently limited. Further, as I have already stated, the making of policy is defined as departing from this status quo. As such, the information gained from experience almost by definition is going to be somewhat different from that required for the specific decision under discussion. The amount of the difference may be small or significant. To the extent that it is significant and to the extent that the expert "stretches" to demonstrate his expertise, he may be more harmful than useful. Still, the knowledge gained from having handled like problems in the past is likely to be better than having to begin to address them *de nouveau.*

- *Brain Storming:* Not only because the Renaissance Man (who knew everything there was to know) can't exist today, but also because the vast majority of the interesting and important public policy issues are people-based (meaning they are likely to be value-laden and opinion-oriented), human inputs from several sources are very likely to be added to whatever contribution empirical information can make. At the very least, open discussion of an issue with experts in areas related to it will provide the greatest possible amount of data for the decision choice.

Gathering to discuss an idea or issue can range from the formal and structured situation of a prepared briefing to a more impromptu meeting. Regardless of the formality, though, there are lots and lots of reasons that such a procedure is apt to be unscientific, inadequate, and biased. Clearly, there can be no more information available to such a session than the combined inputs from everyone in the room. There is no guarantee that those present are the right people, are well prepared, or care enough about the subject. Seldom if ever does anyone stop the meeting to go look up or check a fact. Policy brain storming, by definition, would mean that a decisionmaker gathers with his lieutenants to discuss a strategy for addressing an issue. Generally, these meetings are such that some degree of candor is necessary. Usually, the degree of candor required would suggest that one might not want strangers in the meeting, at least until a trial position had been thoroughly investigated by some inner circle. But if only those in the inner circle can get into such a meeting, there is real reason to doubt whether the technical expertise or experience necessary will be forthcoming or the best possible. Another real-world example of Catch-22!

Further, as I noted in Chapter 4, there is a natural tendency to acquiesce to the leader (or senior person) in the room for all decisions, including technical ones. Certainly, many of the political appointees in the federal establishment have professional credentials, but these people seldom limit their opinions to their area of training—for understandable reasons. In the end, it is this person who will be burnt by a bad call. So, it is often up to them to set the goals (and relative importance) of the subject being discussed. This "right-to-rule" posture, legitimate or not, may do serious harm and diminish the usefulness of a brain storming session. Similar skewing of the results can come to pass with an aggressive person who tends to dominate a brain storming session. These are the types of abuses that Delphi was designed to overcome, but its obsessive formalism makes it too cumbersome for practical use.

On the other hand, frank discussion, well prepared, and rewarded by management will tend to bring out both the competitive and cooperative spirits of a policy team and, over time, bring to the fore a smoothly functioning decision unit. Guarding against the worst foibles of group dynamics will go a long way toward making this practice still the most useful for policy setting.

- *Persuasion:* One of the ways of handling a policy dilemma is to conceptualize a situation so that the need for a decision is obviated. Because there are clearly dozens upon dozens of factors which could combine to define what was going on in a specific situation at any particular period in time, it is not realistic to suggest details as to how to redefine a situation that would be applicable to such a wide spectrum of possibilities. Instead, let me, in an exemplary fashion, suggest two general strategies: selling and threats.

Selling a position, idea, or strategy might be one way to proceed to change a situation so that one did not have to face an issue directly. One might want to do this if the development of a particular issue might cause political embarrassment or difficulty or when the decision about how to address an issue is obviously going to be extremely complex and problematical. In such a situation, diversionary or prophylactic selling could be used to head off a messier confrontation. Say two energy technologies are about equal from the standpoint of energy supply, but one is considerably favored from an environmental perspective. One might participate in the selling of the environmentally favored technology early on, even though there is no real interest in the technology, merely to avoid the need for considering an energy/environmental trade-off.

In a similar fashion, threats could be used to avoid a conflict by using raw political power to do away with the need for analysis. Again in the area of energy and environment, an environmental group might threaten or bring to bear political action to get its way, making it unnecessary to battle on technical grounds about the merits of an issue.

- *Common Sense:* Regardless of the decision method agreed upon (formal or otherwise), when all is said and done, somebody has to make a decision. At that stage, no presently available technique can supplant good horse sense. In the private sector (excepting such aberrations as neoptism), there is generally a succession of experience and roles which one is expected to pass through which not only permits a person to gain more experience, but tests judgment and the ability to make "good" decisions. Unfortunately, no such neat ladder is available (outside the Civil Service) in the public sector where the ultimate decisionmaker is often a political appointee. There are several ways one might compensate for this lack of management experience. Getting lieutenants who are proven good managers in the public sector (and letting them do their jobs) is probably the best solution. If one is not concerned with a specific decision, experience suggests that the decisionmaker possessed of good common sense either delegates responsibility (officially or unofficially) to people who can handle the situation, or has a short reign.

The decision model suggested by combining these factors is obviously incomplete and does not in any way require that one completely abandon rigorous analysis. Clearly, analysis can augment the factors noted above which tend to depend more on human ingenuity. If the policy level requires inputs from the technical level with frequency and vigor, then formal structure and methods will tend to appear that combine both. The existence of people-oriented practices in the process will prevent formal techniques from becoming the be-all-and-the-end-all they often appear to become, however. What about these formal techniques, though? What can be done for the long run?

DOES ANYTHING SURVIVE?

If the metamodel on which systems analysis is built is flawed, if the information is inadequate for the use of technical rigor, and if the same decisionmaking process historically used before the advent of computers and systems analysis is still the best for most policy issues, of what use are all the sophisticated analytic techniques?

- *Defense:* Such analyses are needed, if for no other reason, because lots of people by now are convinced that techniques like systems or decision analysis are useful. Not having such analyses therefore stigmatizes one as having analyzed a problem inadequately.
  Snobbery is a potent weapon and in the technical world is sometimes used to intimidate. The "Bead Game"[7] of models is often used to suggest to those who might oppose a position: "It must be

so, look at how complex the techniques have been to develop the position." In this light, the sophisticated techniques are a form of posturing and set the stage for more practical aspects of the decision-making process.

Furthermore, there has to be a cadre of analysts available to read the work of other groups who make use of such techniques. Even though it might be pretty generally conceded that the output is worthless, no decisionmaker would want to pass by something which he had a chance to review and which might come back to haunt him later. This is especially true if it costs him little to order an analysis done. He has the analysis, and so is protected from the criticism of not using the "latest" techniques, but really feels no compulsion to use the results unless they are useful to his position.

- *A Known Perspective:* Another argument in favor of a rigorous approach to policy analysis is that if the method is well understood, then the results obtained can also be understood against this backdrop. If such results are added into the brain storming session noted earlier, then the analyses might make a useful contribution, although how useful would obviously depend upon the situation.

The purpose of an analysis then becomes the structuring of an argument in terms that are mutually agreed upon. Such a service might be useful in reducing the level of conflict by narrowing the specific things the combatants will discuss.

One problem is that the analysis itself often becomes the focus, or one of the foci, of the policy debate, thus enlarging rather than narrowing the combat zone. For example, in the days of the Energy Research and Development Administration (ERDA), an Annual Plan was mandated by Congress which had as its purpose a description of the energy future and, against this backdrop, a plan for research which would result in making America less dependent on others for the energy supplies suggested by such a future. The Plan itself became a target of debate, as did the techniques used to produce it. The support team of contractors who did the actual modeling and much of the analysis felt the heat so intensely that to protect themselves and their "professional reputations," they included as a part of one of their reports to the ERDA a section which essentially said that the model was not adequate for the use to which it was being put.[8]

More important than the difficulty of introducing analytic techniques or resulting documents into the policy foray that make the argument worse is the problem of dealing with the fact that structuring the argument by using a particular analysis or technique automatically gives some credence to the tool or technique being used. The controversy surrounding the book *Limits to Growth,*[9] which we alluded to earlier in the section on communication, called into question results which not only suggested a Cassandra-like warning of global doom, but which specified that this doom would be in the form of environmental pollution. The ensuing debate, which was carried out around the world, did not really zero-in on the problems of how to solve the fundamental global issues which come to the fore regardless of what resource constraints appear, such as the very real institutional problems introduced by how the nations are made up culturally, what their individual sovereignty means, the different levels of economic development, and so forth. Instead, the debate was concerned, rather superficially, with the issue of pollution levels introduced into the world by industrialization and development. Possibly this narrow focus was all that was intended. But to the extent that it was not, there is some question as to the utility of the model and the subsequent analysis. Calling attention to an issue is only of service when it highlights the right issue in an illuminating fashion, regardless of how loud the call.

There is no additional argument made in favor of presently available rigorous techniques. In spite of their very great deficiencies, they are all we have and using them can give a decisionmaker useful information. However, as we suggested throughout the preceding chapters, if the data, theory, and so forth are flawed, then the introduction of information from such a system could do real harm to the decision process. The recent popularity of discovering "counter intuitive" results from running computer models should make us uncomfortable not because models are predicting things and results that experienced people in the field wouldn't or didn't think of (a suspicious happening if frequent), but because the people are, as a consequence, judged incorrect and the models correct!

Impact Analyses. Much of the action in the policy community is reactive in nature. By this I mean that issues are eventually formed in terms of "if this is to be the case, then this will be the result and I do or do not want that to happen." Based on this paradigm, if undesirable results are forthcoming, a suggestion is made that the analyzed situation or policy be altered (if possible). Such analyses are called impact analyses, meaning that they are designed to measure the effects of a policy in terms of how it would change the status quo. These impact analyses appear to at least get away from the problems associated with forecasting the future, as they merely suggest that one accept a particular forecast as a given (somebody else's idea of the future) and then measure the future impacts of a specific set of policies (energy policy on environmental future, for example). Similar impacts can be measured by accepting a particular forecast as a reference (as opposed to expected) case and perturbing the forecast by introducing a particular policy. In this case, the forecasted future can be anybody's. The existence of two cases, differing only in terms of the introduction of this particular policy, allows rigorous analysis of the impact of the policy on the system being studied.

Lincoln Moses, former head of the Energy Information Administration at DOE, suggests in a recent paper that this practice and its expected benefits should be questioned, though:

> Check out an often heard "quasi-theorem" which states (approximately) that though one might be quite cautious about accepting some forecast of the future, he can have more confidence about "impact," the difference between two forecasts that differ only in that one of them involves a particular policy intervention whose impact is to be addressed.
>
> The proposition has intuitive appeal. It is in the spirit of comparative measurement, matched controls, paired experiments and the like. On the other hand, it is not appealing in full generality, for a "policy intervention" might work to make some essential features of the model less "valid" for the second scenario and the "impact" could be worse than one of the forecasts.
>
> The principle is important. It would be desirable to identify and state which *is* true along these lines, and then offer a proof, or a way of assembling information which would sooner or later tend to confirm (or disconfirm) it.[10]

In short, Moses suggests that the structure, data, or logic problems inherent in any model which purports to predict the future are likely to be found also in any model which merely attempts to forecast the impact of a perturbation.

Amusement. Finally, if a decisionmaker has prurient interest in what others think he "should" do, or if he wants some ego-supporting attention given his monarchical sense of people asking him what his "goals" or "win strategies" are, then having analysts around is fun. The choice as to whether he has to listen to them still remains with him, however.

In formulating arguments in favor of keeping many of the analytic tools we have around today, I am reminded of the days when the automobile was in its gestation period. The early designs of the auto and the early sales literature were designed to gently draw the general populace away from the horsedrawn toward the horseless carriage. We are in another similar period of transition where it is becoming widely realized that the very sophisticated techniques of the past have gone too far in promising to "solve" our policy dilemmas (whereas the previous transition was to a push-button policy system). Some of the results obtained while chasing this will-o-the-wisp are ludicrous indeed and we have noted many here. There is some reluctance, though, to throw out the whole attempt and start over. One strong argument against such a move is that there is no clear set of methodologies to replace what we have now. Yet I suggest that there are some very common sense things which could be done to buttress the policy analysis field while it goes on looking for better ways to carry out its business. I have gone so far as to suggest that there are even some so-so reasons for not phasing out all the sophisticated techniques and their proponents-practitioners immediately. There is a clear message, however, that they should take themselves seriously so that others will trust their formal analyses. In the next chapter, I want to investigate a few things which might be done to speed up a transition to a new policy analysis era.

NOTES

1. Department of Energy analysis (unpublished).

2. In modeling terms, the technique of mathematical programming has developed a solution called a "saddle point." This solution is usually the one which yields the maximum gain for the minimum expenditure of resources. Consequently, it is referred to as a mini-max solution.

3. Office of Environmental Assessments, *Technology Assessment of Solar Energy (TASE)*. U.S. Department of Energy, February 1981 (forthcoming).

4. "Environmental Readiness Document—Wood Combustion," DOE/ERD-0026. Office of Environmental Assessments, U.S. Department of Energy, August 1979. "Engery Conservation and Indoor Air Quality." Office of Environmental Assessments, U.S. Department of Energy, December 1979.

5. *Annual Environmental Assessment Report (AEAR)* (Washington, DC: U.S. Department of Energy, 1977).

6. The Washington Post, August 19, 1980, p. B-5.

7. Herman Hesse, *Magister Ludi* (The Bead Game) (New York: Random House, 1969).

8. "Creating Energy Choices for the Future: A National Plan for Energy Research, Development and Demonstration," ERDA-48. U.S. Energy Research and Development Administration, 1975. See also "U.S. Actions Needed to Cope with Commodity Shortages," Comptroller General Report to Congress, B-114824. U.S. General Accounting Office, 1974; and "The Relationship of Energy Growth to Economic Growth Under Alternative Energy Policies," BNL 50500. Brookhaven National Laboratory, March 1976.

9. Dennis Meadows et al., *Limits to Growth* (Washington, DC: Potomac Books, 1973).

10. S. I. Gass (ed.) "Validation and Assessment of Issues of Energy Models." Workshop sponsored by the Department of Energy and the National Bureau of Standards, January 10-11, 1979. NBS Special Publication 569; U.S. GPO 003-003-02155-5.

CHAPTER 6

POLICY SKILLS AND
INSTITUTIONAL CHANGES

Summing Up

I shall make an attempt in this final chapter to formulate some guidelines and strategies that might be used to improve the art of policy analysis, to make it more useful to those who may need such analyses to make policy decisions, and further, to make some specific suggestions for those who teach it to budding analysts. This attempt could be thought of as ambitious by the more generous. Others, not so kindly, might think of the exercise as more in the nature of foolhardy. To reduce the risk of being so cast, I have made the recommendations selectively modest. I also recognize explicitly that whatever comes to pass will happen over a protracted period of time.

I see these longer-run changes as occurring in at least four areas: (1) the teaching of policy analysis with an expanded and more focused curriculum; (2) the design and operation of policy shops within the public sector whose focus is on delivering a product rather than enhancing formalism; (3) the gradual evolution of new programs and techniques to structure policy issues for more meaningful analysis; and (4) the explicit incorporation of organizational and institutional modes of thinking into formal analyses. Much of this adjustment will have to come within the institutions whose business it is to train the analysts of the future. The discussion presented earlier has implied some guidance to these teachers; this chapter will attempt to handle the suggested improvements in a more straightforward fashion.

We shall move from the set of guidelines suggested for teaching policy science to the actual forming of a policy analysis unit in the public sector. Although experience normally forces such units to respond in certain ways or become useless, they would be more efficient if they were pragmatically and realistically structured in the first place. In this section, as with the one on teaching policy science, I repeat some topical areas, suggestions, or observations noted in previous chapters. The purpose is to emphasize the required changes and institutions that will have to be carried out and the form of this change to most effectively bring the needed improvement to pass. The first section made some suggestions as to how one might go about teaching policy analysis. These directions may take some time to effect, particularly in the schools which are more traditionally based. The section on setting up a policy shop may or may not take place in the organization of the future and may or may not be properly classified as a longer-run modification. It depends upon the organization and the policy leaders in that organization. The next section is an attempt to specify improvements that might be used to improve analysis in the resource areas of the public sector, specifically incorporating improved regional perspectives at the federal level.

The chapter then proceeds to see if there is any technique or methodology that might be further developed to be useful in the policy arena, especially in the area of resource-related (as opposed to human policy) issues. Because this book has been concerned with trading off these resources among themselves, the methodology investigated is more heavily weighted toward being useful for problems of a resource nature. Formally, the method evaluated is a variant of a concept developed in the field of ecology called "carrying capacity." The section reviews various attempts to use this concept and presents a sophisticated model based on the idea. It concludes with the suggestion that, at present, the data base does not exist for fully implementing the model but describes a first stage attempt at a methodology.

It is noted at this point that one of the difficulties with most of the formal analytical methods and policy analysis is that they usually do not explicitly integrate numerous institutional and organizational variables. Among the reasons for this is the fact that the logic on which such decisions are made is very different indeed from that of the empirical analyst. These decision rules are then reviewed. The chapter ends on a hopeful note. The paradigm of carrying capacity, although not really useful in the sense of being able to support a full formal model, provides a structure for analysis that can be used, provided there is a supporting data base. Finally, the chapter investigates a system called PASS—an information system that captures such a data base and the analytic structure used to make such a system more useful for policy purposes.

SKILLS NEEDED BY THE ANALYST

Recently, a group of us who have done policy analyses for the public sector (either as bureaucrats or consultants) attempted to delineate the skills we saw as useful or necessary for anyone who would set out to make the art of policy analysis their vocation. As with the earlier lists, this collection of statements is meant to focus thought rather than be exhaustive.

Communications. Depending on the situation, the policy analyst has to be able to communicate his findings and ideas to another person, as it is seldom that analyst and final decisionmaker are one and the same. This will require knowledge of how to write clearly and precisely; less in the nature of a term paper, though, and more in the style of a memorandum (decision or information). Oral skills for briefings or hearings are also required, as is the ability to use or reorganize good visual ones. Such mundane skills are not usually taught in most policy science programs, and consequently have to be acquired at present through on-the-job training. In the meantime, the trainees' policy analyses are possibly inadequately transmitted to those who might use at least part of this work. This deficiency has two costs: the decision process is possibly diminished by the lack of the analyst's input; and the analyst himself may be thought badly of and his analysis mistrusted because he cannot communicate effectively. Consequently, he becomes a drain on the system rather than an asset.

Management skills. Most curricula for preparing policy analysis seem to portray each analyst as the "Lone Ranger." Considerable emphasis is placed on the analyst's technical ability to carry out analyses of issues on his own. In reality, because analysis staffs in the public sector are usually people-short and money-rich (at least in a relative sense), the analyst finds himself doing tasks more reminiscent of a manager than a technician. For this role, he needs to be able to write and evaluate proposals, to handle personnel matters (in-house and contractual), and to prepare and monitor budgets. Again, these skills are usually learned after the fact, not in a college classroom.

Problem solving. Clearly, today's analyst should be thoroughly versed in most or all of the techniques available for policy analysis. This proficiency is needed not only so that he may carry out or monitor the use of such techniques in his own analyses or those of his contractors, but also to be able to comprehend and comment on the work of others, particularly those who are adversaries of the position his agency is supporting.

In addition to the straightforward ability to use technical skills, the analyst should be trained to constantly put a "reality" test on the outputs of his analysis. Experience, coupled with a familiarity with the problem, should give him some idea of the expected result of his calculations. Although results which are the opposite of so-called "conventional wisdom" are often found, normally they should be treated with suspicion. For most situations under analysis, the data, information, and model quality or analytic technique are sufficiently primitive that sophisticated results, particularly those that are counter to research insight, are often difficult to sustain.

Finally, the analyst himself has to be a self-starter, aggressively going after information, insights, opinions. He should build his own network of contacts and have tested to his own satisfaction the quality of the information obtained. The number of issues handled in an average public policy shop and the short time for the performance of their analysis and presentation leaves little left for constant individual handholding on the part of the analyst's manager.

Political understanding. Nothing frustrates the analyst or those he works for more than to have naive or simple-minded work put forth for consideration in the fast-moving world of policymaking. Such efforts sometimes sour the new analyst against doing careful work in the future or turns off policymakers who must consider the analyst's inputs as part of their own decision process. Political sensitivity is not meant to be any more than acknowledging the realities of a specific analysis in much the same way one would consider restraints of place, time, information, and other resources that might be a part of the decision process. One should also be able to coordinate with others outside the group and negotiate a final organizational position. This skill has been called "vision" by a colleague of mine. In his mind, the analyst should be able to relate the question he is working on to a larger set of issues and happenings so as to avoid a myopic view of the issue he is studying. The vision in the perspective determines a context for decisionmaking.

Implementation. For many issues, it is not only necessary for the analyst to understand how to perform the analysis to answer the question at hand, but it is important that he envision how particular solutions would actually be implemented. Extreme solutions, having little or no chance actually to be carried out, are usually evident to the decisionmaker and, again, brands the analyst as academically oriented, a zealot, or impractical. These impressions should be avoided in the writeup of the analysis. More conceptual findings should be labeled as difficult to implement and at most offered as possible goals to shoot for.

Team building and operation. As noted earlier, many of today's policy issues are too complex and require too broad a knowledge base for the analyses to be handled by a single individual. Consequently, analysts are usually asked to provide inputs into a larger effort and to work harmoniously with or as a team leader. Team building and supporting skills (running meetings, work sessions, preparing outlines, setting policy options, meeting deadlines, and so forth) are not usually part of the academic world that fosters individual term papers, theses, speeches, and the like. Consequently, these more social skills have to be acquired on the job.

Evaluation and planning. Finally, the talents required of a policy analyst often begin or end with the ability to analyze an existing, ongoing program and to plan future directions for its progress. These abilities are also not usually a part of the empirical kit bag of an analyst, although the logic he has learned should help.

REAL-WORLD SKILL REQUIREMENTS AND ANALYSIS

The partial list of abilities an analyst should have is far beyond those of a simple technician. Of relevance to this discussion here, these skills may suggest deficiencies or incompleteness in the current heavy emphasis on teaching analysis techniques, as their applications have to be so heavily buttressed by such a massive dose of social and other nonanalytic talents. Obviously, not all of the facets of policy analysis as it is practiced have been covered. However, one purpose of this chapter is to begin to sensitize those who teach the policy sciences and public administration to the fact that the realities surrounding public policy analysis as practiced are often very different from those portrayed in the academic or theoretical literature. In the spirit of assisting changes in this situation, let me suggest two types of modifications—one in teaching policy science, and another in organizing to practice it. These suggestions may already be known to many readers, but I repeat them here and urge that more emphasis be placed on their adoption.

- *Training:* The teaching of policy science and analysis is a recent phenomenon. In fact, there are relatively few schools across the country where students can major in such fields, and most of these are at the graduate level. More characteristically, policy sciences are covered in a department or school of public affairs or public administration. Practical considerations dictated by the individual institution may not allow policy instruction to be a part of a formal curriculum, but at least a few courses which address policy should be taught in the social sciences, engineering, economics, and public administration departments. Although the specific topics taught in any one of these places would depend upon the department and the school, it seems clear that a certain minimum set of concepts, methods, data handling, and practicalities should be covered.

- *Teaching Not Preaching:* Policy analysis came into vogue in the Fifties and Sixties and developed through extensive use of the concepts of systems analysis and operations research. These were the days of "whizkids" at the Pentagon, a resurgence of faith in the solutions offered by science and technology, the New Frontier, and the slogan, "If we can get you to the moon, we can . . . (the reader is to supply the appropriate words)."

  It is the opinion of many, then and now, that the officials who make public policy are inept, relying on guesses—or worse, on falsified or slanted information—to make decisions. An oft-repeated theme has been that the practitioners of policy analysis should move aside and let the new policy science specialist, armed with methods and models, show public officials how analysis and decisionmaking should be done.

  My plea is that instead of building more abstract and rhetorical arguments for how analysis ought to be done, more time should be spent in preparing future analysts to perform in situations in which actual decisions are made. This is not to say that no time should be spent in improving the state-of-the-art in practical policy analysis, but only that less niggling and armchair philosophizing should be done in this field.

- *Case Studies:* The teaching of business administration, pioneered in such places as Harvard, makes extensive use of case studies of actual business situations tailored for the classroom. Similar courses in the field of public administration exist, but there appear to be few in the area of policy analysis.

  One possible reason for this paucity of case histories on the evolution of public policy is that this sort of history is often subject to "laundering" for public consumption. The behind-the-scenes dealing, the repetitive analyses often focused on irrelevant minutiae, the glaring errors of analysis, the influence of personalities, the politics of the issue, the happy coincidences, the sheer bad (or good) luck, are left out. And yet, as we have noted above, these events so often are principal elements that influence specific policy decisions.

  Two improvements seem to be warranted. First, a series of candid case studies should be prepared so that the parties involved are not embarrassed, but with full disclosure of the details of how a policy was analyzed and decided on. Business schools have often augmented their case studies with the formal technique of mock business experience. Possibly some similar form of role playing in the public sector curriculum could be equally useful to students. Second, a meaningful work-study program where students become involved in a more realistic policy process should be developed.

Since many policy issues are politically delicate and full disclosure is not readily available even after a considerable length of time, and because the working through of the issues requires a certain degree of trust (along with commitment to the goals or ideals of the group) on the part of those involved, case studies and on-the-job training before the analyst is part of a "team" will not be easy to implement. And yet, if we do not begin to move toward this situation, we shall continue to be guilty of teaching analysts to seek change in the system without ever understanding many of the realities that have significant influence on that system. They shall continue to be strong in (and misled by) the theory of how policy "works" or be doomed to normative pronouncements of how it should work. An argument could be made that the existence of normative utterances is a result of ignorance of how things happen and of reactive frustration at not being able to find anyone who will explain the process or rationale involved.

In the end, the people who pay for the inadequacies of the educational system are those who are taught by it. If the educators are to revolutionize the system by themselves, they are almost surely doomed to frustration and failure. Chief among administrative realities is that all large bureaucratic systems are deliberately designed to resist change, particularly the type of change which is driven by frontal assaults.

- *Techniques:* In spite of our complaints that students are taught to an excess that policy analysis can actually be done in a purely analytical fashion, I believe they should be well grounded in those analytical techniques that are fundamental to practicing their art. The reasons have been outlined above. However, a few curriculum improvements of the type also mentioned in previous chapters might be considered with additional warning. Many schools, in an attempt to soften what had appeared to be an overly rigorous, engineering perspective to policy studies, have introduced a course or two aimed at giving the student a broader purview—giving them a glimpse of the so-called "big picture." Care has to be taken that this worthwhile trend does not go too far, and that students not turn out to be better grounded in how to make use of an analytical result rather than in how to do the analysis.

More to the point, research should be undertaken to devise better methods of teaching and performing policy analysis, so that the less quantifiable but more dynamic and realistic factors can be melded into the analysis. Parallel, or perhaps subsequent to instruction in rigorous techniques, less rigorous methods need to be taught. Guidelines for decisionmaking, as contrasted to pure methodology, might be experimented with. As already noted, in spite of the analytical assaults sometimes mounted on complex issues, the key elements on which the issue is decided are often of a political nature. Superb analysis may go wanting when decision alternatives are not clear-cut. As stated earlier, more attention should be paid to presentation of results and to understanding the needs of particular policymakers. Term papers, theses, or articles—time-tested teaching devices—could be replaced by issue papers and decision memoranda based on samples from the policymaking world.

- *Formalism:* Attempting to discover order and structure in one's endeavor is a feature of the scientific approach; the constant seeking of a natural law or set of underlying principals to explain the occurrence of a set of phenomena, thus allowing generalization and prediction.

Unfortunately, in policy analysis, the attempt to catalogue problems, techniques, and analytical methods can lead to excessive formalism. Structuring a problem into well-defined categories may make for empirical neatness and may be required to permit the analyst to utilize a particular set of analytical tools, but such structuring may not result in a useful approach to providing policy support for decisions on actual problems.

Our goal should be to teach the new analyst not to structure an issue analysis merely to fit a "pet" technique in his kit-bag, but to reduce it to those few significant variables upon which a decision could be based, and then to decide which one of the analytical tools most aptly fits the issue at hand. Expressing this point a bit differently, we need to give more emphasis to the problems of reducing real-life complexities to manage abstractions: why, how, when, where, and so forth.

The teaching of policy science should therefore include not only a firm grounding in techniques but a realistic assessment of how these techniques are really *apt* to be used, rather than how they ought to be. There should be a greater emphasis on how decisions are really made, not from the perspective of telling "war stories," but to place techniques in the context of living organizations, institutions, and individuals. Finally, more realistic case studies, role playing exercises, and internships will have to be set up to shorten the entrance shock of nonanalysts. In the end, the two things which will have the most impact will be better qualified teachers of policy science and—the most valuable teacher of all—experience.

Setting up a Policy Shop

Having made some suggestions on what should be done to improve the teaching of policy analysis, let us turn to a description of how such analyses should be carried out in the public sector. A better understanding of how a policy analysis group should be organized and operate might make it easier for those who teach or for those who are learning to relate the technical details of analytical methods to actual performance. Unfortunately, even here the real world refuses to yield to the neatness one might desire when describing how such analyses are performed.

In truth, I might be judged guilty of what I have accused others of, namely, describing what ought to be rather than what is. My only defense is that many policy operations are a mix of all of the functions I will describe. My exposition, therefore, is primarily to improve understanding and to suggest directions for future improvements. Sketched here is what I believe is necessary, in an institutional sense, to operate an effective policy analysis group or shop. At the outset, to be highly effective, policy analysis has to be performed by a captive in-house group, augmented as required by outside specialists in particular areas. There should also be those within the organization who at least keep up with, if not produce, new methods and new data sources, or else a policy shop becomes intellectually bankrupt and outdated relatively quickly. In general, there are at least three levels of effort required in an effective policy shop: policy analysis, impact assessments, and methods and data research. Let us examine these levels more closely.

- *Policy Analysis:* The analytical group should be almost totally involved with identifying and analyzing issues and producing the responses, briefings, and reports which communicate their work to decisionmakers. The group should be fully engaged in issue analysis and yet have a large enough staff to enable a sufficient division of labor, with experts in the various discipline areas that must be covered to adequately serve the policy level.

  Much of their time will be spent keeping abreast of the continually changing public policy climate, attending meetings, participating in task forces, and reporting on issues of concern to the policymaker. They are constantly communicating, either orally, in formal briefings, or in writing. Their expertise allows them to respond to simple queries on policy issues efficiently, although this is clearly not the most exciting part of their job. They prepare issue papers that consist of a statement of the issue, a paragraph on background, several alternative actions that could be taken, an analysis of the impacts of these alternatives, and a timetable for action.

  Finally, the policy analyst is expected to prepare comprehensive reports on major current issues, examining the issue in-depth. Although most of the work to prepare these studies could be handled by an analyst (given sufficient time), in practice it often is not the case. Even if analysts are experts in the area, they often have to seek help, which can range from requesting information from a colleague to contracting for the preparation of background papers and the assemblage of pertinent data. Further, issues have an unpredictable flare-up factor; controversy or interest in an issue may become so intense that the analyst is unable to keep up with the output demanded. The analyst, however, is held responsible for preparation of the analyses and presentation of the findings, regardless of the sources of the information used in the analysis.

The individuals who make up policy groups are usually motivated less by the drive to make professional contributions than by being in on the decisionmaking process. They build up a network of analysts and other contacts in a variety of other organizations, realizing that this network is an essential element in their efficient response to a broad range of issues.

- *Assessment:* Longer term, incisive impact assessments should be obtained in another section of a policy shop. Staff in the assessment group have the responsibility for carrying out the more complex in-depth analyses which are the essential grist for the policy analyst. At times, assessments force issues into the open. A well-reasoned, documented assessment can bring to light an issue not currently under consideration and focus it for the policy analyst to consider. Topics chosen for assessment require experience, sensitivity, and a degree of clairvoyance. Ideally, no assessment would be undertaken unless it was in support of a policy analysis. However, because the analyst often suffers from shortening of vision (policy myopia being an occupational hazard) brought on by the brushfire realities of the job, and because there is a purposely defined mismatch between the time lines of policy analysis and impact assessment, the interaction of policy needs with assessment outputs is frequently charged with serendipity. Although continual communication between the policy and the assessment groups is needed, this is less likely to focus on specific assessments than on sensitizing the assessment people to the form and content of an assessment that is to contribute to a relevant policy issue.

Assessments can be large interdisciplinary projects taking weeks or even years to complete and requiring a considerable expenditure of resources, or they can be short enough to feed directly into the policy stream. The output of assessment work generally has a wider audience than that of the policy analyst.

Whether the people who work in the assessment shops actually prepare assessments is a question of style and workload. It would be my preference to have those who manage specific assessments also to publish in the same area. Directors of government policy shops are readily aware that manpower shortages can often reduce the staff to contract managers. If the professional contract managers also do research, however, the continual development of their talents has several obvious advantages. These researchers command greater respect from the people who are performing contract work for them. There is also less chance of shoddy, poorly reasoned work sliding by, both because the research manager is more apt to be on his professional toes and because the contractor is apt to sense this, too. If the assessments manager is a recognized expert in a relevant field, he is also an asset not to be overlooked by the policy analyst who is often searching for experts with whom to consult.

One important function of the assessment group is to act as a repository of methods, data, and information that have been used in previous studies or that is being developed or researched. The availability of previous works, new and improved methods, and data resources means not only that the capability to respond rapidly to policy issues is enhanced, but that the quality of such response is improved with each new assessment adding to the knowledge base.

- *Research:* Few areas receive more theoretical attention and lead to less skilled application than policy research. Because resources are always scarce and the rewards from research distant and uncertain, the natural tendency, short-sighted as it may be, is to undercut research and focus on more pressing and immediate matters. If policy-oriented research is tied to the policy shops and if the projects undertaken satisfy policy needs or assessment requirements anticipated in the future, then the research has a high potential for immediate and longer-range payoff. Most of the research in an active policy shop ought to be directed toward methods development, data manipulation, or aimed at insights into comparative analysis, presently a difficult field to quantify for complex issues.

CONCLUDING REMARKS: SETTING UP A POLICY SHOP

The symbiosis suggested by melding the three areas of policy analyses, assessment, and research into one shop has obvious and significant benefits. Its greatest danger is that all the groups will be drawn into fighting brushfires. The opposite problem of having the activities focused on research projects is not as great in an active shop, but cannot be ignored.

One method of handling these problems is to place these requirements in separate units of the organization, based on the strategy that the functions require different skills and that their separation is therefore logical. On the other hand, by some mixing of staff from the different units on specific projects, the dangers of overspecialization is minimized and individual analysts are able to do some intellectual dabbling in order to keep their skills sharp. Unfortunately, no single approach will fully overcome the inherent organizational barriers to cooperation among separate units in a policy shop.

I have attempted to address some of the current shortcomings in the practice and teaching of public policy analysis and to suggest ways to achieve more productive and effective analyses through changes in these practices. Since highly trained people are involved in public policy analysis activities, both inside and outside of the government arena, there exists an excellent opportunity for preparing young analysts for the type of public policy work they are most apt to engage in. The result could be that the initial work they produce is more useful, and the disappointment and disillusion they now tend to experience would be much reduced. A few steps have been indicated toward more honest teaching and organization which could minimize the wasted talent and productivity. In the end, the big gainer is the public, which will get the quality of analysis that it feels it is currently paying for.

Specific Attempts at Institutionalizing Policy Methodologies

Moving from the generalizations which started this chapter, I want to delve into a few specific attempts to improve the art of policy analysis per se. The first section made some suggestions as to how one might go about teaching policy analysis. These directions may take some time to effect, particularly in the schools which are more traditionally based. The section on setting up a policy shop may or may not take place in the organization of the future and may or may not be properly classified as a longer-run modification. It depends upon the organization and the policy leaders in that organization. The next section is an attempt to specify improvements that might be used to improve analysis in the resource areas of the public sector—specifically, incorporating improved regional perspectives at the federal level.

The introduction of human inputs and the cumbersome ways people organize and interact with each other means that negotiation and compromise must be factored into the rigidity of analyses. Ofttimes, the policy level does not have the luxury of such time, as we have already noted. In Chapter 3 I suggested that the analytic tools are wanting. Is there any technique that can be useful for resource analysis that has not been reviewed thus far? For the next several pages, I shall look at such a concept and one that appears, at first examination, to be very suitable for resource-based policy analyses: carrying capacity.

Growth and Carrying Capacity: The Evolution of a New Paradigm[1]

Virtually every system in the world today, natural or man-made, is faced with problems of accommodating some degree of future growth and development. The evolution of our current demographic structure in the United States, for example, is the result of a variety of powerful economic and resource factors. This growth has at times strained local resources and resulted in a deterioration of local conditions. Many strains can be exemplified by the way we have handled our waste products. This waste, especially when relatively excessive, is referred to as pollution.

If pollution can be simply described as having too much of a substance at a particular time in a particular place, it becomes obvious how the high density of people in a specific place would increase the likelihood of such a condition. The failure to consider the finite assimilative capacity of the environment leads to excessive use or congestion of the natural systems and an overloading of its carrying capacity.

CARRYING CAPACITY AT A CONCEPTUAL LEVEL

The concept of carrying capacity developed historically in connection with the study and description of the growth and dynamics of natural populations. Because of this origin, the term is generally understood to mean the population limit of a species in a given ecosystem or regional habitat.

The earliest popular description of this term as related to human population was by Malthus in the nineteenth century and may be expressed in exponential form as

$$N(t) = N_o e^{kt}, \qquad [1]$$

where N is population size at any time, t, N_o is the initial population, k is the growth rate per time period, and t is time in appropriate units. This growth model approached no upper bound or population limit, but continues to grow at accelerating rates until catastrophe occurs.

This equation was designed to describe the change in the size of natural populations which are both in contact with one another and that have an upper bound on population density. This upper bound on population density was called the population carrying capacity (K) and was thought to be the result of density-related negative feedback, caused by such things as resource shortages, disease, or predation triggered by high population density.

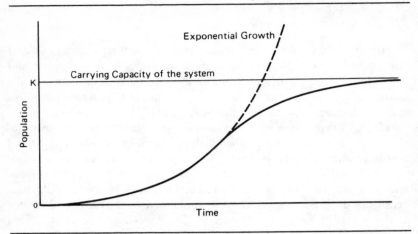

Figure 6.1 Population growth

ECOSYSTEM PROPERTIES

If the concept of carrying capacity is to be useful, it must enable the analyst to assess and evaluate the impacts of various proposed certainties on environmental quality and other factors. This requires insight into and understanding of the behavior and interaction of ecological and human systems, the ways in which the health of support systems can be measured, and other changes monitored. If carrying capacity is framed primarily in terms of the ecosystem, then rendering it operational as a basis for policy analysis will require corresponding algorithms to be developed that are applicable to the human environment and to other interest areas, such as energy. An extremely important requirement to making this concept operational is to specify the limiting factors in an environment to human growth and development. A limiting factor, you will recall, is the requirement that is present to the minimum extent necessary to the needs of a species in a particular ecosystem.

The search for limiting factors when one discusses carrying capacity in human terms becomes somewhat problematical because man's culture and technology often allow him to adjust the ecosystem to redefine limiting factors. But man can usually only modify ecosystems for a limited period of time and in a relatively limited fashion. In the end, he is still subject to the global ecosystem's carrying capacities and the mobility of resources that can also act as limiting factors.

THE LINKS BETWEEN THE HUMAN SYSTEM AND THE ECOSYSTEM

An essential ingredient in the vitality of any system, human or otherwise, is that the limiting factors to growth within the ecosystem are not overused. If overuse occurs, the system suffers stress and undergoes change. Readjustment of the ecosystem to such stress can be accomplished in several ways. In the simplest case, the stress is only temporary and within a short period of time will return all of the system characteristics to the previous equilibrium. A more severe trauma may cause some redesign of the system characteristics, resulting in a new equilibrium state with some likely attendant adjustment to the relevant carrying capacity. In some cases, the trauma can be enough to severely damage the system, causing a sudden degeneration to a very different ecosystem equilibrium with much lower levels of carrying capacity. For example, if people depend too much on the use of any regional limiting factors for too long a period, they may produce a damage to the encompassing ecosystem— pollution of media, lower plant growth due to resource shortages, starvation, or too many domesticated nonfood animals. The limiting factors for human ecosystems are akin to the resources that technology and agriculture transform into man's products. They are not limited, however, to the more classical definitions of resources applied in manufacture, but include all limiting factors of an ecosystem that can be affected by man. Thus we must include as generalized resources the media of the ecosystem: air, water, and land; labor and capital; as well as crops, ores, and fuels.

The carrying capacity theme consequently becomes much more complex when applied to human activities. It seems clear that rather than defining carrying capacity as a certain level of population or some other point criterion, it must be defined in terms of a rather complicated function or set of functions, including a number of regional characteristics and economic parameters, and making explicit the possible trade-offs implicit in the definition. This requires a representation of the set of social trade-offs between the citizen's concept of, say, environmental quality and the degree to which that society desires or needs to utilize the production and assimilation capabilities of the natural environment. In examining the critical interrelationships between human and economic activity, we must be concerned with a number of resource limits and environmental factors that may act as constraints or dampening forces on the dynamic interaction of population growth, related socioeconomic activity, resource base, and the environment as an assimilator of waste. This simplified paradigm of carrying capacity is diagrammed in Figure 6.2.

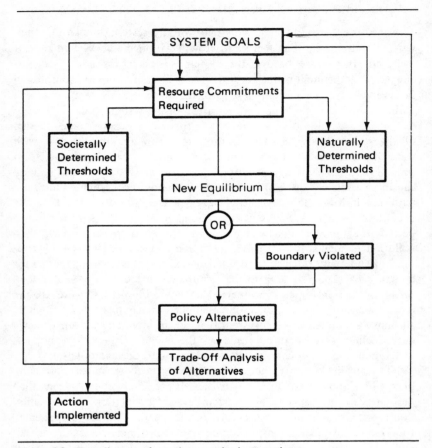

Figure 6.2 Flow diagram of carrying capacity in operation

If Figure 6.2 were a closed system, carrying capacity would be seen as the ability of the system to produce desired outputs (goods and services) from a given resource base while at the same time maintaining desired quality levels. For an open system, the definition would further have to allow for import of both resources and goods and services, and the export of output and residuals. The diagram yields four relationships that are relevant to the overall measurement of carrying capacity:

(1) Resource-production functions: the capacity of available resources to sustain rates of resource use in producing the system output.

(2) Resource-residual functions: the capacity of the environmental media to assimilate wastes and residuals from production and consumption certainties at acceptable quality levels.

(3) Infrastructure-congestion functions: the capacity of infrastructure and the distribution and delivery systems to handle the flow of goods and services and resources.

(4) Production-societal functions: the capacity of both resources and production outputs to provide acceptable quality of life levels.

Working from these four relationships, then, human carrying capacity is defined as the level of human activity that a region can sustain at acceptable "quality of life" levels.

The high degree of interrelation among resources, environmental media, and desired quantity and quality states for human and associated socio-economic activity underscores the fact that trade-offs must inevitably be made among desired production-consumption levels, resource uses, and a clean, healthy, and pleasant environment. From this perspective, carrying capacity must be interpreted as a variable socially determined within our understanding of economic, social, and environmental values and their relative contribution in maintaining acceptable quality of life levels. This dual perspective is required to give an operational meaning to the definition of carrying capacity. Figure 6.2 illustrates that the working use of carrying capacity definition requires a series of adjustments to reconcile the capacity limits related to quality levels of the natural environment and the desired levels of consumption of goods and services by society. Each set of decisions is tested for the availability of resources as well as against the natural and social thresholds of an area. If they pass, the plans proceed to implementation. If not, new policies must be promulgated and tested. If passed, these policies may actually adjust to the overall goals of the system.

As the foregoing discussions and examples indicate, description and analysis of environmental carrying capacity must be performed within properly identified and dimensioned domains. The domains of key concern are spatial and temporal. The problems arise in that the dimensions and boundaries of these domains in human environments do not neatly map onto or correspond with the dimensions in natural environments. This gives rise to the additional problem of making social and environmental trade-offs.

ENVIRONMENTAL-SOCIAL TRADE-OFFS

In summary, it seems clear that rather than defining carrying capacity as a certain level of population or some other point criterion, it must be defined in terms of a rather complicated function or set of functions which would include a number of regional characteristics and economic parameters, and that would make explicit the possible trade-offs implicit in the definition. The adjustments between future desires or social capacities and resource capabilities in operationalizing the normative definition of carrying capacity are partly technical questions where analytical models can usefully be applied, and partly value questions where social and political mechanisms are required.

Some basic problems are likely to plague most efforts to base decisions on carrying capacity analysis. A recent article by Rice Odell[2] summarizes some of these limitations:

(1) Any identification of an area's carrying capacity or holding capacity is an invitation to use or fill that capacity.

(2) It is very hard to come by scientific and other data that are both reliable and refined.

(3) Since all regions are part of a larger, indeed global, system, a carrying capacity assessment limited to specific boundaries is apt to be arbitrary and inadequate.

(4) It is important to decide how long a given level of population, or of environmental quality, is to be maintained.

(5) The carrying capacity of a region is likely to be highly flexible.

(6) The ultimate drawback of the carrying capacity concept, perhaps, is its limited usefulness in making the ultimate land-use choices that are necessary—choices that must be framed not only in ecological terms but in social and economic terms as well.

For analyses of resource-based systems and policies attendant to them, carrying capacity just seems to make good sense. It is clear, though, that it will be very difficult to come up with the data to actually build a model as complex as such descriptions imply. The principle, however, seems to have conceptual utility. In fact, it has underlay several recent analyses done at the Department of Energy. These analyses were done at different levels, national and regional, and seem to demonstrate the widespread utility of this method of approaching a problem.

APPLYING THE PRINCIPLE: SYNTHETIC FUELS AS A CASE STUDY

The Bishops and Crawford study made reference to several earlier discussed models and studies which formally attempted to use the carrying capacity concept. But the basic principle is so general that almost any resource-related methodology that trades one variable off against another could be said to be making use of a form of carrying capacity analysis. Possibly this is an accurate description, though. For example, studies were done recently by DOE to see if there was sufficient carrying capacity at the national level to accommodate the synthetic fuels program proposed by the federal government. Later in the year, a more specified analysis was done to see whether the Piceance Basin in Colorado could carry the 400,000 BPD projected by the same nationally set goals. We will now examine these studies in some detail.

INTRODUCTION TO THE SYNTHETIC FUELS ISSUE

Possibly one of the more dramatic steps taken in recent times to deal with the energy problem has been the creation of the Synthetic Fuels Corporation in 1980. As a first phase, this institution expects to encourage the production of two million barrels per day of equivalent synthetic fuels, 400,000 of which will be from oil shale. In line with President Carter's 1977 Environmental and Energy Message, the production of energy is to be done in an environmentally acceptable fashion. Consequently, during the formulative stages of the proposal for a Synthetic Fuels Corporation, an important part of the analyses was the expected environmental impact. To look at this question, an interagency task force was formed. Here is a summary of its findings in the environmental area.[3]

Deployment of synthetic fuel facilities to produce gaseous and liquid products from coal, shale, and biomass of approximately 1.5 million barrels per day by 1995 appears feasible in terms of successfully resolving critical environmental constraints. This success assumes that most effective environmental control technologies and practices are applied in these new facilities, and that full utilization of operational monitoring information is made to identify and resolve unforeseen problem areas and uncertainties. The greatest areas of regulatory uncertainty concern impacts of yet-to-be-defined regulations. Such regulations include visibility, short-term nitrogen oxide ambient standards, extension of prevention of significant deterioration (PSD) regulations, hazardous waste standards, toxic product regulations, and occupational safety standards.

Any production level requires resolution of a number of institutional constraints, including permitting delays and the acceptability of the facility to the local populace. The greatest potential impediments for first-generation technologies include long time delays, facility size limitations, and local citizens' unwillingness to change the character of their community.

Since July 1979, the synthetic fuels program proposals of the Carter Administration have undergone significant modifications. The program year for which the development goal was to be reached has been changed from 1990 to 1995. The original goal for synthetic fuels was set at 1.5 million barrels per day by 1990; the later one, two million by 1995. The plan is now proposed to have two stages to ensure, among other things, better environmental protection: an initial stage emphasizing applied research and development, including environmental research, followed by a second stage that would accelerate deployment of those synthetic fuel technologies judged most ready for commercialization within environmental, health, and safety protection requirements. These program changes have significantly expanded the scope of technologies to be analyzed, and have assumed that the numerous environmental R&D efforts will be successful in solving principal health and safety concerns for technologies prior to the initiation of the second stage of the accelerated deployment plan.

Assuming that the most effective demonstrated environmental control technologies and management practices are applied to each process, the following supplementary findings were made:

(1) The locales potentially suitable for siting appear well distributed across the several major U.S. fuel resource areas. The 1995 technology deployment proposal of 1.5 million barrels per day appears feasible. This would require careful planning to resolve some environmental impediments, but no major exclusionary regulatory constraint is obvious at the moment. Those technologies that would be most susceptible to an absolute constraint are direct liquefaction processes (potential worker and public exposure to toxic and carcinogenic substances in wastes and products) and oil shale in situ conversion processes (potential for ground water contamination). Risk that environmental R&D programs cannot fully satisfy all existing and expected regulated control demands exists, but is deemed to be acceptable. Most of these risks should be identified by operational monitoring data by the mid-1980s, with appropriate control solutions made as the technology undergoes accelerated deployment in the second stage of the strategy. Consequently, the need continues for intermediate and long-term environmental, health, and safety monitoring of all technologies at all scales of development and commercialization, emphasizing data concerning equipment reliability, sources and extent of fugitive emissions, and the ultimate fate of solid waste compounds.

(2) Uncertainties in permitting process-times and institutional barriers appear to be resolvable at the program level. Site-specific impacts may influence local attitudes, preclude some locations, or cause significant size or process modifications; these cannot be assessed prior to site-specific feasibility and engineering studies.

(3) To foster the best control technology and engineering practices, detailed state-of-the-art environmental control guidelines and standards should be established as early as possible, and should be followed by monitoring activities and R&D strategies to support responsive upgrading of the control equipment and engineering practices. Some yet-to-be-defined regulations, if promulgated in their most stringent forms, appear capable of severely limiting a number of synfuel technologies. At the time of this assessment, these regulations include air quality emission control measures for visibility, changes in the original PSD regulations, extension of PSD limiting increments to other pollutants, short-term nitrogen oxide ambient standards, development of hazardous waste tests and regulations, toxic product regulations, and occupational safety standards. Because states are emerging as the primary environmental regulators, often with authority to prescribe more stringent standards than the Environmental Protection Agency, they may pose substantial constraints on siting alternate energy facilities in some parts of the country.

SCOPE OF ANALYSIS

For this analysis, each technology was reviewed in terms of known environmental problems that must be controlled, potential environmental impacts that require further characterization research, probable environmental control technologies, and determination of risk areas that may prove to be insurmountable by an environmental impacts control and mitigation plan. Environmentally and ecologically oriented legislation and regulations were also reviewed to determine probable implementation trends, the most likely future stringent form of the regulations, and the probable cumulative impact on synthetic fuel technologies. Because yet-to-be-defined regulations are perceived as the greatest impediment to accelerating private development, recent changes and trends were also noted.

Environmental impact analyses for probable coal and oil shale resource locales were carried out to see which regional concerns were most likely to affect technology deployments. These analyses combined and extended the separate technology and regulation analysis results discussed previously. Topic areas considered on a regional basis included air quality, water availability, water quality, community development, and ecological disturbance. Regional carrying capacity thresholds were defined to delineate limits to technology development.

TECHNOLOGY ANALYSIS

Technologies considered in the analysis were the conversion and supporting technologies for production of fluids from coal, oil shale, biomass, and urban wastes. Support industries included increased coal mining and product transport. In terms of major pollutants and resource demands, the large coal conversion and oil shale retorting plants do not produce water demands or air and water pollutants with hazard levels above those of known facilities. Therefore, major pollutant impacts in a locality can be expected to be of the same order of magnitude as those that have been studied in other major industrial facilities.

Trace pollutants are not well characterized or regulated for any industries. Some increased trace concentrations could exist in some synthetic products from coal and shale and may require product upgrading. Additionally, heavy distillate products from synthetics have demonstrated mutagenic activity and potential carcinogenic compounds. This is of particular concern for direct coal liquefaction heavy distillates that may require special transport considerations and special fugitive emission practices and production treatment.

In situ processes (both coal and oil shale) provide a potential for leaching and aquifer contamination; control processes require further study. Also, mining in the proximity of an in situ retort may require increased worker safety provisions and exposure characterization.

A major concern for surface oil shale processing is the high volume of shale that must be retorted and, when spent, disposed of. These wastes, if a portion is replaced in the mine area, could also lead to contaminant leaching. If the wastes are disposed of aboveground, large areas will be used, contours will be changed, and long-term revegetation may be untenable.

Coal mining and similar oil shale mining concerns will be increased. These deal primarily with worker safety and health; impacts on watercourses, especially after mine closing; and surface mine vegetation and local contour reclamation. Due to the size of the supporting mines for a large-scale conversion facility, site-specific ecological concerns can be aggravated.

Biomass alcohol production and residue collection can lead to erosion. The alcohol production facilities include some increases of air emissions (particulates) and water effluents (oxygen depletion). Urban waste processes must also control increased toxic trace air emissions.

REGULATORY ANALYSIS

Each major environmental and health regulatory area was analyzed to determine present and potential future impacts of deployment of the synfuel technologies. By applying stringent environmental controls and practices, the technologies appear to be able to meet current regulations. Areas of greatest uncertainty at the time were:

- Regulations to be promulgated but not yet defined. Of particular concern were visibility, short-term nitrogen oxides (NO_x), and modified and expanded PSD regulations of the Clean Air Act; hazardous waste regulations of the Resource Conservation and Recovery Act; product and byproduct process restrictions possible within the Toxic Substances Control Act (TSCA); and occupational safety standards and surface water and ground water protection regulations.
- Regulations not now anticipated that may arise from ongoing environmental monitoring and R&D activities that determine the existence of an unanticipated critical environmental problem. For example, in situ processes may be subject to possible regulation through the Safe Drinking Water Act. Direct liquefaction products have a potential for increased control because of TSCA concerns. Also, the handling and transport of highly aromatic heavy crudes and fuel oils will present special problems with respect to spill containment and cleanup requirements.

A major increased risk of the synthetic fuels program is that any accelerated deployment plan will lead to greater commitment of facilities, which may in turn meet unanticipated costs and time delays due to the need to redesign and/or retrofit control technologies, if and when an environmental problem results in a new regulation. In the extreme, a severe environmental problem not amenable to retrofitted controls could lead to abandonment of marginal facilities. While there is no risk-free solution to this uncertainty, one step that reduces the probability of a major unanticipated regulatory dislocation is for all regulatory and permit conditions to press for stringent, state-of-the-art control technologies and management practices based on data and information sources kept current for New Source Performance Standards (NSPS), best available control technology (BACT), lowest achievable emission rate (LAER), best available technology (BAT), and National Pollutant Discharge Elimination System (NPDES) rulemaking.

REGIONAL CARRYING CAPACITY

The carrying capacity approach was then implemented in the attempt to estimate whether there were sufficient sites available on which to locate the number of plants necessary to generate the level of synfuel production called for in the government's proposal. The factors studied to determine siting availability included: air quality, water quality and quantity, ecological, and socioeconomic.

To carry out the analysis, the nation was divided into five regions: Four Corners, Rocky Mountain, Appalachia, Northern Plains, and Midwest. Each of these in turn was analyzed in terms of typical plant size of 50,000 BPD. Its location was set within a radius of a hundred miles of a coal field of sufficient size to sustain a plant of this size for its lifetime.

Detailed air dispersion modeling of 50,000-barrel-per-day plants (typical size plant chosen for analysis) indicates that siting in PSD class II areas can be done within the PSD increment for SO_2 and TSP. Rough terrain areas may be an exception to this; resolution will require specific locale data and modeling. Because of these relaxed restrictions, the areas having no constraint (or having high siting ease) due to air quality considerations were numerous. This is especially true of eastern areas that are not in rough terrain.

WATER CONSIDERATIONS

In addition to physical flows, institutional constraints and opportunities and water quality were covered. Because of the difference in water usage and permitting procedures, the results for the western and eastern areas were different. In the West, physical water flows and the institutional aspects of water rights caused both regions to be somewhat constrained. Yet for the great majority of the Northern Plains Area and for the oil shale areas, the constraint was judged moderate or less. In the coal areas of the Four Corners/Rocky Mountain resource area, more restrictive siting constraints were noted.

In the two eastern regions, the great majority of areas had little or no water constraints. However, when constraints did exist (south central

Illinois, eastern Kentucky, southeast Ohio), they were considered more severe than for the Western locales and were primarily due to water quality.

The constraint analysis was not undertaken in a simple-minded go/no-go fashion. As we discussed in the conceptual section on carrying capacity, human technology and institutions can often augment nature's assimilative capabilities. Few, if any, areas can be thought of as absolutely limited from an air or water availability sense, but some locations may be either so expensive to make usable or so difficult institutionally or organizationally to realize their availability that these sites are effectively unavailable.

Other variables are also important for locating large synfuel facilities in various areas across the country. One might be called socioeconomic, the other ecological. The socioeconomic carrying capacity is largely determined by an area's ability to raise the financial wherewithal to build and support the public sector infrastructure for the incoming populace. The ecological measure is a more complex composite index of wildlife and habitat factors suggesting the resiliency of an area to synfuel-type activities.

In the Northern Plains Area, the low population density throughout the coal resource area indicates that potentially adverse boomtown impacts appear to be the greatest constraint (although the area is also judged to have ecological constraints) that would slow growth. In the Four Corners/ Rocky Mountains area, ecological criteria appear to be a common constraint, especially in Colorado. Ecological concerns were judged to be so pervasive in this area that over 85 percent of the area was placed in the highest constraint category. This suggests that there may be a need for increased consideration of alternative sites for individual facilities and detailed site reclamation determinations. A lesser constraint factor is boomtown considerations; however, this factor will impact most development locales.

In the Mideast, prime agricultural areas and urban sites are the most prevalent secondary impact causes. For Appalachia, ecological concerns play an increased role, together with urban locales.

This macro-level carrying capacity analysis could not, under any definition, be called a model or formal analytical technique. On the other hand, it clearly is a recognizable approach to analyzing the policy issue at hand. The technique applied to arrive at the estimate of each of the area's carrying capacities for each of the studied variables was very different. Further, several judgment calls had to be made, meaning that the resultant findings were often subjective. The biggest drawback was that the analysis was quite broad-based. Later in the same year that this analysis was done, hearings were being held on the potential for oil shale development in the Piceance Basin, Colorado. Again, a rudimentary carrying capacity paradigm was used to perform the analysis.

SYNFUELS AND OIL SHALE:
A SECOND CASE STUDY

In the summer of 1980, a Senate Budget subcommittee headed by Senator Gary Hart held hearings in Colorado to ensure that there was consensus on the feasibility of producing the Piceance Basin's share of the proposed 400,000 BPD in an environmentally acceptable fashion. The hearings were prompted by a recent study done by Exxon which suggested that:

> Considering the readiness of technology, size of resource base, and financial capabilities of the private sector, a goal of meeting the potential synthetic fuels demand of 15 million barrels per day by 2010 would be highly ambitious—but not beyond achievement by a determined America.

> The output of a cost effective 15 million barrel per day industry would include some eight million barrels per day of shale oil.

Senator Hart was interested in ascertaining if the carrying capacity of the Piceance Basin was sufficiently great to sustain such an industry size. A number of interesting things were discovered while researching that question. The analyses were focused on capacity issues related to air quality, water availability, and the negative socioeconomic impacts that might occur.

A peculiar historical trend of analyses was noted in each of the areas. For the air quality and water availability areas, we saw better estimates concerning carrying capacity as the availability of data and quality of analytical methods improved over time. In addition, an upward revision in the oil shale production carrying capacity level which the Piceance Basin could support was also observed. In the socioeconomic area, a similar trend was noted. The estimate given will most likely continue to narrow as more is learned about the production technologies and the geographic area over time. Our current socioeconomic impact assessment methods and data, however, are not as reliable as those of the first two areas, and such trends were not noted.

OIL SHALE: AIR CARRYING CAPACITY

A number of studies conducted since 1976 have examined the air quality impact of oil shale. At first glance, several of these reports appear to be considerably contradictory; some say there can be essentially no significant oil shale development, while others predict the potential for a substantial industry. A closer examination of these reports suggests an interesting hypothesis. Early estimates, based on whatever information was available, tended to be conservative. As the body of information on oil shale has grown over time, these conservative assumptions have been modified, usually yielding higher projections for the size of the industry. Another important factor is that generally, the focus of these reports has been to identify the impact of a single plant or an assumed level of development (e.g., 200,000 barrels per day) rather than to determine the maximum level of development possible (i.e., a more traditional carrying capacity measure) due to air quality regulatory constraints. This means there is likely to be a range of estimates, none of which, however, is aimed at the maximum carrying capacity of a region. A brief review of these studies is informative.

A 1976 report for the Energy Research and Development Administration gave perhaps the lowest estimate for oil shale development when it stated, "control levels beyond the best available technology will be needed for particulate and SO_2 emmissions from synthetic liquid fuel plants." Using the TOSCO II process as a prototype, the study noted a single 100,000 barrel per day plant could not be sited without a significant reduction in particulate emissions and a marginal reduction in SO_2 emissions.

DOE published studies in July 1979 and June 1980 on synthetic fuels. The 1979 study concluded that "air quality considerations would not preclude construction of judiciously sited and efficiently controlled" oil shale technologies, up to the 400,000 barrel per day Administration proposal. The 1980 study also concluded that the 400,000 barrel per day level was practical from an air quality perspective. No upper limit was determined.

Several EPA papers have also examined the air quality impacts of oil shale development. A 1976 memorandum, originating in EPA's Denver Office, stated a 200,000 barrel per day capacity was feasible. A November 1979 analysis based on the Colony and Union oil permit applications also identified 200,000 barrels per day as acceptable. In a paper presented this past spring in Golden, Colorado, officials of this same office raised the estimate to 400,000 barrels per day. These limits were projected as due to PSD I areas.

A draft report of another EPA/Region VIII study concluded that about an 850,000 barrel per day capacity could be sited (due to the PSD Class II increment for particulates). Finally, in his July 17, 1980 testimony before Senator Hart, the office projected air quality constraints starting at the 1.1 million barrel per day level (due to ozone). Based on the earlier EPA analysis (Spring 1980), the Office of Technology Assessments stated that the Clean Air Act "could limit production in Colorado to 400,000 barrels per day." A summary of the outcome trend of these reports is presented in Table 6.1.

One should be careful not to read too much into the apparent trend these projections present. They can indeed be seen to represent a shifting opinion as to how much capacity can be safely sited, but curve extrapolation is not justified, as explained below.

Several factors probably contributed to the increase in siting capacity projections. First, and probably most important, is the fact that in 1976, when these projections started, oil prices were too low to allow synthetic fuels to compete successfully in the marketplace. Therefore, interest centered on the feasibility of one or two demonstration plants, not an entire industry. Projections at that time, and to a lesser extent at later times, reflected the authors' opinion that *at least* (not at most) a certain capacity could be sited. Second, the technology has evolved in two directions. Both controls for specific shale technologies have improved, and inherently cleaner, second generation shale oil technologies have entered the projections. These improving technologies, however, may not continue to evolve at the same rate. A third area of change, which is likely to continue changing with time, is modeling practices. The oil shale areas are typically located in irregular terrain, the most difficult to model. The actual areas have been modeled differently in several studies. Development of better models will likely occur over the next few years, and this will affect the capacity deemed acceptable.

A third category of factors which have varied over time could perhaps best be termed "details." After the major decisions are made concerning what process will be modeled, what control technology will be assumed, and what model will be employed, a number of less conspicuous assumptions must be made. These include the source of power for the facility, the "cleanliness" of fuels burned on-site, the height of emission stacks, the ducting arrangements (minor air emission streams can be combined and emitted through a single stack), the plant configuration, and terrain assumptions.

TABLE 6.1   Summary of Air Quality Studies

1976 (ERDA)

o   Based on TOSCO II
o   PSD Class II limits for PM
o   Controls beyond BACT needed to allow a single 100,000 BPD facility

September 1979 (EPA)

o   Based on extrapolation of first permits
o   Flattops PSD I SO_2 is limiting factor
o   200,000 BPD

Spring 1980 (EPA)

o   Based on EPA short-range models and announced plans
o   Flattops PSD I SO_2 is limiting factor
o   At least 400,000 BPD

June 1980 (EPA)

o   Based on long-range puff models and extended plans
o   PSD II TSP may limit industry size
o   But Flattops PSD I also close to limit
o   At least 890,000 BPD

July 1980 (EPA)

o   Extrapolated from June data and announced plans
o   Ozone in first size limitor for health NAAQS
o   Colorado development limits due to NAAQS are:

        —— Ozone/0.9 million BPD
        —— NOx/3.1 million BPD

    due to PSD I are:

        —— SO_2/1.7 million BPD
        —— TSP/5.4 million BPD

Given all of these variables, it is remarkable, I believe, that the recent projections from different government organizations have been as close as they appear. Although air quality modeling is as much art as science, and is inherently inaccurate, it is the best tool we have to predict future impacts of plants and prevent degradation of our air resources.

In summary, over the past four years various studies have predicted that sitable oil shale capacity using best available air pollution control technology could range between less than 100,000 barrels per day to over 1 million barrels per day. The trend, with respect to time, is toward a larger projected carrying capacity.

WATER AVAILABILITY

The issue of water availability for oil shale development in Colorado is also a complex one because it too is a function of so many different parameters. To compound the issue even further, as important as the purely physical aspects of water availability are, the institutions governing the allocation, storage, and distribution of water resources are often even more telling.

In the long term, availability is a function of average annual surface flow and ground water that can be recharged, less that amount of water which is currently being utilized, demands set by lower Basin rights, and all projected future energy and nonenergy demands in the Upper Colorado basins. Long-term availability is not the only consideration necessary for a determination of water availability, since oil shale facilities require a continuing water supply during low flow as well as high flow conditions. For this reason, short-term or instantaneous supply is a function of unallocated surface flow, drawn from impoundments and reservoirs and ground water, less existing demands, lower basin rights, and a factor to allow for inability to redistribute water from impoundments.

Addressing each of these individual features which, taken together, will ultimately determine the net availability of water for oil shale development in Colorado, will require information from numerous studies. Several such studies already exist. The most current and complete are those of the Colorado Department of Natural Resources, including its section 13(a) assessment.

WATER REQUIREMENTS FOR OIL SHALE

The first key factor I will discuss is water requirements for oil shale. I believe that there still exists in some quarters a common misconception that there is not enough water to support energy development in the West. This issue is addressed in a study sponsored by DOE/EV and completed in 1979, titled "Predicted Costs of Environmental Controls for a Commercial Oil Shale Industry," and is often cited in other comprehensive assessments such as the Office of Technology Assessments report of June 1980, referred to in the air section above. The range of water requirements for four different oil shale technologies in that study was: Paraho Direct, 5,346 acre feet/year; Tosco II, 10,694 acre feet/year; Modified In-Situ (MIS), 5,817 acre feet/year; MIS with Lurgi, 5,656 acre feet/year. These reductions in estimated water requirements hold true for other synthetic fuel technologies, and are a result primarily of (1) projecting more extensive use of dry cooling, which uses air rather than water, and (2) increased recycling and reuse of waste and process waters.

Therefore, the corresponding water requirements for a 500,000 barrel per day oil shale industry, including associated municipal growth, could range from less than 50,000 acre feet/year to upwards of 100,000 acre feet per year. As a comparison, current use by irrigated agriculture in the state of Colorado is approximately 1,200,000 acre feet per year, out of total state of Colorado depletions of 1,800,000 acre feet per year from the Upper Colorado River.

WATER SUPPLY

One of the reasons that water availability for oil shale development is a concern to people in this region, and to the Department of Energy as well, is that the West is a relatively arid region. Although the Colorado River basin is large in area, its flow is relatively small, averaging 13.8 million acrefeet between 1930 and 1974, compared, for example, with the much greater flows of the Columbia and Mississippi Rivers of 180 million and 440 million acre feet, respectively.

In addition, flows vary seasonally, being quite high during the spring snowmelt. These flow variations, which become most critical when the low flow cannot meet all needs, have necessitated the construction of reservoirs or impoundments to mitigate or dampen seasonal fluctuations, and to augment natural supplies during dry years. A number of reservoirs have been built in the region by the Water and Power Resources Service (WPRS), formerly the U.S. Bureau of Reclamation. Table 6.2, from the GAO report, lists some of these reservoirs in energy resource areas which could supply future water allocations to oil shale and other energy developments with their industrial allocations.

Indeed, the construction of additional impoundments in the oil shale region is one of the key assumptions made by the Colorado Department of Natural Resources in their recently completed draft assessment of water-for-energy for the Water Resources Council. This study, funded by the Department of Energy, pursuant to section 13(a) of the Federal Non-nuclear Research and Development Act, and titled "The Availability of Water for Oil Shale and Coal Gasification Development in the Upper Colorado River Basin," addressed a hypothetical baseline scenario in the year 2000 of 1.3 million barrels per day of oil shale, 825,000 of which is to be sited in Colorado, and eight coal gasification plants (or a total of 1.5

TABLE 6.2   Selected Reclamation Reservoirs Located in Energy and
             Mineral Development Areas

Reservoir	Basin	Long-Term Industrial Allocation (acre-feet/year)
Ruedi	Upper Colorado	47,700
Fontannele	Upper Colorado	228,000
Navajo	Upper Colorado	115,250
Powell	Upper Colorado	142,000
	4 Reservoir Total	525,000

Source: GAO, CED-80-30

million barrels per day liquids-equivalent). It concluded that the water demands of such an industry and its associated growth could be satisfied from surface supplies without having to impact other projected consumptive uses in the Upper Basin.

This conclusion was based on a number of assumptions, the most important being that water is to be purchased from existing federal reservoirs and/or that new reservoirs, pipeline, and pumping facilities are to be built to store and transport the water. The study estimated the total capitalized cost of such facilities at $1 billion for a 1.5 million barrel per day industry, or 1 to 2 percent of the capitalized costs of the energy facilities proper. Most of this additional reservoir capacity would be located in the White River basin.

In some respects, this assessment can be considered conservative in its conclusions. The study also addressed an accelerated level of oil shale development of 2,400,000 barrels per day, 1,700,000 of which was to be in Colorado. The body of the report indicated that even this level of development might be accommodated with greater storage development and associated costs. In addition, the projected depletions by nonemerging energy technology uses are expected to increase from the current 3.8 million acre feet to nearly 5.4 million acre feet in the year 2000, and the study imposed strict conditions on the assumption that present uses need not be affected. These include a 500 percent increase in consumption by steam electric power and construction of all currently authorized irrigation projects by 2000. It also assumed no transfers of water rights from irrigated agriculture to oil shale, and assumed that all oil shale developers' water rights were junior to all other rights.

WATER RIGHTS

As we have said, water rights in Western states are, in general, based upon the prior appropriation doctrine, which in turn is based upon obtaining water rights from state engineers or water courts. In the Upper Colorado Basin, conditional water rights, many of which have not been put to use, far exceed the actual flow of the Colorado. I believe that this fact also contributes to the misconception that no water exists in the Basin, since so little of the claimed water is actually being used. In fact, unallocated surface water is available in some of the region, as indicated by a Colorado Department of Natural Resources (DNR) assessment.

Many potential oil shale developers have acquired relatively large holdings of water rights, either in the form of conditional decrees or purchased irrigation rights. The following table, from material gathered for the 1979 Environmental Protection Agency study, "Energy from the West," by the University of Oklahoma, shows estimated existing conditional water rights held by oil shale developers.

Existing Rights	*Estimated Quantity (arce feet/year)*
Colony	171,000
Union Oil	85,000
SOHIO	72,000
TOSCO	39,000
MOBIL	36,000
Superior	17,000
	420,000

Other options for obtaining water are purchase of surplus water from federal reservoirs and construction of new reservoirs, as indicated in the DNR assessment; interbasin transfers, which may be constrained by institutional problems; and the development of ground water supplies.

INTERBASIN TRANSFERS

Interbasin transfers, or diversions of water from one major basin to another, have often been mentioned or proposed as alternatives to increase local water supply. Indeed, diversions from the Columbia and Upper Missouri River Basins to the Upper Colorado have specifically been pointed out as potential suppliers of additional water to the oil shale area.[4]

Intrabasin diversions, or transferring water from one sub-basin in the Upper Colorado system to another (e.g., the Green River basin to the White River basin) are at least institutionally feasible. Such a diversion would be subject to provisions of the Upper Colorado Compact, especially with respect to state shares of river flow, and to prevailing conditions regarding water rights which may already exist.

GROUND WATER

It would be worthwhile to discuss the potential for industrial use of ground water in more detail. Most water availability assessments have limited the available water options to surface water. This is because, in general, not as much is known about ground water as surface flows, which can be easily measured. The Colorado DNR assessment pointed out that estimates of the amount of ground water in storage in the Piceance basin range from 2.5 million to 25 million acre feet. The amount of water which is discharged to surface streams, and recharged primarily by snowmelt, is estimated at from 26,000 to 29,000 acre feet per year. If only an amount equal to the recharge rate in the Piceance basin were developed, it could support as much as 250,000 barrels per day of oil shale development. In fact, mine drainage water in the central portion of the Piceance basin where the current federal lease tracts are located could produce from 6,400 to 18,000 acre feet per year for those two tracts alone.

The recent Office of Technology Assessment report, "An Assessment of Oil Shale Technologies," indicated that the quality of much of the stored water in the Piceance basin is so low (being high in dissolved solids and flourides) that its use for nonenergy purposes would not likely increase. It further estimated that if oil shale developers upgraded this ground water, and utilized 15 percent of the maximum 25 million acre feet, the aquifers alone could supply a 1 million barrel per day industry for 20 years. This rate of consumption would, however, exceed the recharge rate, and result in reduced surface flows in some streams in the Piceance basin. The Colorado DNR assessment indicates that ground water development would produce much less adverse impact on fish and recreation than relying on surface water use alone.

In summary, it appears that sufficient options exist for developing the water necessary for a sizable oil shale industry in Colorado. Uncertainties related to each of these options preclude the detailed identification of the size of an industry that could be supported by available water resources.

SOCIOECONOMIC IMPACTS OF OIL SHALE PRODUCTION

A common theme is evident within all the discussions during the testimony: that we are vitally concerned with the identification and management of environmental impacts associated with oil shale production. Analytical efforts in two of these areas, air quality and water availability, are well along toward specific identification and resolution of the magnitude of the problem. The third, direct and indirect socioeconomic impact, is not as well-defined in terms of the scope of the problem or mitigation requirements. Air and water impacts have been assessed using detailed deployment patterns and engineering specifications, while the financial and management initiatives required to provide adequate social service support need more in-depth analysis of the impacts related to the existing and new in-migrating population.

TYPES OF SOCIOECONOMIC IMPACT

There are two types of socioeconomic impact which need to be addressed. The first is sociopsychological in nature. Rapid growth of rural areas, especially when due to the introduction of high-technology industries, may alter the way in which residents view their community and its characteristics. Often, such growth results in changes in how residents interact with one another, decreases the levels of social control and quality of life, and creates conflicts between new and longtime residents. Social problems such as divorce, crime, drug abuse, and mental illness usually accompany such growth. These sociopsychological impacts are not simply associated with the construction phase of the new industry, but rather are problems associated with the transition to and maintenance of a growing urban area.

The second impact is a more direct result of rapid growth. It is the inability of local and state governments to design and fund an infrastructure mechanism which adequately supports the rapidly growing population. This problem is especially acute during the initial stages before adequate public revenues are generated by the operation of new facilities. Let us look at the magnitude of the problem. According to the oil shale study prepared by the Office of Technology Assessments, the population level for the Piceance Basin associated with a 500,000 per day oil shale industry in 1990 is 280,000; 107,000, or 60 percent, beyond the normally expected growth for the area expected prior to the accelerated energy technology development.

Both of these socioeconomic problems have common elements. Both have a related economic demand placed upon the local public sector. In both cases, up-front capital facilities are required within the geographic area, an area which currently has a minimum infrastructure support capability because of its rural nature. The population and economic behavior which we are discussing is not the classic "boom-bust" situation which has so often occurred in rural areas where a single large plant was added to a small community. Rather, it is a situation where we can expect rapid but continuing urbanization, with the industry base oriented toward expanding, and long-time use of the area resources. These socioeconomic impact problems are therefore cash flow problems associated with an initial low capital base availability to the local government. The ultimate concerns in the socioeconomic impacts area are what quantity and quality of infrastructure support should be provided to the growing population, and on what schedule. What is the associated cost and how can this cost be met?

THE IMPACT ASSESSMENT METHOD

The assessment method used to answer these questions requires estimates of variables related to population growth, employment, and area characteristics. The principal variable for these assessments is the technology mix and social deployment for the oil shale demonstration and production facilities. These parameters allow definition of the labor force required to construct and operate these facilities. Based upon the work force level, indirect employment can be estimated. Also associated with work force is an additional population sector which represents the families of these laborers. Once these parameters are estimated, usually through the use of appropriate multipliers, the level, timing, and cost of the required infrastructure can be estimated. These infrastructure costs can be met through direct revenue, subsidization, taxation, and/or bond sales.

The assessment method mentioned above is also influenced by the character of the geographic area within which the oil shale production industry is located. The size and makeup of the area's historic labor force will influence the level of indirect employment that must be met by new in-migrating workers. The physical topography of the area will affect the residential patterns of the growing population of new worker families, while the economic base of the area will also affect secondary employment generation and growth rate beyond initial unused capacity. Finally, the level of the existing infrastructure support and the level of excess capacity which may exist will influence decisions concerning expansion of the infrastructure system and its cost. For example, the Office of Technology Assessments study projects that the present and planned structure of the communities of the Piceance Basin can support an oil shale industry of approximately 133,000 barrels per day without assistance.

IMPACT STUDIES

There have been several studies which have attempted to examine the magnitude of the socioeconomic impact associated with the oil shale production industry within the Piceance Basin. A number of these are site- and single-plant-specific, examining the impact associated with a particular facility on a particular site. I have been unable to find a comprehensive assessment which examines the impact of all potential oil shale and energy development within that region and focuses on all elements of the analysis—that is, from technology deployment through definition of infrasturcture support cost. Nonetheless, it is possible to provide information which represents the most recent estimate of the socioeconomic impact for oil shale production within Colorado.

The federal government's current target for oil shale production is, as noted above, 400,000 barrels per day in 1990. The *construction* labor force required during the period 1980-1990, normalized to a 1990 production capacity of 400,000 barrels per day, has been estimated as 54,336 labor years of effort. The total estimated *operations* employment over the same period, again normalized at 400,000 barrels per day production, is 57,114 labor years of effort.

This increase in population due to in-migrating workers also stimulates other population and economic growth. There are a series of multipliers which are used to estimate this growth. These multipliers are related to: worker average family size; indirect employment generated; and infrastructure support cost. A wide range of multipliers have been used to estimate family size associated with these new workers. The multipliers found within related studies are as low as 1.2 and as high as 3.8. It is important to note that it may be especially appropriate to segregate estimated family size by the construction and operations phase. Construction workers and their families are often transients and do not establish permanent residence within the geographic area experiencing development. The average number of dependents per construction worker has been estimated as 1.2 per worker; that for operational workers as 2.4 per employee.

Secondary or indirect employment generated by the introduced oil shale industry is also represented by a range of multipliers. These multipliers are as low as 0.4 and as high as 2.0. Once again, as in the case of estimating associated family size, segregation of these multipliers for construction and operations is appropriate, and the range of multipliers that we have seen for both categories is coincidental with the range mentioned above.

Based upon the use of these data, the range of total 1990 population growth associated with oil shale production in Colorado has been from a low of 54,719 to a high of approximately 85,382 for a normalized 400,000 barrel per day case. One cost estimate for the related infrastructure support was prepared by the Colorado State government and represents the incremental per capita cost of infrastructure related to energy production of $4,725 per person. This falls within a commonly used infrastructure support cost range with which we have become familiar of $3,000 to $6,000 per person that studies of other areas have estimated.

FUTURE EFFORTS IN THE SOCIOECONOMIC AREA

The information presented above demonstrates that there is certainly a fairly significant range of specific conclusions concerning socioeconomic impacts associated with oil shale production. Of course, as we move through the demonstration phase to commercialization for the actual facilities, we will learn more about the technologies and their associated impacts; mitigation plans can then be refined.

It is likely that these uncertainty ranges will become smaller between now and 1990. There are several reasons why these data ranges are broad. First, the oil shale technologies are still in their embryonic stage, and we still have yet to learn specific data about their construction needs and operating characteristics, including associated employment. The various multipliers mentioned above should become more specific factors as more is learned about the technologies and the geographic area's reaction. The growth pattern which will be experienced will not be similar to the "boom-bust" situation which often accompanies the introduction of a single plant within a rural area, but rather will be one of rapid growth. As time passes, the exact patterns which we can use as a basis for forecasting will become evident.

The idea of carrying capacity as a conceptual paradigm can therefore once again be seen to have practical application, but cannot be billed as a formal methodology or technique as used here. In addition to the deficiencies already noted, this idea carries with it the notion of comprehensive analyses. Care will have to be taken that one does not succumb to this temptation, though. Besides information deficiencies already agreed to, there is policymaker resistance to techniques which could potentially tell us "too much." Years ago, a procedure called incrementalism was proffered as an alternative to systems analysis. The neat, sequential process suggested by this idea is very appealing to those involved in policy analysis. Let us take a short detour and review it again here before we return to our efforts with carrying capacity constructs.

INCREMENTALISM: AN ALTERNATE APPROACH?

Anyone who has been a participant in the process of initiating change in the public sector knows that to get any sort of cooperation as consensus (or alternatively, not to anger everybody), or to do a complete and comprehensive analysis starting from scratch (rather than whatever the present situation happens to be), is hopeless. As such, there is no other possible action than sequential, small-stage policy implementation. Change (outside of revolution) is incremental not so much because that is the best way to proceed, but because most of the time, it is the only way. Recently, Charles Lindbloom, recalled in an article entitled "Still Muddling, Not Yet Through,"[5] the concept he made popular over a decade ago—incrementalism—by defining it through different levels of incremental policy analysis:

(1) Analysis that is limited to consideration of alternative policies all of which are only incrementally different from the status quo. Call this simple incremental analysis.
(2) Analysis marked by a mutually supporting set of simplifying and focusing strategems of which simple incremental analysis is only one, the others being those listed in my article of 20 years ago; specifically:
   a. limitation of analysis to a few somewhat familiar policy alternatives;
   b. an intertwining of analysis of policy goals and other values with the empirical aspects of the problem;
   c. a greater analytical preoccupation with ills to be remedied than positive goals to be sought;
   d. a sequence of trials, errors, and revised trials;
   e. analysis that explores only some, not all, of the important possible consequences of a considered alternative; and

    f. fragmentation of analytical work to many (partisan) participants in policy making.

This complex method of analysis I have called *disjointed incrementalism.*

(3) Analysis limited to any calculated or thoughtfully chosen set of stratagems to simplify complex policy problems, that is, to short-cut the conventionally comprehensive "scientific" analysis.

In Quade's book,[6] he questions that systems analysis is to be preferred over incrementalism because:

(1) Incrementalism assumes that the costs of analysis and delay (the costs of delaying action, that is, not necessarily the costs of delaying a "solution") are greater than the costs of error; systems analysis tends to assume the opposite.

(2) Systems analysis is more likely to act on the notion of "integrity of design," that is, the systems analyst can be expected to sometimes say, "The consequences of such and such a compromise are likely to defeat the major intent of the program, so if that compromise is a condition of its acceptability, it's better to have no program at all."

(3) The soul of systems analysis fosters foot-in-the-door techniques, that is, commitment to beginnings without much consideration to total costs and benefits should the foot stay in the door nor to the costs of reneging on what looked like a commitment if the door should be slammed shut.

We hold that this response is typical of the systems analyst and again makes clear his fundamental argument of reality versus analytic response to policy.

Throughout this work, I have tried to make clear that there is some argument as to whether systems analysis is necessarily better than an incremental approach. There is also some warranted skepticism as to whether a highly sophisticated systems analysis of most situations requiring policy determinations is even possible. A recent book by James E. Anderson, titled *Public Policy-Making,* makes a similar point.[7] He defines three theories of decisionmaking—Rational-Comprehensive, Incrementalism, and Mixed Scanning. The Rational-Comprehensive theory is the systems analysis technique we have been discussing; Incrementalism is as described above. His feeling is that modern day analysis has to be a mix of the two, but generally, he says analysis techniques are too primitive for general utility and they certainly do not warrant the adulation given them by their proponents. Consequently, their use in any form should engender caution.

Similar doubts may be voiced about the potential for designing and building a formal carrying capacity model. As we noted earlier, thresholds in human systems are not as well-defined as in the plant and animal communities. Many times they are set by laws or other institutional means. At best, carrying capacity may be the basis for a process that makes use of a logic and data base. This is the philosophy behind PASS, the Policy Analysis Screening System. The use of such a data-based information system recognizes the incremental nature of the policy process and permits a mining of the information for use by the policy analyst as he addresses a specific issue. Let me turn to this method now.

A POLICY INFORMATION SYSTEM: PASS

The idea that there is some standardized way to perform policy analysis appears naive to those who actually perform such analyses. By the time the questions of who the analysis is being performed for, the time available, the resources and information at hand, and the location of the analysis unit are addressed and melded with the political situation at hand, it becomes easier to understand why policy analysis is more often thought of as an art than a science. It is not the purpose of this section to dwell on the difficulties of doing policy analysis in a rapidly changing political environment in order to conclude that no routinization is possible; on the other hand, it is equally hard to believe that every policy analysis situation is so unique that nothing can be done to anticipate the ever demanding requests for information from the policy level.

There is still considerable argument about what should be the measurement of success or legitimacy of a particular policy. The economic community has convinced several policy analysts that the proper measure is the ratio of the costs of a specific policy or program to its benefit. Regardless of how attractive this simple display appears to be, there has historically been a great deal of difficulty with measuring (as we noted in Chapter 3) the benefits as accurately as the costs. The difficulty with measurement, however, does not excuse the analyst from doing the best possible job of comparing the various costs (monetary, resource, environmental, employment, and so forth) with what is being purchased for that cost (cost effectiveness analysis). The principal difference between the two techniques is that the successful cost/benefit analysis speaks to the full efficacy of a decision or set of decisions; cost effectiveness merely measures how much of a particular measurable output is purchased per amount of money spent.

Rather than dwelling on the methods, let me instead turn directly to examples of policy analysis done by the Office of Environmental Assessments to see if these experiences will help us to develop a paradigm for more rigorous and routine assessments in the future. In the earlier section, we looked closely at a national policy issue concerning the creation of a Synthetic Fuels Corporation. We also looked at a regional issue in our review of the analyses done of the carrying capacity of the Piceance Basin. To round these out, I have chosen a local issue—conversion of oil-burning plants to coal. The local decision chosen relates directly to the interruption in Iranian oil exports following the fall of the Shah.

In response to the Iranian oil curtailments, 11 power plants located along the East Coast were identified for immediate possible conversion from oil to coal. The total fuel use of these plants is equivalent to about 128,000 barrels of oil per day. (The projected potential oil savings for these plants after conversion has been identified as 90,000 barrels/day; one or two plants would not be converted.) Because the location of the plants was near major population centers, an analysis of the impact of these oil-to-coal conversions on air quality was performed by the Office of Environment. The findings were:

- All but one of the 11 plants are located in counties having *officially designated nonattainment areas* for SO_2 and/or TSP (6 for primary standards, 4 for secondary standards).
- A review of *actual air quality data* shows primary TSP standards are exceeded near every plant and primary SO_2 standards are also exceeded near 3 of the plants.
- A first order calculation of potential ambient impact of the plants indicates that each can significantly aggravate existing air quality problems unless controlled by high efficiency particulate matter control equipment (i.e., ESPs with 95-99% efficiency).
- In view of these facts, EV provided the following conclusion:

> The estimated oil savings from these 11 potential oil to coal conversion plants of 90,000 B/D (without environmental considerations) would actually tend toward zero when environmental considerations are taken into account. This is because *all* of the potential coal conversion facilities, if converted, could lead to violations of primary health standards, without stringent pollution control equipment.

Again, for this analysis the components are much the same as for the national analysis. The analyst looked at the assimilative capacity of the regions; the regulations, particularly the Clean Air Act; and finally, the technology was examined in terms of the expected energy impact of the policy.

There is enough of a thread of similarity among the analyses (regardless of the scope of the issue) to suggest that there may be a way of reducing the technique to a routine to enrich future assessments. In the next section, we shall define such a process.

A Design for Policy Analysis Support: PASS

As a first step in the design, let us generalize the types of questions normally addressed by an environmental impact analysis of an energy policy.

Case one: For a particular technology or mix of technologies, comment on the potential environmental insults of development according to a specified deployment schedule. (Table 6.3)

Case two: For a particular area of the country (e.g., state, air shed, river basin), comment on the feasibility of locating a given energy complex in the area.

Case three: For a set of proposed environmental, health, or safety regulations, comment on their impacts on energy policy and programs.

Case four: For a scenario of national energy/economic futures, provide an environmental assessment.

If the same group of people repeatedly perform all of these types of analyses, surely they develop a style, using a consistent data base. Let us now reduce this process to its essence.

To perform this analysis really only requires that one knows information about four general variables: the controlling scenario (the context), the environmental health and safety regulations (the institutional boundaries), the state of the physical environment (the physical boundaries), and the description of the technologies of interest (the change stimulus). These four variables interact in a relatively straightforward fashion to provide the resulting answers to the environmental/energy issues in question. The form of the assessment will depend on which of the four variables becomes the independent one, but the general logic and information base will remain pretty much the same. Let us look at these four variables in a little more detail, first looking at the conceptual basis for the kind of variables that should be collected and some rationale for how they might be used.

TABLE 6.3 Types of Policy Questions Faced in Energy Environment Analyses

	QUESTION FOR ANALYSIS	RELEVANT VARIABLES
Technology	Given a particular energy technology or mix of technologies, what are the environmental effects of commercializing it to a specified deployment schedule and how significant are they?	• The quality of the local *environment* within which the technology would be implemented • The existing or planned *regulations* that would impact on the technology • The energy/economic *scenario* under which the technology would by implemented
Environment	Given a locality (state, air shed, river basin), what is the feasibility of locating a certain type of energy facility there?	• The characteristics of the *technology* • The *regulations* pertaining to environmental quality in that locality • The energy/economic *scenario* chosen for that locality

Regulations

Given a set of proposed environmental, health and safety regulations, what energy programs are affected and how?

- The *technologies* impacted by the proposed regulation

- The current quality of the *environment* in the localities affected by the energy programs

- The relevant economic/energy *scenario* under which the regulations would be implemented

Scenarios

Given a scenario of national energy-economic futures, what are the environmental impacts?

- The energy outputs and environmental insults of the *technologies* included in the scenario

- The quality of the local *environment* affected by the scenario

- The existing or proposed *regulations*

THE PASS SYSTEM

The conduct of environmental energy trade-off analyses to support policy development has led us to define a set of typical problems taken from actual experience and to characterize the classes of the data used to support these analyses. We have found that all levels of policy analysis—from the simple answering of a letter to addressing complex national or global questions—result in our consideration of energy systems as constrained by regulatory or institutional impacts, with the measurement being made in terms of a set of regional environmental outcome projections. Additionally, we often find for the more complex questions that these results must be set in the context of an overall scenario to show whether this subject is a major or a minor impact as compared to other similar impacts over which there is regulatory or technological control. The PASS areas defined above have been standardized into a fast information retrieval system as a prototype. Even in these early stages, PASS is proving useful for rapid information collection and for setting the bounds on needed analyses in a day-to-day policy analysis environment.

The Policy Analysis Screening System (PASS) is a computerized information-retrieval system developed to support the analyses of the Department of Energy's Office of Environment. PASS provides rapid access to information needed for analyses of environmental issues and policies related to energy development and use. The Office of Environment has amassed a large and complex information base on energy technologies, environmental issues, and environmental and resource regulations. This information, including source documents and quantitative data bases, is now available through PASS.

The ability to obtain complete and accurate information quickly is essential because many requests require responses within days, and some within hours. Under this fast pace of operation, cumbersome methods of accessing and displaying information can leave too little time for interpreting and analyzing it. Furthermore, the danger exists that very recent data will be overlooked.

PASS is structured to meet information needs occurring within many analytical frameworks. Typically, an analyst who is looking at environment/energy trade-offs must consider issues from, as we have just said, four interrelated perspectives: (1) the energy *technologies* involved; (2) the applicable *regulations*; (3) the status of the *environment* in the geographic areas affected; and (4) the energy/environmental *scenarios* under which events are assumed to take place.

The need to consider so many factors requires analysts to seek information from a variety of sources. These include environmental evaluations of individual energy technologies; compilations of regulations issued by federal, state and local governments; statistics on environmental quality in various regions of the United States; and projections of future environmental quality under various energy scenarios. PASS makes this information available on a central computerized system for instantaneous access by many users simultaneously.

PASS contains executive and analytical summaries from many types of documents:

- Judgments on the environmental advisability of commercializing various energy technologies.
- Environmental research and development plans for the various technologies.
- Assessments of the regional environmental and socioeconomic impacts of future energy development.
- Comprehensive technology assessments addressing accelerated commercialization of various fuel cycles.
- Environmental regulation analyses.
- Environmental policy issue digests.

Numerical data bases have been extracted from technology characterization handbooks, environmental impact projections, energy supply and demand forecasts, regulatory status displays, and geographical pollutant emission summaries. Because the system is maintained on a large-scale computer with supporting visual display hardware, much of the tabular material can be rapidly extracted and summarized as tables or as graphics to highlight numerical analysis findings.

The designation of information about technologies, regulations, environmental impacts, and scenarios as the ones that are most often referred to when one performs policy analyses in the energy, environment, and economic areas is the necessary step for designing a formal carrying capacity model. In fact, designing an algorithm with this amount of information might not be too bad. For example, for policy analyses at the national level, the official scenarios stored in PASS automatically become the reference base case against which a policy is tested. If one assumes that the mix of technologies and their stage of development is known, as are the regulations, and the impact of energy changes on the environment, then the model becomes a pretty straightforward impact assessment procedure which, if repeated often enough, would lend itself to computer modeling. In short, the process and the data are available for a form of carrying capacity analysis.

But my above description actually assumes away the more interesting parts of the problem. No federal policy shop is ever going to be able to do analyses only at the national level. The more interesting and relevant implication is usually regional or local in nature. As we saw in the Piceance Basin example, there is seldom enough high quality information available to do a regional or local analysis of any given subject. Policy, as we have already said, deals with new problems that need to be handled outside the status quo. Because of this, it is unlikely that the necessary information would be available to do the fine grain, localized analysis one might like. Under these circumstances, the scenario data can act as boundary conditions for the local analysis or can give some clue as to the expected magnitude of an impact. The information about the locale to provide even a rudimentary base or reference case will have to be obtained elsewhere or developed from scratch.

The description of the energy technologies and their environmental impacts is similarly general. The technologies described are averages of a set of possible process configurations. As long as one is doing analysis of groups of technologies or is interested in average impacts, the data are alright. It is inadequate for specific site or technology analyses, however. The information on regulations and impacts is also apt to be macro in nature. In all these cases, the data in PASS, because of an earlier analysis, may be more detailed, but would tend to be so more by luck than design.

PASS, at this stage in the development, is as akin to a library reference system as it is to a data retrieval system. The user is apt to get only summary data when calling for some particular information and then referred to hard copy manuscript for more detail. Difficulties in handling the vast amount of data and resource considerations kept the system to its present size. These same considerations would have to be taken into account if one were to attempt to move the system from simple information retrieval to simulation modeling. But even this obstacle isn't all that has to be addressed to break the barriers of developing a formal computer model. A rudimentary next stage might look as follows.

AN INDEXING SYSTEM

Although an ideal situation might to be incorporate this information directly into a model, the facts are such that it is unlikely to occur in the near term. As a rudimentary first step, one might construct a series of scalar indices which could be used to rank the relative risk of carrying out a particular energy strategy to a given measure in a particular country. The variables measured might include water quantity and quality, skilled labor force density, air pollution, and ecology. For each variable, a scheme would be devised to create an index and then used to rank, say, all of the counties in the nation in terms of the state of that variable at a point in time. Unlike traditional carrying capacity, the concept of thresholds would not be used but would be replaced by one of relative risk of incurring additional cost (political and economic) to carry out a policy.

By looking at a collection of these maps in a particular region, one could display the counties in the region by the variables collected and compare the whole vector of relative difficulties across the region. No attempt would be made to combine these impacts, however. Although a far cry from a model, this indexing method is a useful organizing and display technique to mine the PASS system in a formalized fashion. Rather than go through the whole technique, let us look at the derivation of the ecological scalar as an example.

THE ECOLOGICAL MEASURE

The analyses conducted by the Office of Environmental Assessments during the past four years have demonstrated the need for an ecological methodology that would show a range or scale from high to low of areas across the country and their associated risk for ecological damage. There are two major problems associated with developing an ecological methodology. One of the problems is in identifying appropriate elements that characterize the ecological conditions of an area. As a result of limited data sets, surrogate ecological elements are often relied upon to build an ecological profile.

Another concern is in calculating the value or weight that should be placed on the ecological elements in a policy analysis. The method must be constructed in a way that gives equal weight to each element and prevents an implicit double counting of any one element. A relatively simple, straightforward approach has merit, in that it provides an opportunity to construct specific equations that may have a higher potential to reflect accurately ecological values. For example, the studies currently underway at the Institute of Arctic and Alpine Research in Boulder, Colorado, offer a model based on three ecological elements: vegetation, soil type, and land form.

In my view, the federal government should develop a system that will quickly identify, at the county level, areas of the country with ecological exclusionary zones which would preclude energy development, as well as determine the risk for ecological damage on the basis of ecological sensitivity and resiliency of a plant or animal species. The objective would be to characterize the ecology in terms of three elements: automatic exclusion from development, ecological sensitivity, and ecological resiliency. These elements seem to provide a mechanism for eliminating areas from consideration for energy development and for assessing the risk of ecological damage in terms of the ecological unit that will receive disturbances in terms of recoverability from a disturbance.

Each element is composed of several variables. An ecological exclusionary zone would consist of a national park or endangered species area. While it is fairly easy to identify the location of a national park and exclude it from consideration, an endangered species habitat criterion creates some problems. It may be difficult to determine the location of an endangered species within a county. Another problem is in the number of species. Would the existence of one endangered species receive the same weighting as the presence of several endangered species within the same geographical area?

Perhaps other areas would also be treated as absolutely exclusionary. Such a list might include the following: wilderness areas; critical habitats of endangered species; wildlife refuges and parks; wild and scenic river corridors; land in the National Park System (e.g., park monuments, national natural landmarks); lands in the state and county park system; scientific research areas (e.g., lands in the International Biosphere Program, National Environmental Research Parks; Society of American Forestry Natural Areas; natural areas managed/owned by universities or government research agencies); privately owned natural areas (e.g., the Nature Conservancy, Audobon Society lands); and other valuable wetlands, estuaries, and riparian habitats; and other areas of special biological or ecological importance (e.g., ecological reserves, plant sanctuaries, and designated coastal areas).

Ecological sensitivity would be characterized by soil type and stream density. The U.S. Department of Agriculture's soil profile would provide information on the productivity potential and composition of soils. Stream density is an important measurement because it indicates the ability of a body of water to recover from disturbances on the basis of the number of tributaries that feed into that body of water. Accordingly, an area of high ecological sensitivity would have a high potential for disturbance susceptibility. Ecological resiliency would be measured in terms of ruggedness (roughness of terrain, steep slopes) and annual rainfall. An area with low resiliency would reflect a low potential for rehabilitation or reclamation.

The SRI group proposed that other parameters that might be considered in the sensitivity and resiliency factors be soil erosion potential, soil salinity, the buffering capacity of soils and water, evaporative stress, annual primary productivity, the time required for rehabilitation to conditions prior to disturbance, flow rates of streams, vegetation response to air pollutants, wildlife responses to human presence, and water availability.

Based on the preceding ecological characterization elements, this approach can be translated into the following mathematical algorithm:

- $PA = f(ES, Pa)$
  Preserved area (or ecological exclusionary zone) is a function of endangered species and national parks;
- $S = f(SD, ST)$
  Sensitivity is a function of stream density and soil types;
- $R = f(A, R)$
  Resiliency is a function of annual rainfall and ruggedness.
- $ER = \dfrac{TA - PA_*}{TA} \quad (1 - S*R)$

  or
- $ER = (1 - \dfrac{PA}{TA}) * (1 - S*R)$

  where

  $0 \leqslant S \leqslant 1$ and $0 \leqslant R \leqslant 1$

The ecological risk equals the total area minus the preserved area, divided by the total area, and multiplied by the fraction of the combined measurements of sensitivity and resiliency. This would, in all likelihood, be scaled to be a percentage.

This information would be translated onto a black and white map with gradations of shadings, illustrating the ecological risk of an area to energy development. The darker areas would show high risk of ecological damage. This technique is also useful as a first order policy screening system which allows an analyst to see, at a glance, which areas are most apt to require further research and where his efforts will likely prove most fruitful given a particular policy initiation.

IMMEASURABLES ONCE AGAIN

We have now come to a point where we have suggested that in handling policy analyses in the resource area, no formal general model exists. Nor is it likely that enough understanding will emerge from the research in the near future to make a more formal model possible. As we have just seen, data, even if available, can be a formidable problem to maintain. The best we can do at present is to use the logic or paradigm suggested by the concept of carrying capacity, and to develop further a sophisticated data base and routinized system to manipulate the information. Before ending, though, I wish to emphasize once again that much of the basis for policy analyses and decisionmaking will likely never lend itself to rigorous analytic handling. Such factors are usually found in the areas of legal, political, or organizational factors.

One recent study done by Battelle Memorial Institute attempted to deal with these factors.[12] In fact, their so-called mapping technique lends little to the algorithms we have searched for here. Still, the following list of questions compiled for building its "maps" is a good first step in doing any respectable policy analysis.

For *legal* constraints or opportunities:

(1) What laws are applicable? What roles do they define for the entrepreneur; for the regulator; and for other concerned parties?

(2) Do the laws which apply to actions of entrepreneurs (economic participants):

   a. Provide an outright prohibition of certain desired ends?
   b. Make for difficulties in achieving necessary intermediate or instrumental goals?
   c. Make it unacceptably burdensome to comply with requirements?
   d. Make certain ventures financially impossible?
   e. Provide clear or unambiguous definition of compliance requirements?

(3) Do laws applying to regulators (governmental partcipants);

   a. Provide a clear definition of regulatory organizations' responsibilities and jurisdiction?
   b. Clarify or confuse agency mandates?
   c. Provide maximal, or minimal, discretionary latitude?

(4) Do laws affecting actions of concerned parties (interest group participants):

   a. Facilitate or limit possible influence over agency decisions?
   b. Provide political leverage over entrepreneurs and regulators?
   c. Limit or constrain opportunities to intervene in the decisionmaking process?

(5) What are the available approaches for changing the law?
   a. Litigation?
   b. Legislation?

(6) What are the costs (time, money, trouble), probability of success, and risks of complying with the legal requirements?

For *organizational* constraints or opportunities:

(1) Are organizational responsibilities clearly, or vaguely, defined? Do responsibilities overlap?; are they inconsistent with each other?; are there gaps in responsibilities?; and are the matters of concern routinely handled or are they irregularly examined?

(2) What are the likely consequences of relying on existing organizational arrangements?

   a. Likely success?
   b. Likely failure?
   c. Delay with an unclear outcome?

(3) What new organizational capabilities are required?

   a. New organizations?
   b. Reform of existing organizations?

      i.   New missions?
      ii. New resources (management, manpower, skills, dollars)?
      iii. New operating procedures (e.g., personnel systems)?

(4) How can required organizational capabilities be secured?

   a. Persuasion?
   b. Legislation?
   c. Litigation?

(5) What are the costs (time, money, trouble), probability of success, and risks of trying but failing associated with each approach?

For *political* constraints or opportunities:

(1) Whose agreement or acquiescence must be secured?

(2) What is required to secure their agreement or acquiescence? (That is, what interests must be accommodated?)

   a. Substantive interests?
   b. Political interests?
   c. Personal interests?
   d. Organizational interests?

(3) What resources does the decisionmaker have available to accommodate interests adequately to secure agreement or acquiescence?

(4) What bargains may be struck?
(5) What are the costs (time, money, trouble), probability of success, and risks of trying but failing associated with each approach?
(6) What are the consequences of proceeding in the face of political opposition?

Summary and Conclusions

We have come to a point, after hundreds of pages of analysis, descriptions, and reporting, which suggests strongly that common sense may be one of the best tools in the policy analyst's kit bag. This trite conclusion, however, cannot be and is not all you are meant to be left with.

We began by reviewing the attempts of the last two decades to bring policy analysis into the policy process. The method was an investigation of some of the underlying assumptions both of systems analysis (and its derivations) and its concomitant implementation. In each case, a series of questions was posed or postulates stated taken from the lore surrounding this field, and we investigated these in the light of experience. In the main, the reader is left with a sense of unease as to whether the paradigm of systems analysis serves the reality of the policy process in a useful fashion.

We then went on to examine in more depth the conventional wisdom that formal analytic methods necessarily improve the policy process. Several postulates were presented and then investigated through the use of case studies in the policy process. The use for formalism looks pretty weak in actual implementation, because several other factors are seemingly more important to how decisions are actually made. The case studies do not, on the other hand, make a case that formal methods are useless. They are merely not a panacea.

To proceed further in this vein, the linchpin of systems analysis—modeling—was looked at in great detail. Problems with form, cost, and documentation were brought out and discussed. Although of great interest to the technicians, these items are not the fundamental ones for the decisionmaker. The real issue is "Can I trust the results—the bottom line that the model suggests?" The material presented on validation and verification should make the decisionmaker very uncomfortable in this regard, because there is *no* way that any absolute response to this question can be given. Protestations that the revealed trust is the state-of-the-art or the best available are small comfort to the person in the position of having to make a very significant policy call.

Having said such things about formal analytic methods, we then stepped back and took a look at the way policy is formulated in the real world and how analysis has actually been used. Although analyses were made a part of the efforts, they clearly did not play a central role—at least to the extent that the early systems analysts might have liked. But this does not mean that all analysis should be abandoned. It does suggest, rather, that a new paradigm might be needed to formally structure such analysis. But we are not going to get into such a situation immediately. A transition is needed. During this time, things such as experience, brain storming, persuasion, and common sense will continue to be used. In no case are we suggesting that one throw out the existing techniques.

The ultimate solution is going to have to be one in which we begin to think about policy issues in ways which are most conducive to addressing concerns that are apt to surface in that field. In this work, we suggest that the most logical one in the general area of population/resources is the ecologist's carrying capacity paradigm. Probably few professionals would find serious difficulty with this model as an organizing principle. In fact, several case studies are presented to illustrate how this principle would work in practice. But it is clear that carrying capacity has, at present, severe limitations in its implementation phase. No formal technique yet exists to use it rigorously. On the other hand, some advances have been made in organizing information to allow the use of the concept while performing analysis. The same information could also provide the background for a formal technique, if one were discovered.

While this drift toward more specialized formal techniques is taking place, there will have to be a concomitant shift in certain organizational/institutional structures to teach policy science less as a technique subject and more as a way to look at problems in the public sector. Policy shops are also going to have to be revamped so that they are less ad hoc bodies that respond to intermittent fire drills.

I believe all this will eventually come to pass. We are now at a point in the transition where, as in all change-related situations, confusion seems to reign. We have suggested that heavy doses of common sense laced with the smorgasbord of techniques available today would be proper. This book has attempted to help point the way through the transition.

In addition to this common sense and a clear understanding of how the policy process operates, there are rigorous analytic or logic-driven techniques that are useful and important in the policy sphere, such as energy and environment. We have just suggested that the conceptual framework of carrying capacity is a useful one for such analyses. I have added a list of questions to the data bases contained in the system called PASS. To this, I suggest that straightforward, special purpose models designed for dealing with parts of issues are also valuable.

Reality forces us to recognize that there are areas which we simply don't understand very well, and that all the formalism in the world can't cure this deficiency. Our standard tracking and analysis practices force us to constantly look back with 20/20 hindsight. This fills us with understanding of the mistakes we made, but gives us little help with the future. Further, unless we can really validate models and their data bases, there is no real basis for a decisionmaker to choose an analytic solution over his own judgment. Because of the inherently impossible nature of validation, this difficulty is one which is apt to be with us for some time.

In no case do I intend to argue for a particular piece of information, for the set of questions on the more qualitative areas of policy analysis, or even for PASS itself. What I am advocating is the development of a framework of the sort suggested here and its adoption by practitioners throughout the resource-based policy areas. This will enrich the data bases, and the imagination used in successive policy analyses will enrich the technique and nudge it toward forcing more and higher quality information into policy formulation in the public sector. And that, after all, is what policy science is all about.

NOTES

1. The sections from here to the end of the chapter are all concerned with the specification, utility, and use of the carrying capacity concept. Because of the length of the section and high level of detail relative to other sections of this chapter, I considered making it a chapter on its own. But its theme belongs in the longer run, along with evolving methods, techniques, and processes. Therefore, I have left it as a part of this chapter in spite of the imbalance. I have made the section a separate one, though.

2. Rice Odell, "Carrying Capacity Analysis: Useful But Limited."

3. Office of Technology Impacts, *Synthetic Fuels and the Environment: An Environmental and Regulatory Impacts Analysis,* DOE/EV-0087, 1980.

4. Although the financial and physical feasibility of interbasin transfer seems high, a number of institutional factors present some rather formidable obstacles. First, there is a Congressionally mandated moratorium (first required by the Colorado River Basin Project Act in 1968) which extends to 1988 on any reconnaissance studies by the Department of the Interior of any plan for the importation of water into the Colorado River Basin. It seems unlikely that any major interbasin transfers could be effected until after this moratorium has ended.

Independent of the moratorium, there are two river compacts which incorporate provisions which would make it difficult to export water into the Colorado system. Neither the Snake nor Yellowstone River compacts allow out-of-basin transfers without approval of the signatory states. No such compact provisions exist on the Upper Missouri.

6. Op cit., Chapter 2, p. 1.

7. James E. Anderson, *Public Policy-Making*(New York: Praeger, 1975), pp. 9-15.

REFERENCES

Ackoff, R. The future of operational research is past. *Journal of the Operational Research Society,* 1979, vol. 30, no. 2.

Almon, C., Jr., Buckley, M., Horowitz, L., and Reunhold, T. *1985: Interindustry Forecasts of the American Economy.* Lexington, MA: Lexington Books, 1975.

Alonso, W. "Predicting best with imperfect data. *American Institute of Planners Journal,* July 1968.

Amitai, E. *Modern Organizations.* Englewood Cliffs, NJ: Prentice-Hall, 1964.

Anderson, J. E. *Public Policy-Making.* New York: Praeger, 1975.

Arrow, K. J. Criteria for social investment. *Water Resources Research,* 1st Quarter, 1965.

Ashley, H. et al. *Energy and the Environment: A Risk-Benefit Approach.* New York: Pergamon, 1976.

Atzinger, E. M., Brooks, W. J., Cherwick, M. R., Elsner, B., and Foster, W. V. *Compendium on Risk Analysis Techniques,* Special Publication 4. Aberdeen Proving Ground, MD: Army Material Systems Analysis Agency, 1972.

Baer, W., Johnson, L., and Merso, E. *Analysis of Federally Funded Demonstration Projects: Final Report.* Santa Monica, CA: Rand, 1976.

Bardach, E., *The Implementation Game: What Happens After a Bill Becomes Law.* Cambridge, MA: MIT Press, 1977.

Battelle Memorial Institute and the University of Michigan. *First Year Report for the Coal Technology Assessment (CTA) Program.* Prepared for the U.S. Environmental Protection Agency.

Baumol, W. and Oates, W. *Economics, Environmental Policy and the Quality of Life.* Englewood Cliffs, NJ: Prentice-Hall, 1979.

Behling, D., Jr., Dullien, R., and Hudson, E. *The Relationship of Energy Growth to Economic Growth Under Alternative Energy Policies.* New York: Brookhaven National Laboratory, 1976.

Bendes, S. and Graham, H. *Environmental Assessment: Approaching Maturity.* Ann Arbor, MI: Ann Arbor Science, 1978.

Boadway, R. Benefit-cost shadow pricing in open economics: An alternative approach. *Journal of Political Economy,* April 1975.

Bordes, B. and Dubuch, M. Motive and methods of policy analysis. In Nagel, S., ed., *Improving Policy Analysis.* Beverly Hills, CA: Sage, 1980.

289

Bradford, D. F. Constraints on public action and risks for social decision. *American Economic Review*, vol. 60, September 1970.

Brewer, G. *The Politician, The Bureaucrat, and the Consultant: A Critique of Urban Problem Solving.* New York: Basic Books, 1973.

Brookhaven National Laboratory. *The Relationship of Energy Growth to Economic Growth Under Alternative Energy Policies.* BNL 50500, 1976.

Buehring, W. A., Foell, W. K., and Keeney, R. L. Examining energy/environmental policy using decision analysis. *Energy Systems and Policy* 1978.

Cazalet, E. *The Methodology of the SRI-Gulf Energy Model.* Palo Alto, CA: Decision Focus, 1977.

Chestnut, H. and Sheridan, T. *Modeling Large-Scale Systems at National and Regional Levels.* Report of a workshop held at Brookings Institute, Washington, D.C., February 1975.

Clean Air Act Amendments of 1977 (P.L. 95-95, August 7, 1977).

Coates, J. F. What is a public policy issue? *Judgements and Decision in Public Policy Formulation.* AAAS Selected Symposium 1, 1978.

Coates, J. and Coates, V. Letter to the editor, *Policy Sciences* 9, 1978.

Cole, H. et al. *Models of Doom: A Critique of the Limits to Growth.* New York: Universe Books, 1973.

Coleman, J. S. *Equality of Educational Opportunity,* Washington, DC: U.S. Government Printing Office, 1966.

Comar, C. L. and Sagan, L. A. Health Effects of Energy Production and Conversion. *Annual Review of Energy,* Vol. I. Palo Alto, CA: Annual Reviews, 1976.

Cremeans, J. and Peskin, J. *Developing Measures of Nonmarket Economic Activity Within the Framework of the GNP Accounts.* Presented at the Southern Economic Association Conference, Washington, D.C., November 8-10, 1978.

Crichetti, C. and Krutilla, J. V. *Preservation vs. Development.* Presented at the Econometric Socity meetings, Detroit, December 1970.

Crissez, B. Public decision-making in the computer era. *Models in the Policy Process.* New York: Russell Sage Foundation, 1976.

Dantzig, G. *The Role of Models in Determining Policy for Transition to a More Resilient Technological Society.* Laxenberg, Austria: IIASA, Distinguished Lecture Series 1, 1979.

Data Resources, Inc. *The Data Resources Quarterly Model, Econometric Forecasting System.* Equation Specifications, 1974.

Ehrenfeld, D. W. The conservation of non-resources. *American Scientist,* 1976, vol. 64 (November-December).

Electric Power Research Institute. *EPRI Workshop for Considering a Forum for the Analysis of Energy Options Through the Use of Models.* EPRI EA-414 SR, Project 875.1, Special Report, Stanford, California, 1977.

Energy Research and Technology, Inc. *A Comparison of Alternative Approaches for Estimation of Particulate Concentrations Resulting From Coal Strip Mining Activities in Northeastern Wyoming.* October 1979.

Ermedinski, R. Questionnaire responses regarding risk taking behavior with death at stake. *Psychological Reports,* 1972.

Executive Office of the President, Energy Policy and Planning. *The National Energy Plan.* Washington, DC: U.S. Government Printing Office, April 1977.

Federal Highway Administration. *An Introduction to Urban Development Models and Guidelines for Their Use in Urban Transportation Planning.* U.S. Department of Transportation, 1975.

Fischhoff, B. Informed consent in societal risk-benefit decision. In *Proceedings of the Society for General Systems Research, 22nd Annual Meeting,* 1978.

Fisher, A. and Krutilla, J. V. Resources conservation, environmental preservation, and the rate of discount. *Quarterly Journal of Economics,* August 1975.

Forrester, J. Counterintuitive behavior of social systems. *Simulation,* February 1971.

Fox, K. A. *Social Indicators and Social Theory.* New York: John Wiley, 1974.

Granessi, L. and Peskin, H. *The Cost to Industries of Meeting the 1977 Provisions of the Water Pollution Control Amendments of 1972.* Washington, DC: NBER, 1975.

Halberstam, D. *The Best and the Brightest.* New York: Random House, 1973.

Halloman et al. *Government Involvement in the Innovation Process.* Washington, DC: Office of Technology Assessment, 1978.

Hamilton, L., Morris, S., and Noosh, K. *Data Book for the Quantification of Health Effects from Coal Energy Systems.* Brookhaven National Laboratory, revised draft, 1979.

Haveman, R. H. Efficiency and equity in national resource and environmental policy. *American Journal of Agricultural Economics,* December 1973.

Health evaluation of energy-generating sources. *Journal of the American Medical Association,* 1978, vol. 240, no. 20.

Heising-Goodman, C. *Quantitative Methods in R&D Decision-Making.* George Washington University Seminar Series, May 1980.

Hesse, H. *Magister Ludi.* New York: Random House, 1969.

Highway Research Board. *Urban Development Models.* Washington, DC: U.S. National Academy of Sciences, 1968.

Hoos, I. P. *Systems Analysis in Public Policy: A Critique.*

Hoos, I.P. *Systems Analysis in Public Policy: A Critique.* Berkeley, CA: University of California Press, 1972.

House, P. W. The developing forecasting hoax. Simulation Councils, Inc., 1977.

House, P. W. *The Quest for Completeness.* Lexington, MA: Lexington Books, 1976.

House, P. W. *Trading-Off Environment, Economics, and Energy.* Lexington, MA: Lexington Books, 1979.

House, P. W. *The Urban Environmental System.* Beverly Hills, CA: Sage, 1973.

House, P. W. and Coleman, J. A. *Realities of Public Policy Analysis.* Draft, 1979.

House, P. W. and Hock, J. *Taking Regional Issues into Account: Regional Impact Analysis Within a National Policy.* August 1979.

House, P. W. and Jones, D. *Getting it Off the Shelf: A Methodology for Implementing Federal Research.* Boulder, CO: Westview Press, 1977.

House, P. W. and McLeod, J. *Large-Scale Models for Policy Evaluation.* New York: John Wiley, 1977.

House, P. W. and Monti, D. *Using Futures Forecasting in the Planning Process: A Case Study of the Energy-Environment Interface.* July 1979.

House, P. W. and Williams, E. R. *The Carrying Capacity of a Nation.* Lexington, MA: Lexington Books, 1976.

House, P. W. and Williams, E. R. *Environment/Energy Tradeoffs as a Process: The*

Development of a Policy Analysis Screening System (PASS). U.S. Department of Energy, Office of Environment, 1979.

House, P. W. and Williams, T. *Using Models for Policy Analysis: A Case Study of an Energy-Environment-Economic Issue.* 1980.

Huettner, D. A. Net energy analysis: An economic assessment. *Science,* 1976, vol. 192, no. 4235.

ICF, Inc. *Coal and Electric Utilities Model Documentation.* July 1977.

Inhaber, H. Risks with energy from conventional and nonconventional sources. *Science,* 1979, vol. 203.

International Institute for Applied Systems Analysis. *Expect the Unexpected: An Adaptive Approach to Environmental Management.* Executive Report 1, Laxenburg, Austria, 1979.

International Research and Technology Corp. *Forecasting, Planning, Resource Allocation: Source Book.* Washington, D.C., n.d.

Kerr, D. The logic of 'policy' and successful policies. *Policy Sciences* 7, 1976.

Knapp, K. W. Environmental disruption and social costs: A challenge to economics. *Kyklos* 1970, vol. 23, no. 4.

Krutilla, J. V. Conservation reconsidered. *American Economic Review,* April 1967.

Krutilla, J. V. The use of economics in project evaluation. *Transactions of the 40th North American Wildlife and Natural Resources Conference,* 1975.

Krutilla, J. V. and Fisher, A. C. *The Economics of Natural Environments.* Baltimore, MD: Johns Hopkins Press, 1975.

Lave, L. B. and Seskin, E. P. *Air Pollution and Human Health.* Baltimore, MD: Johns Hopkins University Press, 1977.

Layard, R., ed. *Cost-Benefit Analysis.* New York: Penguin Press, 1974.

Lee, D. *Models and Techniques for Urban Planning.* Buffalo, NY: Cornell Aeronautical Laboratory, 1968.

Lindbloom, C. E. The science of muddling through. *Public Administration Review* 19, 1959.

Lindbloom, C. E. Still muddling, not yet through. *The Bureaucrat,* Mississippi State University, November/December 1979.

Majone, G. On the nation of political feasibility. *European Journal of Political Research* 3, 1975.

Marglin, S. *Approaches to Dynamic Investment Planning.* Amsterdam: North Holland Publication Company, 1967.

Marglin, S. *Public Investment Criteria.* Cambridge, MA: MIT Press, 1967.

Marland, G., Perry, A. M., and Reister, D. B. Net energy analysis of in-situ oil shale processing. *Energy,* vol. 3.

Matheny, R. W. *Evaluation of Emerging Energy Techniques: A Matrix Programming Approach.* Presented before the American Society for Public Administration, Baltimore, Maryland, April 1-5, 1979.

McAlister, D. DATA. In *Environment: A New Focus for Land Use Planning.* Report on an NSF/RANN sponsored workshop/conference, Boulder, Colorado, 1972.

McLeod, J. How to simulate. *Simulation in the Service of Society,* September 1974.

Meadows, M., Randers, J., and Behrens, W. W., III. *The Limits to Growth.* New York: Signet Books, 1972.

Menkes, J. *Epistemological Issues of Technology Assessment,* National Science Foundation, 1976.

Mettsner, A. *Policy Analysis in the Bureaucracy.* Berkeley, CA: University of California Press, 1976.

Miles, R., Jr. The origin and meaning of Miles' Law. *Public Administration Reviews* 38, 1978.

Mishan, E. J. *Cost-Benefit Analysis,* New York: Praeger Press, 1976.

Moore, G. H. The analysis of economic indicators. *Scientific American,* 1975, vol. 232, no. 1.

Morris, F. and Cals, R. *Institutional Analysis for Energy Policy,* Pacific Northwest Laboratory, PNL-3529, 1980.

Murphy, T., Nuechticlein, D., and Stepak, R. *Inside the Bureaucracy: The View from the Assistant Secretary's Desk.* Boulder, CO: Westview Press, 1978.

Nagel, S. *Improving Policy Analysis.* Beverly Hills, CA: Sage, 1980.

Naill, R. *Managing the Energy Transition: A Systems Dynamics Search for Alternatives to Oil and Gas.* Cambridge, MA: Ballinger, 1977.

Natanson, M., ed. *Philosophy of the Social Sciences: A Reader.* New York: Random House, 1978.

Nath, S. K. *A Reappraisal of Welfare Economics.* New York: Augustus M. Kelley, 1969.

National Commission on Supplies and Shortages. *Government and the Nation's Resources.* Washington, DC: U.S. Government Printing Office, 1976.

National Economic Research Association, Inc. *A Description of the National Economic Research Association (NERA) Electricity Supply Optimization Model,* January 1979.

National Energy Act, October 15, 1978. Composed of five bills: The Public Utilities Regulatory Policy Act (P.L. 95-617), The Energy Tax Act (P.L. 95-618), The National Energy Conservation Policy Act (P.L. 95-619), The Power Plant and Industrial Fuel Use Act (P.L. 95-620), and The Natural Gas Policy Act (P.L. 95-621).

No Time to Confuse: A Critique of the Final Report of the Energy Policy Project of the Ford Foundation: A Time to Choose America's Energy Future. San Francisco: Institute for Contemporary Studies, 1975.

Nuclear Power: Can we do without it? *National Journal* 17, 1979.

Nuclear Regulatory Commission. *Reactor Safety Study—An Assessment of Accident Risks in U.S. Commercial Nuclear Power Plants.* WASH 1400—"Rasmussen Report," in several volumes, October 1975.

Olsen, M. E., Curry, M. G., Greene, M. R., Melber, B. D., and Merwin, P. J. *A Social Impact Assessment and Management Methodology Using Social Indicators and Planning Strategies,* Pacific Northwest Laboratory, PNL-RAR-18, August 1978.

Otway, H. J. and Pahner, P. D. Risk assessment. *Futures,* April 1976.

Perera, F. and Ahmed, A. *Respirable Particles: Impact of Airborne Fine Particulates on Health and the Environment,* NRDC Report, 1978.

Perspectives of Benefit Risk Decision Making. Washington, DC: National Academy of Engineering, 1972.

Peskin, H. and Seskin, E. P. *Cost-Benefit Analysis and Water Pollution Policy.* Washington, DC: The Urban Institute, 1975.

Philipson, L. L. et al. *Investigation of the Feasibility of the Delphi Technique for Estimating Risk Analysis Parameters*, DOT-05-2011411. Washington, DC: Department of Transportation, 1974.

Pikul, R. P., Risselle, C., and Lilienthal, M. Development of environmental indices: Outdoor recreational resources and land use shift. In William Thomas, ed., *Indicators of Environmental Quality*. New York: Plenum Press, 1972.

Quade, E. S. *Analysis for Public Decisions*. New York: American Elsevier, 1975.

Raiffu, H. *Decision Analysis: Introductory Lectures on Choices Under Uncertainty*. New York: Addison-Wesley, 1968.

Romon, D. *Science, Technology, and Innovation*. Columbus, OH: Grid, 1980.

Rose, D., Walsh, P., and Leskovjan, L. Nuclear power—compared to what? *American Scientist*, 1976, vol. 64 (May-June).

Salisbury, R. The analysis of public policy. In D. C. Thompson, ed. *Politics, Policy, and Natural Resources*. New York: Free Press, 1972.

Sen, A. K. *Collective Choice and Social Welfare*. San Francisco: Holden-Day, 1970.

Simon, H. Theories of decision-making in economics and behavioral science. *American Economic Review,* June 1959.

Slovic, P., Fischhoff, B., and Lichtenstein, S. "Rating the risks. *Environment,* April 1979.

Solar Energy: Its Economic and Environmental Consequences, N. G. Dossani, W. D. Watson, W. P. Weygant, presented at the Houston Meeting of the American Institute of Chemical Engineers, April 1979.

Steger, W. *Models I Have Known: A Fifteen Year Assessment*. Pittsburgh: CONSAD Research Corporation, 1978.

Steinbruner, J. *The Cybernetic Theory of Decision Making*. Princeton, NJ: Princeton University Press, 1974.

Stokey, E. and Zeckhauser, R. *A Primer for Policy Analysis*. New York: W. W. Norton and Company, 1978.

Teknekron Research, Inc. *An External View of the Policy Implications of the Draft SO and Particulate Criteria Document,* Draft RM-035-DOE-80, Berkeley, California, 1980.

Testimony Before the Senate Budget Committee. Dr. Peter W. House, Director, Office of Environmental Assessments. U.S. Department of Energy, Rifle, Colorado, August 29, 1980.

Twiss, B. *Managing Technological Innovation.* London: Longmon Group, 1974.

U.S. Atomic Energy Commission. *Comparative Risk-Costs-Benefit Study of Alternative Sources of Electrical Energy*. Washington, DC: U.S. Government Printing Office, 1974.

U.S. Congress, Office of Technology Assessment. *An Analysis of the ERDA Plan and Program.* Washington, DC: U.S. Government Printing Office, 1975.

U.S. Congress, Office of Technology Assessment. *An Assessment of Oil Shale Technologies,* Washington, D.C., June 1980.

U.S. Department of Energy, Office of Environment. *A Summary and Report on Four National Environmental Workshops,* Washington, D.C., 1980.

U.S. Department of Energy, Office of Environment. *An Assessment of National Consequences of Increased Coal Utilization: Executive Summary,* February 1979.

U.S. Department of Energy, Office of Environment. *Annual Environmental Assessment Report,* Washington, D.C., 1977.

U.S. Department of Energy. *Domestic Policy Review of Solar Energy,* TID-22834, February 1979.

U.S. Department of Energy, Office of Environment. *Environmental Analysis of Synthetic Liquid Fuels,* July 1979.

U.S. Department of Energy, Office of Environment. *Environmental Readiness Document–Wood Combustion,* Washington, D.C., 1979.

U.S. Department of Energy, Office of Environment. *Summary and Status of Environmental Development Plans,* Washington, D.C., 1978.

U.S. Department of Energy, Office of Environment. *Synthetic Fuels and the Environment: An Environmental and Regulatory Impacts Analysis,* June 1980.

U.S. Department of Energy, Office of Environment. *Technology Assessment of Solar Energy (TASE),* Washington, D.C., 1981.

U.S. Department of Energy and the National Bureau of Standards. *Validation and Assessment of Issues of Energy Models,* NBS Special Bulletin 569, 1979.

U.S. Energy Research and Development Administration. *Synthetic Liquid Fuels Development,* 76-129/2, Volume II, 1976.

U.S. Environmental Protection Agency. *Community Health and Environmental Surveillance System, 1970-1971,* Washington, D.C.

U.S. Environmental Protection Agency. *Environmental Modeling and Simulations,* EPA/ORD, Washington, D.C., 1976.

U.S. Environmental Protection Agency. *Health Effects Considerations for Establishing a Standard for Inhalable Particulates,* Health Effects Research Laboratory, U.S. EPA, 1978.

U.S. Environmental Protection Agency. *Resources and Pollution Control,* EPA 600/5-79-010, 1979.

U.S. Federal Energy Administration. *Project Independence Report.* Washington, DC: U.S. Government Printing Office, 1974.

U.S. General Accounting Office. *U.S. Actions Needed to Cope With Commodity Shortages,* Comptroller General of the U.S., Report to Congress, B-114824, 1974.

U.S. Government Printing Office, *Opportunities to Fully Integrate Environmental Research and Development into Developing Energy Technologies,* U.S. GPO EMD- 78-43, Washington, D.C., 1978.

U.S. Simulation Modeling Advisory Committee, SCOPE, Simulation Modeling Assessment Project. *Environmental Simulation Modeling and Its Use in Decisionmaking: The United States Experience.* Indianapolis, IN: Praeger Press, 1976.

Van Horn, A. *Utility Simulation Model Documentation,* Teknekron, Inc., April 1979.

Vaupel, J. Muddling through analytically. *Policy Sciences Review Annual* # 1. Beverly Hills, CA: Sage, 1977.

The Washington Post. *Style Plus,* Tuesday, August 19, 1980.

Weinberg, A. *Limits to Energy Modeling,* Institute for Energy Analysis, Oak Ridge Associated Universities, ORAU/IEA-79-16(0), 1979.

Wendt, D. and Vlek, C., eds. *Utility, Probability, and Human Decision-Making.* Boston: D. Reidel, 1975.

White, D. *Decision Methodology: A Formalization of the OR Process.* New York: Wiley-Interscience, 1975.

Wildavsky, A. Richer is safer: Risk assessment in the large. Submission to the National Science Foundation, Draft, 1979.

Woll, P. *American Bureaucracy.* New York: W. W. Norton, 1963.

ABOUT THE AUTHOR

Peter W. House has been involved with efforts to develop analytic methodologies for more than a decade. These are catalogued in, among others, his *The Urban Environmental System: Modeling for Research, Policymaking, and Education* (Sage, 1974); *The Quest for Completeness: Comprehensive Analysis in Management and Environment* (D. C. Heath, 1976); and *Planning and Conservation: The Emergence of the Frugal Society* (with Edward R. Williams; Praeger, 1977). In recent years his work in the public sector has shifted from development and research to the use and application of such techniques—see, for example, *Regional Perspectives for Federal Decisionmaking* (with Wilbur A. Steger; D. C. Heath, 1981). Dr. House is currently Director, Office of Environmental Assessments, U.S. Department of Energy. Several major policy issues in the areas of energy and environment have been analyzed by his office in recent years, and it is this unique confluence of method development and application that distinguishes this present work.